Lady with a Brooch

Lady with a Brooch is a biography and a detective story—with a very satisfying ending. As a Munch scholar, there is so much here that I did not know! I really appreciated the part of the book that focuses on Eva Mudocci's life: her family background, her years as a child prodigy, her education and her musical career with Bella Edwards— all of this is really fascinating, with colorful descriptions of the milieu and the status of woman violinists. And when Munch enters the scene, it becomes even more interesting. Rima Shore has done a thorough job puzzling the bits and pieces of information together into a credible picture, and tells Mudocci's story in language that is very fluent and readable.

—Magne Bruteig, Senior Curator of Prints and Drawings, Munch Museum, Oslo, and author of *Munch: Drawings* (Marot)

It's been a long time since I was as sorry to come to the end of a book as I was with Rima Shore's utterly captivating biography. Beautifully crafted, witty, and even suspenseful, it is both deeply researched and subtly, intriguingly personal. A social history, it is also a moving— and sometimes troubling—portrayal of artists *in extremis*, a study of women musicians negotiating what Shore describes as "the uneven terrain between nonconformity and respectability." Set variously in Paris, London, Berlin, Dresden, Oslo and Copenhagen, this work contains enough intense drama to fuel an opera or a movie. Shore's readers are in for a big treat.

—Stephen R. Lehmann, co-author of *Rudolph Serkin: A Life* (Oxford University Press)

A fascinating biography, elegantly told. Eva Mudocci was not only a highly appreciated violinist and owner of an important violin, but also the subject of celebrated portraits by Edvard Munch and Henri Matisse. Mudocci and pianist Bella Edwards were at the crossroads of early twentieth-century music and art. Their story offers new slants on such leading lights as Henri Matisse, Edvard Grieg, Malvina Hoffman, and Lady Maud Warrender, and on the lesbian communities of Belle Époque Paris and mid-century England.

—Nelly Furman, Professor Emerita, Cornell University, and author of *George Bizet's Carmen* (forthcoming, Oxford University Press)

About the author

Rima Shore, a writer based in New York City, has published in the areas of literature, education, and women's studies, and is the co-author of the *Dictionary of Contemporary Biography* (Penguin). Until 2015, Rima was the Adelaide Weismann Chair of Educational Leadership at Bank Street College of Education in NYC. Also a student of the violin, she has studied for many years with Eva León.

Lady with a Brooch

Violinist Eva Mudocci

a biography &
a detective story

Rima Shore

with a foreword by Sarah G. Epstein

ISBN 978-1-7335602-0-7

Design by Niki Harris Graphic Design, Eugene, Oregon

To learn more, please visit *evamudocci.com*

For Eva León, who inspired this book,
& Karen Weiss, who knew it was a book.

Contents

Foreword

Who is the "Lady with a Brooch"? She is Eva Mudocci, born Evangeline Hope Muddock in England in 1872—an outstanding European violinist of the early 20th century. What has long piqued interest is the fact that she was one of Norwegian artist Edvard Munch's lovers and the subject of celebrated portraits. (Munch, of course, is well known as the creator of the famous painting, *The Scream.*) For the first time, this biography shows Mudocci as a fascinating, complex figure in her own right.

In lively, engaging prose, Rima Shore has written an extensive and detailed history of Eva Mudocci and her accompanist at the piano, Bella Edwards, who gave public concerts and frequented— and often performed at—gatherings of artists and musicians in Europe, especially in Paris, Berlin, and London. The story takes unexpected turns. On December 19, 1908, the unmarried Eva gave birth to twins whom she named Edvard and Isabella. How was this handled in the prevailing Victorian social climate? Was Edvard Munch the father?

Rima Shore, a dedicated scholar, traveled widely over six years, following every lead in order to trace Eva and Bella's lives, careers, families, and friends, as well as the relationship of these two women. The book is the fruit of dozens of interviews, in many countries, which revealed previously hidden stories, letters, documents, and news items. Her extensive notes are testimony to her care in seeking evidence before including details in her account of Eva's life and career.

Readers will be privileged to steep themselves in the atmosphere and mores of the European artistic circles frequented by Eva and Bella—and to acquaint themselves with an unfinished oil portrait of Mudocci that scientists have analyzed. Could it be an unacknowledged work by Edvard Munch? Readers will also discover where the stage name Mudocci came from, and what has happened to the famous Stradivarius Emiliano d'Oro that Eva played for four decades.

As a longtime collector of the prints of Edvard Munch, I've been curious about Mudocci for many years. I am delighted to have learned so much about the life and times of the gifted woman whose beautiful face is reflected in *The Brooch—Eva Mudocci*, as well as in our lithograph, *The Violin Concert*.

Sarah G. Epstein
Washington, D.C.

Mudocci's World

Musicians
Lyell Barbour – pianist
Henri Deering – pianist
Frederick Delius – composer
Bella Edwards – pianist and composer
Edvard Grieg – composer
Carl Halir – violinist
Joseph Joachim – violinist
Rose Lynton (born Evangeline Hope Muddock, later known as
    Eva Mudocci) – violinist
Carl Schneider – violinist
Arma Senkrah (born Anna Harkness) – violinist
Arthur Shattuck – pianist
Christian Sinding – composer
Ludwig Straus – violinist, violist
Eugène Ysaÿe – violinist

Singers/Actors/Dancer
Emma Calvé – singer
Isadora Duncan – dancer
Leon Lion – actor
Oda Nielsen – actor
Gertrude "Toto" Norman – actor, theater journalist
Marcia Van Dresser – singer

Artists
Clement John Heaton – stained-glass artist
Malvina Hoffman – sculptor
Christian Krohg – painter
Henri Matisse – painter, printmaker, draughtsman
Edvard Munch – painter, printmaker, draughtsman
Kay Nielsen – illustrator
Jelka Rosen – painter
Janet Scudder – sculptor
Stephan Sinding – sculptor
Theodore Spicer-Simpson – sculptor

Writers
Mildred Aldrich – journalist, novelist, memoirist
Georg Brandes – literary critic
Radclyffe Hall – novelist
Henry James – novelist
Louis Levy – poet, novelist, journalist
Henri Nathansen – playwright, stage director

Art/Music World "Supporting Cast"
Sarah Epstein – collector, scholar
Harald Holst Halvorsen – collector, art dealer
Johan H. Langaard – museum official
Tove Munch – museum patron
Poul Rée – art dealer
Reidar Revold – museum official
Winnaretta Singer (aka La Princesse de Polignac) – patron, amateur organist
Waldemar Stabell – radio journalist, painter
Rolf Stenersen – collector, biographer
Richard Tetlie – collector
Maud Warrender – patron, amateur singer
Hermann Wolff – concert manager

Levy Connections
Birgitte Andersen – mother of Johannes Louis Levy
Clara Larsen Levy – first wife
Johannes Louis Levy – son

Margrete Ericksen Levy – second wife
Morten Levy – grandson
Robinson Levy – son
Niels Ott – son
Olga Ott – mother of Niels Ott

Mudocci Connections

Harry Brander (born Gustav, Price of Vasa) – suitor of Eva's
    grandmother; pen name used by Eva Mudocci as poet
Alice Dew-Smith – friend, writer
Kai Ellson (born Edvard Ludvig Kay Ellson Muddock) – son
Louis Ellson – fictitious father of Isobel Weber
Emily Hann – aunt
Harriet Rich Hann – grandmother
Robert Hann – grandfather
William Henry Hann – great-uncle
Lucy Knupffer – friend, author of unpublished biography
Carl Johan Lemvigh-Müller – physician; with wife Alice, foster
    parent to Mudocci's twins
Otto Lund – Kai Ellson's psychiatrist
James Edward Preston Muddock (aka Dick Donovan) – father
Louis Muddock – fictitious husband of Eva Mudocci
Lucy Hann Muddock – mother
Carl Schneider (aka "Uncle Tom") – violin teacher, benefactor
Bent Weber – grandson
Isobel Weber (born Isabella Estella Ellson Muddock) – daughter
Janet Weber – granddaughter
Sven Weber – grandson

Munch Connections

Karen Bjølstad – aunt
Andrea Ellingsen – niece
Daniel Jacobson – neurologist
Mathilde "Tulla" Larsen – ex-fiancée
Christian Munch – father
Inger Munch – sister
Elisabeth Munch-Ellingsen – great-grandniece
Laura Bjølstad Munch – mother
Jappe Nilssen – friend, art critic

Introduction

In 1982, at the opening of an exhibit entitled "Androgyny in Art," a woman in her early forties lingered near *The Brooch*, taking in Edvard Munch's exquisite 1903 portrait of British violinist Eva Mudocci. In a gallery set in motion by circulating visitors, it was the woman's stillness that caught the attention of Sarah Epstein, a noted American Munch collector and scholar.

Epstein had been captivated by Munch's evocative images since coming upon his work in 1950 and realizing that he would be her "artist for life." She had spent decades studying the Norwegian artist, interviewing scores of people who had known him, and acquiring as many works by Munch as she and her husband Lionel could afford. Over time, she and her family amassed the largest private collection of Munch's work outside of Europe. All of the drawings and prints in the "Androgyny in Art" exhibit had come from their collection. Epstein knew many of the people at the opening, but not the pensive woman who remained standing in front of *The Brooch*. Curious, she walked over, introduced herself, and asked whether the lithograph had special meaning for her.

"Yes, it does," the woman responded and identified herself, in a faded British accent, as Janet Weber. "The lady with the brooch was my grandmother," Epstein recalls her saying, matter-of-factly,

Edvard Munch, *The Brooch—Eva Mudocci* , 1903, lithograph, 23-7/8 x 18-1/4 in. (60.6 cm x 46.4 cm). NATIONAL GALLERY OF ART, WASHINGTON, D.C., EPSTEIN FAMILY COLLECTION

"and I have reason to believe that Edvard Munch may have been my grandfather."

For a Munch scholar, this was extraordinary news. After breaking off an engagement with a Norwegian woman named Mathilde "Tulla" Larsen in 1902, the artist had never married. Moreover, coming from a family plagued by tuberculosis and mental illness, Munch had more than once declared himself, in journal entries, unfit for fatherhood. He was thought to have died without issue, and his possessions, including more than one thousand canvases and many thousands of prints, were left to the city of Oslo. News of possible Munch children—and grandchildren—could shake up the art establishment of Norway and reverberate beyond its borders.

Sarah Epstein was keenly aware of this history, and was fascinated by Munch's fraught relationships with women. She certainly knew of Munch's liaison with Mudocci. Over the years, all the Epstein family dogs had been named for Munch and his circle, and one golden retriever was called Eva Mudocci. But information about Mudocci was sparse. It seemed likely that the artist and the violinist were lovers, but resulting offspring had been mentioned neither by Munch's biographers, nor by the many acquaintances of Munch whom Epstein had interviewed.

The two women exchanged contact information and, over time, struck up a friendship. Sarah—known to her friends as Sally—invited Janet to visit her Washington, DC home, where the walls are covered with Munch's drawings, prints and paintings. A prominent place in the living room has been given to *The Violin Concert*—a lithograph of Eva Mudocci and her accompanist, Bella Edwards. As she shows guests through her spacious home, Sally enjoys recounting the history of particular prints and paintings. She asked Janet whether she might mention their meeting to guests, and Janet agreed.

Decades later, Sally Epstein hosted a Norwegian delegation that included Jon Gelius, a correspondent for Norwegian

Broadcasting. As they paused in front of *The Violin Concert*, she recounted her conversation with Mudocci's granddaughter. Gelius was intrigued. The year was 2012, a time when Munch's usual prominence in Norway, where his image appears on currency and postage stamps, had been magnified by the upcoming 150th anniversary of his birth. The artist's international profile was raised dramatically in May 2012, when a pastel version of his most celebrated image, *The Scream*, set a record by selling at auction for an astronomical sum—$120 million. Gelius thought the moment ideal for offering a fresh angle on Munch's life to his television audience.

In the summer of 2012, Jon Gelius filmed an interview with Janet Weber at Sally Epstein's home. Janet said that she thought she might be Edvard Munch's granddaughter—the result of a liaison between the artist and her grandmother. She explained that Eva Mudocci, who never married, gave birth in 1908 to twins: a girl and a boy. The girl was Janet's mother. During the broadcast, Gelius put to her the question he thought would be uppermost in viewers' minds: was the artist aware of the twins' existence? "I don't think Munch ever knew," Janet replied, and explained her reasoning: "I think if he did, it would be hard not to have some correspondence."

When she thought the interview was over, Janet remarked that of course these days DNA can be tested, so it should be possible to know with certainty whether she was indeed Munch's granddaughter. That remark became the headline.

In Norway, the broadcast fueled intense speculation. Few artists can claim the vast stretches of a nation's collective imagination that Edvard Munch occupies in his homeland. His work has particular power and poignancy for his countrymen, who have their own take on the slanting rays and ominous fjords, the crimson skies, the unrelieved sense of isolation that fill Munch's canvases.

Word of Janet Weber's appearance soon spread beyond Norway. In London, a *Guardian* reporter approached her. To Janet's dismay, the resulting article led with the headline: "Edvard Munch was my grandfather, says Surrey-born nun." Janet was indeed a member of a religious order, but considered her vocation irrelevant to the story. She was also distressed by the sub-head: "Janet Weber believes her grandmother had a fling with *The Scream* painter and is willing to undergo DNA tests to prove it." To Janet's way of thinking, "fling" did not remotely describe her grandmother's tender relationship with Munch. The article mentioned that Mudocci's granddaughter, born in England, had spent the past forty years in the United States. On August 21, 2012, the United Press International newswire service picked up the story, and American media outlets took note. That is how, sixty years after her death, the neglected violinist Eva Mudocci emerged into the glare of twenty-first-century media.

Part I

Viva fui in sylvis,
dum vixi tacui,
mortua dulce cano

I once lived in the forest,
in life I was silent,
in death I sweetly sing

Inscription on a sixteenth-century violin

1

English Rose

She began life in Brixton—a placid English village of country lanes and thatched farmhouses that grew into a middle-class suburb during the late Victorian period, when trains and trams linked it with central London. Born Evangeline Hope Muddock in 1872, Eva Mudocci spent her first years at Nutley Cottage, her maternal grandparents' home. Eva's mother was Lucy Mary Muddock, née Hann, an accomplished singer and piano teacher, and member of a musical family that had produced a couple of composers and nearly enough mustachioed string players to populate its own chamber orchestra. Hann family concerts were a staple of cultural fare across England's Midlands.

Eva's father, James Edward Preston Muddock, was arguably Britain's best-known mystery writer in the years before Arthur Conan Doyle introduced readers to Sherlock Holmes. A self-styled adventurer, Muddock had traveled in India, China, and Australia, and found himself in the United States during the Civil War. When he returned to England, he launched a literary career, claiming that he was encouraged to do so during a chance encounter with Charles Dickens. Over the course of his career, Muddock's sensational, serialized detective stories, featuring Glasgow gumshoe Dick Donovan, won a loyal following. He also wrote ghost stories and ventured briefly into science fiction, conjuring a submarine that encounters a lost civilization in America.

This was a family with more surnames than souls. Given names were even more plentiful. When she appeared as a singer, Eva's mother went by the stage name Lucy Lynton or sometimes Mary Lynton, making use of an old family name. Eva's father would later borrow his popular detective's moniker, Dick Donovan; he also went by the name Joyce Emmerson Muddock. But at the time he wed Lucy, thirty-year-old Muddock had not yet won renown. The bride's parents may not have been pleased with Lucy's intended, but the timing of Eva's birth—nearly a month earlier than might be expected, given the wedding date—suggests that they had little choice. It was not a promising match. Muddock had been married once before. His mental health was fragile and his professional prospects uncertain. The newlyweds did not set up their own household.

Despite his quick pen and ready store of adventures, Muddock's financial condition was woeful. Two years earlier, in 1870, he had taken over proprietorship of the *South London Courier*, filling its pages with his own tales, but could not make a go of it. In 1872, announcements in Kemp's *Mercantile Gazette* and *London Gazette* made it known that the newspaper editor and proprietor James Edward Muddock of Nutley Cottage, Gresham Road, Brixton, was "out of business." Persons with an interest in the matter were directed to attend a "general meeting" on October third to seek satisfaction. As if born a creditor, baby Eva made her appearance six days later.

Muddock soon left his in-laws' home—if indeed he had ever actually lived there—and in 1880 took a third wife, Eleanor Rudd, apparently without taking the trouble to divorce the second. This was not unheard of in Victorian England. The Divorce Act of 1857 had made it possible for a man to divorce his wife only if he could prove that she was an adulterer, and it was not uncommon for disgruntled husbands to simply walk away. They did not need to walk far. Many, including Muddock, carried on their lives in close proximity to the families they had abandoned. In most cases, the legal risks for the male bigamist were trifling, the consequences for the forsaken wife grave and enduring.

Over time, the new Mrs. Muddock gave birth to ten children, including three sets of twins. The two families had no contact despite living in the same region, sometimes no more than five miles apart. As Eva grew up and began performing in the 1880s and 1890s, she seems not to have known her half brothers and sisters. If she ever met her father, the encounter left no documentary traces, but she was aware of his literary accomplishments and in interviews made reference to her paternal forbears.

Grandfather Hann died when Eva was a toddler, and the family moved from Brixton to an attached brick house at 6 Disraeli Road in nearby Putney. For a time, she was the lone child in a household of women. After the unceremonious suspension of one marriage, Lucy Muddock was in no position to enter into another. Census records suggest that she was reluctant to claim the status of deserted wife. In 1881, enumerators recorded her as Lucy Hahn, using a Germanic spelling of her maiden name, and described her as the widowed mother of eight-year-old Eva Hahn.

Lucy Muddock was hardly the only abandoned wife of that time and place to call herself a widow. In 1881, desertion cast a pall on a woman's reputation and colored virtually every social and economic transaction. A deserted English wife had no legal identity separate from that of her absent husband and no legal right to her own children, even if the wayward husband died. She was not entitled to support. She could not sue, dispose of her own property, or even make a will. Only after new legislation passed in 1886 was a deserted wife entitled to maintenance, and then only if she had remained demonstrably faithful to her husband, even if said husband was known to be an adulterer. The situation of deserted wives was so desperate that in the late Victorian era, it became a cause célèbre, inspiring such works as Thomas Hardy's *Tess of the D'Urbervilles*.

From her early years, Eva was guarded, sensitive, painfully shy. She learned the bohemian ways of the musicians and artists who populated her extended family and frequented the Hann household, but mastered the art of projecting primness to the outside world. In time she would learn, perhaps from her mother's example, that one could have intense, unconventional relationships so long as personal and public personas were kept strictly separate. Candor was a luxury she could not afford; silence—a virtue.

Eva's maternal grandfather—the most distinguished in a long line of Robert Hanns—was a violinist who spent years as concertmaster of the Covent Garden Orchestra and was acquainted with the likes of Felix Mendelssohn and Niccolò Paganini. Eva remembered her maternal grandmother, Harriet Hann, as a beautiful, olive-skinned woman with black hair and large hazel eyes—"the perfect heroine of her own romantic tales." Eva was intrigued by her grandmother's stories. During Harriet's teen years in a coastal town near Brighton, she had been wooed by a suitor fifteen years her elder—Gustav, Prince of Vasa. Gustav was the dashing, exiled crown prince of Sweden who had taken the name Harry Brander, studied in Scotland, and befriended Sir Walter Scott. Hann family lore had it that the besotted couple ran off together but were swiftly separated by their horrified parents.

Not long after Grandfather Hann died, the family welcomed a young man with Alsatian roots who had grown up in Paris. The young man stayed, and over the next quarter century became a pivotal member of the household. In the 1881 British census, he was listed as Carl Schneider, a German-born "nephew" in the household that was headed by Harriet Hann and also included Harriet's grown daughters, Lucy and Emily, her eight-year-old granddaughter Eva, and a servant named Louisa Chapman. In that year, Schneider was twenty-seven; Lucy Muddock—a decade older. For Harriet Hann's family, the census offered an opportunity to recalibrate ages: it made Schneider several years older and Lucy several years younger. The Hanns were hardly alone in making such adjustments. Families often took liberties in their reports to census enumerators, sometimes to preserve the dignity of unmarried daughters, sometimes to get around unmentionable aspects of family history.

Like other members of the household, Schneider went by several names. British naturalization papers listed his full legal name as Charles Louis Eduard Schneider. He went by Charles in France, Carl in England, and Karl in Germany. Young Eva called him by one of the few common male names he did not claim. To her, he was Uncle Tom.

Young Carl Schneider had studied violin at the Paris Conservatoire under a famous teacher, Hubert Léonard. In the aftermath of the Franco-Prussian War, his parents moved to London, where Carl continued his studies with Ludwig Straus, an eminent Jewish violinist from Austria who had made England his home. When Carl's parents returned to the Continent, in about 1874, he moved in with the Hanns. It is not clear whether he was in fact a relation, as census documents claim, a talented violinist referred to the Hanns by a musical acquaintance, or simply an artistically inclined young man who was welcomed as a boarder when Robert Hann's death left the family in financial straits.

Eva was a small child when Carl Schneider joined the household. She began piano lessons at age three and quickly showed promise. Schneider soon gave her a scaled-down violin, and, when she took to it with miraculous ease, devoted himself to developing her gift. For the next two decades, he would be her sole teacher.

From the start, Eva was encouraged to perform. She recalled as a child playing concerts for an admiring audience of stuffed animals, with a portrait of the great Spanish virtuoso Pablo de Sarasate propped up in the critics' circle. Before long, she was playing in the drawing rooms of family acquaintances, sharing the spotlight with diminutive sopranos and velvet-clad declaimers. This early training was meant to build emotional stamina and inure her to public scrutiny. Over time, Eva gained poise and polish, but never completely conquered stage fright.

In 1882, the nine-year-old violinist, using the stage name "Miss Rose Lynton," gave her first public recital at the Athenaeum Club, performing pieces by Henri Vieuxtemps and Charles-Auguste de Beriot that showed off her agile bow technique and precocious facility with double stops (playing simultaneously on two strings). *The Strad* later recalled that that the reception given to the "little violinist" at her debut was "most enthusiastic." Three years later, in December 1885, she was one of several featured performers at a "Grand Concert" at Royal Victoria Hall. In May 1886, she gave her first full-length solo recital at Prince's Hall, playing works by J.S. Bach and other composers—with an emphasis on those who were themselves legendary violinists, and whose works were meant to spur and showcase virtuosity. The journal *Truth* reported that an "English girl, Miss Rose Lynton, who is only thirteen years old, announced a formidable programme of violin music, including Bach's 'Chaconne.'" The highlighted selection was the final movement of Bach's *Partita No. 2 in D minor*—a fifteen-minute tour de force for unaccompanied violin that was at once so arduous and so well known to audiences that only the most confident adult performers were attempting it in public. Then, in her mid-teens, Eva began playing on the Continent, making a Berlin debut at the eight-hundred-seat Sing-Akademie concert hall. She performed Joseph Joachim's *Hungarian Concerto* with the Berlin Philharmonic.

The return of Miss Rose Lynton to London's concert stage in 1891, at age eighteen, was aggressively promoted by her agent, Daniel Mayer. This was to be Eva's debut as an adult artist. Mayer's advertisements of upcoming concerts in spring editions of *The Music News* listed Miss Rose Lynton's recital at Prince Albert Hall alongside those of eminent musicians, such as violinist Eugène Ysaÿe and pianist Ignacy Paderewski. Expectations were high, with *The*

Miss Rose Lynton, c. 1888. WEBER FAMILY COLLECTION

Strad predicting that Miss Lynton would find "a place in the front ranks of violinists."

The buildup was more than the anxiety-prone young performer could live up to. A review in *The Musical News* began with praise that readers would have recognized as faint, calling Miss Lynton's performance "most successful," then declaring her rendition of *Chaconne* more "an ambitious attempt" than "a finished piece." *The Strad* leapt to her defense, but in the process ceded her place in the "front ranks of violinists": "We may conscientiously state, whatever may be the opinion of other people, that [Miss Rose Lynton] is no longer a 'prodigy,' but a finished artist who has every right to take a place amongst the leading *lady violinists* of the day" (emphasis added).

Eva soon set off on a tour of England and Scotland, and *The Strad* conveyed news of her triumphs, including an alarming report that her performance in Glasgow's City Hall had "literally brought the house down." The review concluded pointedly that the "vociferous cheering" that greeted her solos "will be good news for some of Miss Lynton's London critics!" Miss Rose Lynton had become a flashpoint in the violin wars that broke out in print in the early 1890s as Fleet Street's fledgling musical publications competed for readers. A veneer of high propriety rarely disguised writers' snide tone or anonymous correspondents' efforts at one-upmanship. A reader calling himself "A Voice From East Bombay" responded to *The Strad*'s reports of Miss Rose Lynton's tour: "I notice that at one of the Concerts she played a Caprice Fantastique by Wieniawski. Would you kindly let me know where this piece is published? I did not find it in any of the catalogues." Presumably, "Voice" was calling out the violinist, and the reviewer, for diminishing Wieniawski's "*Grand*" *Caprice Fantastique*. Other correspondents, writing on a range of subjects, were less subtle. To one, *The Strad* responded: "We can not print your letter as you have transgressed all limits of 'decorum.' We must ask our correspondents to use polite language to one another, even if it be upon such a fiercely discussed question as the 'value of Experts' opinion.'"

Fueling the violin wars was a vogue for the instrument that produced legions of would-be virtuosos—especially among girls and women. The movement of female violinists from the drawing room to the concert stage reflected, in part, the celebrity of a few individuals, particularly the woman often called the "female Paganini"—Wilma Norman-Neruda (also known by her married name, Lady Hallé). Her renown inspired thousands of parents to arrange lessons for their daughters. Some girl violinists, like Eva, grew up in musical families and were trained exclusively at home, avoiding the significant costs of musical education. Others enrolled at the Royal College of Music, which had begun admitting women in 1872, the year Eva was born. The number of female violin scholars quickly grew until they accounted for half of the College's enrollment. Many aimed for careers as soloists, a lofty but unsurprising ambition given that in both concert halls and theater pits, orchestras remained the exclusive province of males.

As parents' expectations rose, music teachers arranged countless recitals in hopes that sympathetic reviewers would provide glowing notices. Quite a few music writers obliged, but others pushed back, lamenting the proliferation of violin "geniuses." As one critic wrote in 1893, "Like the roses in summer, so lady violinists continue to come and go. Most of them are heard once, they appear, they play, and no sooner have they made their final bow than they are forgotten again and another fair fiddler takes their place." One rose unlikely to wither, in the view of *The Strad*, was Miss Lynton, who in the same article was said to have "fairly electrified her hearers" during her Midlands tour. Such treatment made her a tempting target for competing publications.

Miss Rose Lynton was not without gifts, nor was she a purely local phenomenon. Her performances in Germany won recognition for "faultless bowing," "large and round" tone, "marvelous technique," "wonderful dexterity," and "deep insight into the spirit of the composition." The *Berliner Fremdenblatt* music critic wrote approvingly that her playing possessed "manly strength." The *Berliner Börsen-Zeitung* found her performance of Bach's *Chaconne* "worthy of all praise, as it united grandeur of style and excellent technique." These qualities, as well as her unusual beauty—her graceful bearing, dark curls, and intense blue eyes—helped to set Rose Lynton apart in a very crowded field.

It probably did not hurt that Carl Schneider had engaged an aggressive London concert agent for his student, or that Schneider was a close friend of Eugene Polanski, the founding editor of both *The Strad* and *The Violin Times*. In 1890-91, during its first year of publication, *The Strad* mentioned Rose Lynton nine times. As is often the case with prodigies, reviewers understated her age ("probably about a dozen summers," one wrote when she was well into her teens), and overstated her place in the pantheon of violinists. Indeed, the index of *The Strad*'s first volume listed articles about legendary virtuosos Arcangelo Corelli, Ole Bull, Joseph Joachim, Pablo Sarasate—and Miss Rose Lynton. In the April 1891 edition, a full-page portrait of Miss Lynton was offered for sale along with those of violin immortals. The following year, *The Strad* offered readers a second full-length portrait of the violinist—now as an elegant young woman holding her instrument.

As she approached her twentieth birthday, Miss Rose Lynton was one of a handful of very popular young women appearing regularly in London's recital halls. She had undeniable talent and an appealing stage presence—and she had something else just as important. It was no ordinary violin that Rose Lynton held in the full-length publicity photograph featured in *The Strad*. She was playing the fabulous 1703 Golden Emiliani—widely considered one of the premier instruments to come out of Antonio Stradivari's workshop.

Miss Rose Lynton portrayed in *The Strad*, 1891. FLATEN MUSEUM, NORTHFIELD, MINNESOTA

In some ways, the Emiliani was a mixed blessing. Performing on this amazing instrument added to Miss Lynton's cachet, but at the same time inflated the expectations of audiences and critics.

Most Stradivari violins have names, recalling individuals who played or owned them. Eva's 1703 instrument honored the Italian violinist, Cesare Emiliani, who performed on it in the mid-nineteenth century. By virtue of its distinctive varnish, the violin became known as the Golden Emiliani. After Emiliani's death, the violin passed through the hands of wealthy collectors and then came to Ludwig Straus—the teacher of Carl Schneider. Straus was one of Victorian England's most esteemed violinists, as well as a leading viola player. In the latter part of his career, he was best known as concertmaster of England's popular Hallé Orchestra. The Emiliani accompanied him on tour throughout the British Isles and on the Continent, staying safely stowed in train compartments while Straus played cards with his friend, conductor Charles Hallé, and other men from the orchestra. But as the years passed, ceaseless performance and touring took a toll, and in 1891, the sixty-six-year-old violinist wrote to Hallé that his doctor had advised retirement. "Never would it have occurred to me," Straus wrote, "to leave an association that contented me so fully, had not my health, during the past three years, been so uncertain, and my joints so unmannerly." From time to time, he continued to play in public, but his days as concertmaster were over.

As Ludwig Straus was winding down his career, Eva was beginning hers as an adult performer. A generous and open-hearted man, Straus had developed a special bond with Eva's teacher—his protégé, Carl Schneider—and passed to him the precious Emiliani with the understanding that it would be entrusted to Schneider's gifted student. Straus possessed another rare violin and was content to play it during his last years.

Ludwig Straus handed down more than a violin. For virtuosos, lineage matters. A rising star inherits the technique, and often the sound and sensibility, of her teacher—and her teacher's teachers.

The fingertip bow grip, easy bearing, and stance of Eva Mudocci (*left*, 1901) resemble those of a virtuoso she greatly admired, Eugène Ysaÿe (*right*, c. 1903).

Eva's teacher, Carl Schneider, had been trained by two eminent violinists—Straus in London and Léonard in Paris. Both men were associated with the Franco-Belgian school of violin performance, which prized emotional expressivity and valued refinement over power, feeling over fireworks. Eva absorbed that aesthetic. In photographs, her stance and bow grip resemble those of the great Belgian virtuoso, Eugène Ysaÿe. Both held their bows practically with the tips of their fingers, a grip that favored flexibility and finesse rather than power. They kept their wrists relatively relaxed. In contrast, virtuosos trained in the Russian tradition, such as Jascha Heifetz, gripped the bow with nearly the whole hand and used a higher wrist, resulting in more intense pressure and, in forte passages, more sound.

Mudocci shared a common violin lineage with some of history's greatest virtuosos, but she lacked the depth of training that those violinists enjoyed. From the first time she picked up the violin as a young girl until she left England in her early twenties, Mudocci had a single teacher, and he is not counted among the great violin masters. Carl Schneider earned a living as a performer and teacher, but was most successful as a pedagogical entrepreneur. In 1890, he joined Eugene Polanski in establishing the College of Violinists, advertised as "the only institution founded solely for the advancement of violin playing." Schneider used his connections in the violin world, and especially its publications, to help his young protégée. He clearly had the background to train a fine violinist. Whether he had the training and temperament to prepare a world-class virtuoso was another question.

As the nineteenth century drew to a close, Rose Lynton breathed her last. In 1894, Evangeline Hope Muddock packed her Stradivarius and left London, shedding the identity of angelic prodigy. Another quarter century would pass before she again called England home.

Eva's grandmother, Harriet Hann, had died three years earlier. Now Carl Schneider—no longer as the Hanns' boarder or as Eva's teacher, but as virtual head of the household—closed the London house and relocated the family to Germany. He bought one of the imposing villas that even today dot the slopes of the Elbe, the stately river that winds through Dresden and much of central Europe. The price tag was 30,000 German marks (about $225,000 today). Schneider used his own funds; Harriet Hann's entire bequest would have covered less than a quarter of the cost.

To reach the house in 1894, the family would have traveled by train from Berlin to Dresden, and then by horse-drawn cab five miles eastward to the König-Albert-Brücke, a suspension bridge known as the Blue Wonder. A marvel of turn-of-the-century engineering, the bridge had been completed the previous year, making Loschwitz a more convenient site for a permanent

Drawing room, Linden Villa, c. 1901. WEBER FAMILY COLLECTION

home. The ride from the bridge to the village center took just a few minutes. From there, they would have ridden uphill along a circuitous road, then continued on foot up a steep, cobbled path to the lovely, large house with terraced gardens, a caretaker's cottage, and a stately old tree that inspired the name Linden Villa.

For Schneider, who had grown up in France and Germany, the move to Loschwitz was a kind of homecoming. For Lucy Muddock, it was a chance to begin again without the stigma attached to the lifelong status of deserted wife. If, as seems possible, Herr Schneider and Mrs. Muddock had become a couple, her legal situation would have precluded their marriage. Linden Villa would have offered a haven away from the prying eyes of Victorian London.

In the same year that he bought the house, Schneider wrote his will, naming Lucy Muddock as his "universal heiress," entitled to his entire estate, and her daughter Eva as the contingent beneficiary. Provision, in the form of a monthly allowance, was made for Emily Hann, Lucy's older sister. All of them were listed as residing at Linden Villa. Schneider stipulated that the bequest to Lucy "shall have the quality of reserved property," without restriction. In other words, Lucy was to be treated as if she were Schneider's spouse. The will further stated that the bequest would be free "from the administration of her husband" and recorded Lucy's declaration that Muddock "left her about 20 years ago, that she has never heard from him since and that she does not know his place of abode."

For twenty-one-year-old Eva, the move to Linden Villa offered a break from a grinding routine, and a way to weather the vocational crisis that often faces aging prodigies. She had outgrown her saccharine English rose image and the repertoire designed to display precocity, but she was unsure what would come next. She was emotionally fragile. In London's contentious violin world, she had received warm praise, but also stinging rebukes. She would later recall being tormented by painful memories of England, in particular the death of her grandmother and the fatal cancer that had disfigured beyond recognition her beloved nanny. A letter written a decade after the move alluded to "something that is too sad—too disgusting—too horrible"—an event not named or described—that haunted Eva and made it difficult for her to even visit England. For these reasons, and perhaps others that left no documentary trace, the depression that would recur periodically throughout Eva's life now attacked her with particular ferocity. She considered giving up the violin altogether.

Linden Villa offered a reprieve from all of this. It was a restful place, a radical change of scenery with the comforts of home. Its setting was rustic; its drawing room, furnished with formal upholstered furniture and a grand piano, was not. Days were filled with music, reading, and visits to Dresden's exceptional art collections. Evenings were spent gathered around the dining table or sitting on the balcony, watching Dresden dissolve into darkness. Chimes from the local church, a short walk down the hill toward the village, marked the hours. In this way, three years passed until Eva, at twenty-four, was ready to make a name for herself, literally, on the European musical circuit. Miss Rose Lynton became Madame Eva Mudocci.

If her old stage name called to mind a refugee from a melancholy Midlands ballad, the new one conjured the heroine of a tragic opera, a mysterious woman of the world, at home nowhere and everywhere. In the years that followed, Eva Mudocci encouraged this impression, cultivating a style—and a way of speaking English—that made her hard to place.

A handwritten note on an early concert program explains that Eva's European impresario thought up her new stage name. The impresario was Hermann Wolff, a leading concert promoter of the day based in Berlin. Wolff's client list and professional network included the leading lights of Europe's fin-de-siècle musical world (Pyotr Tchaikovsky, Anton Rubinstein, Hans van Bülow, and others). Wolff was willing to represent a gifted young woman, but believed that to win an international following, she would need an alluring, enigmatic persona. Female violinists with plain-Jane names would lack box-office appeal, especially in English-speaking countries.

Mudocci was no doubt an Italianized version of Muddock, but an additional source is suggested by the use of Roman numerals in catalogues of rare violins. Wolff was intrigued by puzzles and anagrams. He had already supplied an exotic aura to Brooklyn-born virtuoso Anna Harkness, reconfiguring the letters of her first name and reversing her surname to arrive at the more mysterious Arma Senkrah. And so, it seems altogether possible that when he came up with the name Mudocci, Wolff had in mind the date associated with Eva's celebrated 1703 violin: MDCCIII.

A name change alone would not transform a prodigy into a fully developed concert artist. Like many violinists making this leap, Eva needed additional seasoning. As Rose Lynton, she could piece together programs from showy airs and caprices; Eva Mudocci would need a wider, more coherent repertoire and a higher taste level to please the refined audiences of European concert halls and salons. Like scores of other young violinists of her day, Eva made a pilgrimage to Berlin to audition for her era's most revered violinist, Joseph Joachim, at the Königliche Hochschule für Musik (Royal Music Conservatory).

Admitted in October 1897, Eva attended the Hochschule for the next three years. For the first time, she was performing simply as Evangeline Muddock and competing with Europe's most promising musicians. Joachim supervised Eva's studies but left her daily instruction to the eminent Czech violinist, Carl Halir. For Eva, Halir would have been an inspiring but challenging mentor, and perhaps that is why she was assigned to him. When it came to repertoire, he was more broad-minded than Joachim; for example, he championed the Tchaikovsky violin concerto, which Joachim disdained and Eva loved. But in style and technique, he was conservative, valuing musicianship over virtuosity or originality. He was more interested in the composer's intentions than in the performer's feelings. Halir could help Eva develop a bigger sound and impose discipline on the more personal, idiosyncratic style of performance she had embraced as Rose Lynton.

Eva and her fellow students followed a rigorous course of study and spent countless hours practicing. In addition, they were exposed to the parade of musical giants who performed in Berlin in the century's last years. The Berlin Philharmonic, led by Artur Nikitch, was at the epicenter of Europe's musical world. The soloists who graced its stage, as well as the stage of the Sing-Akademie, included overlapping generations of legendary virtuosos. Between 1897 and 1900, Hochschule students could hear Joseph Joachim perform concertos by Wolfgang Amadeus Mozart and Ludwig van Beethoven, Pablo Sarasate play Camille Saint-Saëns, and Eugène Ysaÿe play J.S. Bach. They could compare interpretations of the Mendelssohn violin concerto by the mature artist Wilma Norman-Neruda and the up-and-coming Franz Kreisler. This convergence of genius represented a unique moment in violin history, and Eva and her friends were taking it all in.

Studying at Joachim's Hochschule was a prestigious stop on a violinist's career path, but did not guarantee stardom. Over several decades, Joachim trained so many performers that in 1899, at a jubilee performance in Berlin marking his sixty years on the concert stage, 140 musicians crowded into the string section to honor their master. Eva was among the current students chosen to join the orchestra. This was the only time in her career that she appeared in a major venue as Miss E. Muddock.

The biographical note on a 1918 concert program claimed that Eva Mudocci was Joachim's "favourite pupil." This was a stretch. Joachim's star student during Eva's time at the Hochschule was a young German named Carl Klingler, who had been trained by Joachim from age seventeen. But it is not hard to believe that Joachim was attentive to Eva—owing not only to her potential as a soloist, but also to her personal tie to Joachim's close friend, Ludwig Straus. By the time Eva enrolled at the Hochschule in late 1897, Straus was in poor health; he died during her time there. But Eva would not have needed a letter of introduction. She had been entrusted with a much more impressive token of Straus's esteem—his Golden Emiliani Stradivarius.

In Berlin, Eva struggled with shyness, but she attracted friends and admirers, and for the first time in her life, found herself in a setting that combined work and fellowship. She had weathered one major setback—the depressive episode that in her early twenties nearly ended her career; now, five months into her Hochschule studies, another crisis followed. In February 1898, forty-five-year-old Carl Schneider took ill. The telegram summoning Eva from Berlin said only that "Uncle Tom" was in grave danger. She set off immediately for Dresden—a three-hour ride on the express train. Meeting her at the station, her mother confirmed the suspicion that had accompanied Eva's train ride: Uncle Tom was dead. Together, negotiating brittle snow, they made the climb up the cobbled path to Linden Villa.

After the funeral, a distraught Eva returned to Berlin and resumed the daily round of lessons and practice, but she was devastated by the loss of the man who, since childhood, had provided inspiration and guidance. She found solace in the company of a new friend—a Danish pianist named Bella Edwards. They met when Eva, after returning from Loschwitz, moved into the boarding house opposite the Hochschule where Bella was living. "Bella had already lived at this pension for quite a time," their friend Lucy Knupffer wrote decades later in an unpublished account of Eva and Bella, stitched together from their own written recollections. "From the windows of her room she had watched the comings and goings at the Hochschule with interest and had been much attracted by the lovely gipsy-like girl, who used to hurry to the college, carrying a violin case."

2

An Astute Pairing

When they met in Berlin in 1898, Eva was twenty-five and Bella—thirty-three. Eva was enrolled at the Hochschule. Bella had completed conservatory training in Copenhagen and Paris, and had already been recognized for her interpretive powers and elegant technique. Like many female pianists of her day, she was engaged primarily as an accompanist and had toured with well-established musicians. In 1898, Bella performed in Copenhagen with Russian violinist Issay Barmas.

Bella continued to hone her skills. She had come to Berlin to study privately with Karl Heinrich Barth, a pianist in his early fifties who had left the concert stage and devoted himself to teaching. "I was terrified of him," pianist Arthur Rubinstein said of his boyhood lessons with Barth, a big, stern man with an Old Testament beard. Barth could reward diligent practice with a tender look and a shy smile, Rubinstein recalled, "but God help me if I arrived unprepared for a lesson!" Students making the climb to Barth's fourth-floor studio would sometimes pass sobbing predecessors coming down the stairs. It is unlikely that Bella was among the distraught. She was, to begin with, older and more experienced than most of Barth's students, and she had been toughened by years of rigorous training and performance.

As Eva prepared to move on from the Hochschule, it was proposed that she and Bella team up for public performances. According to their friend, the distinguished Danish scholar Georg Brandes, "it was Joachim who united the two ladies musically." Impresario Hermann Wolff agreed to arrange concerts for the duo.

It was an astute pairing. Musically and temperamentally, their strengths were complementary. Before enrolling at the Hochschule, Mudocci had been trained exclusively by her gentle uncle. She had played the expected virtuoso pieces in performances that were praised as much for their emotional complexity as for their technical prowess. Bella Edwards's musical training was broader. She had studied piano under J.P.E. Hartmann in Copenhagen and Ludovic Breitner in Paris, and composition under Edvard Helsted. With more than a decade of solid conservatory training behind her, she had gained a composer's insight into musical structure. She introduced Mudocci to a wider repertoire, including the works of leading Scandinavian composers. Over time, the duo became known for renditions of works by two Norwegians—Edvard Grieg and Christian Sinding.

Mudocci prided herself on being a writer and painter as well as a musician; Edwards was said by contemporaries to be entirely devoted to performing and composing. Mudocci could be assertive about her musical preferences, but she was naturally diffident and never completely overcame stage fright. In a 1903 letter she wrote: "Do you know what a child of pain music is? How one suffers, how for weeks before an important concert one is sick with nerves?" With intimates, Eva could be lively and engaging, but when she performed, she turned inward. She believed that her artistic gifts had divine origins, and on the stage, she would often close her eyes, playing as if moved by otherworldly forces. Bella Edwards was more outgoing and self-assured, projecting greater confidence. She was determined to connect with the audience, and understood that inspiration would not suffice. "You have no idea what it feels like to play in front of a large audience," she once wrote to a friend.

"[W]hen I play from the depth of my soul, there is seldom a single human being who understands my music, but when I play as I have been taught, my music has greater effect, more impact, and then I am successful. And that is how it is for all of us." Bella's discipline and emotional stamina made her a good match for Eva Mudocci.

There were other differences. Eva valued sincerity; Bella—irony. Eva admired propriety and polish and held on to some of the starchy thinking absorbed in London parlors; Bella was known to speak her mind with comic effect, reserving her sharpest wit for people she thought pretentious. Bella kept her feet on the ground, even as Eva, drawn to spiritual pursuits, drifted toward higher elevations. Eva was prone to bouts of melancholy; Bella, as her sister once wrote, brought "sunshine and light" wherever she went.

Like a tightly wound metronome, Eva oscillated between the prim idealism learned from the Victorian tales of enchantment that captivated her as a girl in England, and the fin-de-siècle enthusiasm for world-weary disenchantment that appealed to her as she came of age on the Continent. More pragmatic and predictable, Bella applied to their relationship the same skills that made her a gifted accompanist: she could follow Mudocci's mood swings while keeping a steady tempo for both of them.

Neither was prescient about disruptive trends in the arts. Eva Mudocci was born in the same year as writer Gertrude Stein, but whereas Stein cultivated younger friends and collaborators, such as the composer Virgil Thomson, Mudocci and Edwards allied themselves with the generation whose time was passing, such as Grieg and Sinding. They adored the music of romanticism and kept a polite distance from the more radical musical inventions of their day. They disliked jazz.

Their tastes in the realm of art were similarly old-school. Both considered painters misguided when they abandoned more traditional styles for fauvist or surrealist experiments. Lucy Knupffer wrote that at an exhibit, Bella Edwards once asked Henri Matisse about his painting of melons, only to be told that in point of fact, it was a portrait of his wife. The Knupffer manuscript suggests that, looking back on Edvard Munch's career, Mudocci and Edwards were ambivalent about the path he had taken: "He had studied in Oslo under Christian Krohg, who had introduced him to the naturalistic school of painting. Munch, however, felt more inclined to express his own, rather troubled feelings, using a very sensitive technique."

Eva and Bella's dislike of trendiness in art took a mischievous turn. In Paris, they had become close friends with Arthur Shattuck, an American pianist with conservative tastes, known at home and in Europe for cerebral performances of J.S. Bach. Shattuck was also an accomplished amateur artist who often made drawings—sometimes serious, sometimes comical—of fellow musicians and other people he encountered during his travels. His memoir described how Eva and Bella helped him submit his own faux-surrealist canvases to the Salon des Indépendants under an assumed identity. Eva decided that he must be Icelandic and proposed the name Adam Andrika. The three friends were amazed and delighted when visitors to the exhibit took the canvases seriously.

With Bella, new possibilities opened up for the shy young violinist from Brixton. The daily hours of practice were less lonely. There were concerts, dinners, evenings of café conversation. Holidays were more cheerful. They made frequent trips to Denmark, often at Christmas, to visit Bella's large family and spend time with her circle of fascinating friends. In the summers, they traveled together to Loschwitz or to Brighton to spend time with Eva's mother and aunt.

Eva Mudocci, c. 1900. WEBER FAMILY COLLECTION

Bella's father Samuel Edwards, an engineer, had come to Denmark in the 1850s with his wife, Isabella Denton Edwards, to direct the Danish Gasworks. Samuel was of Welsh and Isabella of Scottish extraction; both had been born in Liverpool. They first lived in Flensborg, where Bella was born, then moved to Frederiksberg. They raised their seven children in a graceful house at 28b H. C. Ørstedsvej, near the Gasworks. Samuel was said to have a pleasant singing voice, but Bella's parents were not musicians. In 1883, at age eighteen, Bella auditioned for the Gade Academy of Music (later known as the Royal Danish Academy of Music) and earned a scholarship to study piano and composing. She enrolled the following January, joining a class that included more than one future star. She graduated two years later, and in her early twenties, over her mother's strenuous objections, left home to continue her training at the Paris Conservatoire. On her own for the first time, Bella found lodgings in the bohemian Latin Quarter, and soon felt at home.

According to Knupffer's account, Bella had been, since childhood, a free spirit—a tomboy who insisted on wearing trousers and joining in the games of her four older brothers. As a young woman, and perhaps earlier, she called herself "Teddie." She grew into a tall woman with a broad forehead, deep-set eyes, and a firm, wide mouth—an elegant, substantial presence at the piano. She was a popular figure at the Gade Academy of Music and, over time, made a place for herself among the men and women of Scandinavia's intelligentsia, whose philosophers, actors, composers, and writers formed a close-knit community. Bella was a close friend of the theatrical star Oda Nielsen—sometimes called the "Sarah Bernhardt of the north"—and was very fond of Oda's son, Kay Nielsen.

Men found Bella charming and she took pleasure in their company. In letters written over many years, male friends addressed her with playful affection: "My little white elephant, for that is what you are my sweet Bella," wrote composer Ludvig Schytte, who had been a teacher at the Gade Academy and must have known that "little white elephant" was the affectionate name given to Bella by her father. "Wonderful Bella," wrote composer Fini Henriques, whose brother had married one of Bella's sisters. "Dear tempting and attractive Bella," another genial correspondent, Paul Nielsen, wrote. Other letters reflect the tender regard for Bella of the Norwegian composer Christian Sinding and the Danish diplomat Ferdinand Prior. Bella could be drolly flirtatious in her own letters, writing to Prior, "I hope you are tanned and herculean after your holidays in Saint-Malo." All of these men apparently appreciated Bella's warmth and humor, but no man was more captivated by her than Norwegian composer Edvard Grieg.

Edvard Grieg. Photograph by Elliott & Fry
studio, London

In October 1895, four years before Bella met Eva in Berlin, she gave a piano recital in Norway's capital with her friend, the singer Margrethe Petersen. A number of Edvard Grieg's works were on the program, and the young musicians were thrilled when the composer came backstage after the performance to congratulate them.

Grieg had met Bella once before at a reception hosted by his publisher, and was eager to renew the acquaintance. Fifty-two and long married, he arranged to spend the next few days with the thirty-year-old pianist. There may have been an affair. In the exchange of fervent letters that followed, Grieg expressed pleasure that Bella had written of their time together as a "three-day relationship with no regrets." Or, there may have been an intensely romantic, platonic encounter. It appears that much of their private time was spent at the piano, talking over Bella's interpretations of Grieg's compositions and discussing how his songs should be performed. Bella—who often accompanied singers and had a pleasant alto voice—sang Grieg's famous song "The Swan," accompanied by the composer.

Bella Edwards was thrilled to share the composer's piano bench; Grieg seemed to have in mind more commodious furniture. The letters he sent her from November 1895 through January 1896 made it clear that he was in the grip of intense infatuation. "You have taken all my heart," he wrote soon after leaving for Germany. He understood that Bella was awed by his stature—at least metaphorically. (She towered over the five-foot-one composer.) And he was not above tempting her with the promise of musical tutelage. In November, he wrote from Leipzig, "How sweet you are when you write: *we* sang 'The Swan'! Yes, you dare say that the tones vibrate in the depth of your soul—that is true. I just wanted the technical expression to be better, and you shall and must acquire this. Couldn't I have the pleasure of playing a bit with you in Copenhagen, when you return home in January-February?"

Grieg's song was based on a poem by Henrik Ibsen about a swan who, near death, breaks a lifetime of silence. "The Swan" was performed frequently by Grieg's wife, Nina—a lyric soprano whose rendition was said to entrance Henrik Ibsen and move Pyotr Tchaikovsky to tears. One rapturous critic wrote, "That mysterious alchemy of spirit possessed by Nina Grieg is a rare quality. And in her case one feels that it may have been part of the fine communion that existed between the composer and his wife."

But Grieg was beyond such considerations. He was, as he wrote to Bella, like "a schoolboy in love." He wrote of his lifelong search for happiness, professed his passion, and begged Bella to meet him again. He proposed coming to Copenhagen. When Bella's admiring, reserved responses failed to match his ardor, Grieg assumed that she was worried about being seen with a married man. "With regard to Copenhagen," he wrote, "I think there would be no need to worry. Over an extended period I have had various workrooms there so hidden away that nobody, not even my closest friends or my wife, have known where they were."

Bella's letters kept Grieg off balance. Judging by his responses, she thanked the composer for "the most wonderful hours" of her life and looked forward to a lifelong bond, but would not agree to a rendezvous. In one reply, Grieg chided, "You mustn't speak about never separating, you, who don't want us to meet!" In another, he was indulgent: "If this is my last letter, then thank you very much for all the beauty I saw in your eyes. It is not your fault if Eros is not capturing you as deeply as me." In the next, he complained, "Your lack of courage has been like a cold bath on my burning passion," adding that he would put off a planned visit to Copenhagen until she was elsewhere. "The way I now feel, I couldn't stand a day, an hour, being in the same place as you without seeing you and talking to you, just the two of us. The pain of longing would kill me." Finally, Grieg put an end to their correspondence: "I cannot answer your letter without opening all the wounds! Therefore, just this: Do not write any more!" For the composer, it was a brief epistolary relationship, with regrets.

Bella would have had many reasons to rebuff the advances of a besotted, married, middle-aged man pleading for trysts in hidden studios. But history often edits out nuance from the lives of complex women who appear in accounts of famous men. "Edwards was rumored to have lesbian tendencies," Grieg biographer Lionel Carley wrote, "a factor which goes a long way to explaining her unequal relationship with Grieg."

During Eva's last year at the Hochschule, she and Bella shared lodgings. In late 1900, they packed up their Berlin studio, and by January they had moved to Paris. In a Saint Germain residential hotel at 9 rue de l'Université, they found cozy fifth-floor lodgings decorated in an understated English style. Bella was happy to be back in a city she knew well—one that indulged her exuberance and prized her wit. Her French was effortless; Eva's was halting. As a teenager, Eva had made visits to Paris with Carl Schneider and had been taken to play for the city's most influential violin masters, but she had spent little time there as an adult.

It is hard to imagine a place and time more exhilarating for emerging artists. Everyone seemed to be in motion. Eva and Bella crisscrossed Paris on foot, despite construction crews that were throwing barricades and dust in their way. When walking was impractical, colorful horse-drawn cabs were plentiful; at the same time, there were not only electric trams, but also the metro, whose first line had just begun operating. The streets were noisy, as were the drawing rooms and cafés. Fin-de-siècle Paris had carried into the new century a commitment to salon culture, which valued conversation and contemplation over pageantry and pronouncement. American writer Edith Wharton called the French salon of the early twentieth century "the best school of talk and ideas the modern world has known." Meeting up frequently was a non-negotiable of salon culture, she said, "based on the belief that the most stimulating conversation in the world is that between intelligent men and women who see each other often enough to be on terms of frank and easy friendship."

Salon culture also shaped the musical world, which contrasted sharply with Eva and Bella's German experience. In Berlin, the scale was huge. Conductors preferred venues with the grandeur to inspire awe, and programs with the sweep and technical rigor to overwhelm audiences. In Paris, musicians were composing and performing music meant for smaller settings. The salon musicians performing in Paris's recital halls and drawing rooms often built programs around familiar themes. The era's more innovative composers were experimenting, to be sure, but were not well represented at the *heures de musique* held in the homes of super-rich, pretentious patrons. These receptions were ideal settings for piano and violin entertainment so long as the selections were brief and recognizable. Bella once told a Danish interviewer that some Parisians are so dedicated to socializing that they view music as "a necessary evil." She added, "It's very common to see well-heeled families in their boxes at the opera playing bridge during performances, pausing only to listen to the most famous pieces."

Mudocci and Edwards had arrived in the densely networked musical world of Paris as unknowns, but they made the most of their ties to Hermann Wolff and Joseph Joachim. On May 8, 1901, they made their Paris debut at the Salle des Agriculteurs, a hall that was, despite its name, one of the city's most prestigious recital venues, described by pianist Arthur Shattuck as "the ugliest concert hall in Christendom," whose "only redeeming feature was its perfect acoustics." Their afternoon program included Grieg's *Sonata for Violin and Piano in C minor*, which became, over time, Eva and Bella's signature piece. Critics received the newcomers warmly.

Salon culture played to their strengths. In the years that followed, German reviewers sometimes resisted the duo's expressivity, but French critics consistently praised their blend of artistry and feeling. Parisian audiences appreciated performances not only for their displays of virtuosity, but also for their emotional poignancy and contemplative qualities. Pieces like Jules Massenet's "Meditation" (from the opera *Thaïs*) were ideal choices for intimate settings, and Bella Edwards published her own "Meditation" for violin and piano, praised by one critic as "laden with beautiful melody and delicious changes." It was a perfect vehicle for Eva, highlighting a characteristic trait of her playing—resonant, sustained chords.

Eva and Bella were soon on their way to becoming minor celebrities. Days were spent building a repertoire of sonatas and suites sufficiently varied and novel to please refined Parisian audiences (see Appendix). The duo would come home from outings to the music publisher Durand, across the Seine at 4 Place de la Madeleine, with stacks of sheet music to try out, keeping those that interested them and returning the rest.

Their social circle widened. Through Bella, they had ready entrée into Paris's Scandinavian colony. In addition, they arrived with a letter of introduction from Joseph Joachim to Frederick Delius, the English composer who had known Joachim since boyhood and was living in France. Eva and Bella exchanged visits with Delius. They soon met other musicians, artists, and writers, and began inviting them to their studio for samplings of their repertoire.

They prided themselves on unstinting hospitality. Gustav Hetsch, a leading Danish music critic, recalled how warmly they welcomed him and his wife in the spring of 1901.

> Miss Bella would prepare a delicious cup of tea and put out boxes of chocolates for us. Miss Eva occasionally served us old cognac or rum, which she would pour into rare antique glasses. Then one of the ladies would arrange a soft cushion behind my neck in the comfortable armchair I occupied, and the other would offer me a Philip Morris. . . And then they started playing, and everything got even more fabulous.

HOFFOTOGRAF HARALD PAETZ EFTERFOLGER

Bella Edwards and Eva Mudocci, 1901. Photograph by Harry Paetz, Royal Danish Library, Copenhagen

Hetsch recalled that it was difficult to pry the two musicians out of their studio. Only after a long day of rehearsal would they venture out. An evening at the Opéra-Comique would be followed by a "little get-together" at the Café de la Régence that would turn out to be not at all "little." Bella would hold court from one of the café's black leather banquettes, peppering polite conversation with irreverent remarks. If the walk back to the Left Bank took them through the Place du Carrousel, the vast cobbled expanse that stretched from the courtyard of the Louvre to the Tuileries Garden, Bella was known to throw her arms around a friend and break into a polka.

The high-spirited Bella was also pragmatic and determined to build their reputation. Hetsch recalled Bella's description of Eva as "too much of a dreamer and romantic" and "too much the artist" to manage her own career. "It would be a sin and a shame if Eva did not become the artist that nature and environment have destined her to be," Bella told Hetsch. "Without in any way wanting to compare myself to her—because I am fully aware that her talent is on a different level than mine—I dare say that she can't succeed without me."

Bella took charge of negotiating contracts. In the summer of 1901, the duo traveled north, launching the first of the tours that would bring them celebrity across Scandinavia. When they returned to Paris that autumn, they found new lodgings at 19 rue las Cases, just off a pretty square that, then as now, was poignantly out of proportion with the massive Gothic Basilique Sainte-Clotilde that overlooked it. They never tired of hearing the chimes from Sainte-Clotilde's steeple and loved pointing out to visitors the winged statue of composer César Franck—the church's one-time organist—that stood in the church garden.

This was the 7th arrondissement—the Left Bank, but hardly its most bohemian corner. Their modest flat was in the heart of the district called le Faubourg Saint-Germain, long the fashionable refuge of the nostalgic, insular French nobility, anchored by Sainte-

Clotilde, where titled Paris prayed. For Bella, le Faubourg was quiet enough for intense work, yet an easy walk from the cafés and conversation of the boulevards Saint-Michel and Montparnasse. For Eva, there was spiritual solace close at hand; she had not been raised as a Catholic, but made frequent visits to the church. The location answered perfectly Eva's desire to combine radical independence with total respectability.

Respectability exacted a price. The very phrase le Faubourg came to signify upper-crust snootiness, evoking what one of its denizens called "the poetry of snobbery." Its gatherings were typically daunting and colorless. As Eva and Bella's American friend Arthur Shattuck recalled, hostesses would pointedly refrain from introducing guests to each other. Newcomers were left to mill about, trying to "casually fall into conversation with anyone that looked least likely to bite your head off." Shattuck added, "The attitude always was that your presence was nonexistent, or too contemptible even to be noticed."

Along with the poetry of snobbery came the vile rhetoric of anti-Semitism. When Eva and Bella moved to le Faubourg, France was in the throes of the Dreyfus affair, which had begun in 1894 with a false accusation of treason against a Jewish officer in the French army. The controversy ignited in France anti-Semitic feelings that had smoldered since the 1886 publication of Édouard Drumont's two-volume rant, *La France Juive*, which pointed to Jews as the cause of virtually every problem facing the country. Hate speech became tolerable, even chic. In 1899, a writer known as Gyp, when asked her profession while testifying in court, did not hesitate to reply, "Anti-Semite." In the social stratum most likely to engage Eva and Bella for drawing-room performances, such bigotry was rampant. And so, it is noteworthy that in the first interview she gave as a touring virtuoso, Eva Mudocci identified herself as a woman with Jewish roots.

Wherever the duo performed in these early years, Eva piqued curiosity. Audiences wondered who the ethereal Madame Mudocci might be, and where she had come from. In February 1902, the Swedish music journal *Svensk Musiktidning* introduced Mudocci and Edwards to its readers. Noting that "more detailed biographical information about the two artists is as yet unknown," it reported, on the basis of an interview with the violinist, that Mudocci's mother "had a German father and an English mother, who [both] also had Jewish blood in their veins."

The account is curious, given public records that offer no evidence of Jewish lineage. It is of course possible that the interviewer misconstrued Eva's comments or made an assumption based on her appearance. But if Mudocci was accurately quoted, if she did indeed introduce herself to the Scandinavian public in this way, it was a bold choice. The bigotry unleashed by the Dreyfus affair was by no means limited to France. In Sweden, it tended to be less virulent than in some other countries, but anti-Semitic sentiments had surfaced there in public discourse and parliamentary debates. In Norway, a country that Eva and Bella often toured, a constitutional ban had excluded Jews from the country for much of the nineteenth century. This was the context in which Mudocci claimed Jewish lineage. Was she principled or naïve? Did she calculate that an interview published in a Swedish journal was unlikely to reach Paris? Or had she taken to heart Hermann Wolff's advice that an emerging female violinist needed to create an exotic persona? Was she eager to place herself in a line of descent from legendary Jewish violinists, such as Joachim and Straus?

Perhaps the impressionable violinist identified with the circle of Copenhagen artists and writers she was meeting through Bella, which included several prominent Jews: towering scholar Georg Brandes, whose very name brought free-thinkers to their feet in Scandinavian taverns; dramatist Henri Nathansen, who would later write a biography of Brandes; and a rising writer and journalist named Louis Levy, whose reports from European capitals made him known to a wide Danish readership. Eva had grown up in the company of Carl Schneider's bohemian friends and would have felt at home among these intellectuals. All three spent time in Paris, and judging by their writings, all were taken with the charming violinist.

To be sure, the lens of later history magnifies the import of Eva's Swedish interview. At the time, it may not have been momentous for her. The article appeared, after all, in a language that her Parisian patrons did not know. And in 1902, Eva and Bella were more deeply immersed in performance than in politics. Nevertheless, the question of Jewish heritage was destined to resurface.

For the next several years, Eva and Bella were caught up in daily practice and the business of arranging and preparing for performances and tours. Those preparations were arduous; even performances at private receptions could be logistical nightmares. In a letter inviting the pair to perform at a soirée in his mansion, one high-society host asked Bella to please bring along a piano.

On the first Sunday of each month, Mudocci and Edwards held candlelit "at-homes" in their small studio. Their performances in European recital halls were well received, and they had begun filling a scrapbook with appreciative reviews. In a typical 1903 review in *Die Musik,* a critic praised a Berlin performance, gushing over "the violinist's entrancing temperament and musical expression."

These were hectic, exhilarating times. Writing home to her mother, Eva reported on recent performances ("The concert in Trocadero was for the freemasons. . . .We played Grieg's C moll [minor]"), described encounters with celebrities (opera star Emma Calvé, painter Christian Krohg), and sent "love from Teddie"—as she called Bella. She wrote home in a major key, but was not entirely free of the gloom that had descended after Carl Schneider's death. As letters of this period reflect, she constantly feared that loved ones would fall ill. Eva would panic at the first sign that Bella might be coming down with a cough or fever. This was not entirely irrational. Paris had long been considered a center of medical excellence, but decades would pass before antibiotics were available. Nevertheless, considering her youth, Eva was unusually alert to the precariousness of life.

As for the two women's close relationship, it raised few eyebrows. Eva and Bella were accepted as an ideally matched musical duo. Press accounts of their careers would occasionally include sly winks, telling readers that the "inseparable friends" work together "day and night." Mudocci and Edwards sometimes encouraged the public's view of them as inseparable. Bella once told a Danish interviewer that either of them could speak for the duo, saying, "*Eva og jeg vi er et.*"—"Eva and I, we are one." But Bella and Eva were discreet, and in any case, at that time and place, an unconventional liaison was no scandal. Disgrace came with breaking the social compact that compelled decorum and collective denial. Later in the decade, a heterosexual interlude, with its visible consequence, would threaten Eva's reputation and career in a way that persistent rumors of homosexuality did not.

3

A Proposition & A Request

Eva Mudocci and Edvard Munch met in Paris in the spring of 1903. In the ordinary course of events, their paths might not have crossed. To begin with, they came from different countries and different circumstances. Born outside of London, Mudocci was raised in a somewhat bohemian, musical household, and was destined from the start for a life in music. Munch grew up a thousand miles away in Kristiania (as Oslo was then known). His mother died of tuberculosis soon after Edvard's fifth birthday; thereafter, he was raised by his father, a pious physician, and by his mother's sister. At age sixteen, Edvard enrolled in a technical college to study engineering, where he excelled in the sciences and in scaled and perspective drawing. Then, at eighteen, to his father's dismay, he turned abruptly to a career in art.

Munch and Mudocci did not speak each other's languages. Edvard liked to produce random, amusing English phrases, but never gained more than a primitive knowledge of the language. When they met, Mudocci knew little Norwegian. Their common language was German, which both knew imperfectly.

They were at different points in their careers. Munch, a decade older, had spent time in the 1880s in the studio of the day's leading Norwegian painter, Christian Krohg, absorbing the aesthetics of naturalism and impressionism, and producing skillful landscapes and portraits. Then, while still in his twenties, he began showing canvases that he called "soul painting," using bold lines and hues, simplified forms, and audacious subject matter to convey inner experience. By the time he met Eva Mudocci, Munch had already exhibited many of the works for which he is now best known, including *The Scream* and *Madonna*. At home in Norway, his work was regarded warily, branded as "eccentric fanaticism, delirium-drunk moods and fever-sick hallucinations." Worldwide fame would come to him only posthumously, but he was exhibiting frequently and gaining recognition outside of Scandinavia.

Mudocci, in 1903, was relatively unknown. By the First World War, she would become a musical celebrity. Not only Edvard Munch but also Henri Matisse would create multiple portraits of her; at least two sculptors and a stained-glass artist would make likenesses as well. Christian Sinding would dedicate a sonata to her. But when she met Edvard Munch, thirty-year-old Eva had just relaunched her career. She had only recently shed the identity of Miss Rose Lynton, blossoming English prodigy. As the more enigmatic Madame Eva Mudocci, she was just beginning to establish a reputation on the Continent.

Geography did not favor a meeting. Since 1901, Eva Mudocci and Bella Edwards had lived and worked in Paris, where salon culture suited perfectly the refined, intimate performance style for which they were becoming known. The two women often spent evenings cultivating wealthy patrons who might engage the duo for at-home musical receptions. Eva and Bella would frequently leave home to go on tour or vacation with family, but they always rushed back to Paris.

For Munch these were peripatetic years. Unappreciated at home, he was working hard to establish himself in Germany, where artists and critics were more receptive to his edgy subject matter and brutal technique. France held fewer attractions. To be sure, Munch felt the pull of the graceful, gritty city that was Europe's artistic center of gravity. Eager to promote his work there, he had made sporadic trips to Paris, but his French was limited, as was his social network, and he was constantly prevailing upon an unlikely source—his friend, the British composer Frederick Delius—to help him connect with the city's art dealers and gallery owners. At times he rented space alongside the many artists who filled Parisian studios, but he could never quite find his bearings in the city's bistros or galleries, and had no use for the kind of stuffy soirées at which Mudocci and Edwards often performed. The cafés of Monmartre were more to his taste, but Munch found scant comfort in the company of Frenchmen. His appearances in Paris were so fleeting that he became known in the city's art circles as the "Norwegian ghost." In the early years of the new century, he was more often to be found drinking prodigious quantities of wine and brandy in German taverns or brothels.

For all of these reasons, an encounter with Mudocci was hardly inevitable. This is how it happened.

In Paris, Eva Mudocci and Bella Edwards were constantly seen together. Some acquaintances, perhaps many, assumed that they were lovers. Most were not troubled by this notion; lesbian relationships were hardly unknown in turn-of-the-century France. But Jappe Nilssen, a Norwegian living in Paris, was not among the untroubled. In 1902, he wrote to his friend Edvard Munch proposing that Edvard seduce Eva to rescue her from Bella's clutches.

How, precisely, Jappe Nilssen phrased this plan is not known. After Munch's death, the letter was destroyed by his sister, Inger Munch, who considered it too scandalous to see the light of day. But Inger did make her own record of the letter, no doubt cleaning it up for posterity:

> There are two women living here in Paris, the pianist Bella Edwards and the violinist Eva Mucicci (*sic*). Eva M. is unlucky. Bella Edwards has complete power over her. They live together in a relationship. I have a proposition and a request for you. They are coming to Norway to give a concert. Do you think that you could pay attention to Eva, flirt with her a little, so that perhaps her feelings may become natural?

Jappe Nilssen was among Munch's oldest friends. A decade earlier, the two men had spent countless evenings together drinking and debating at Kristiania's Grand Hotel with a group of self-declared radicals that also included artist Christian Krohg and his wife, painter Oda Krohg. The Kristiania *bohème*, as they became known, had brought back from Paris an ideological allegiance to free love and an erotic energy that, in the provincial, claustrophobic Norwegian capital, quickly became overheated. At the center of sexual intrigue was Oda Krohg, who was linked romantically with several men of their circle—including the much younger Jappe Nilssen. It was a disastrous match. Jappe was suspicious, tormented; Oda appeared in public with conspicuous bruises and claimed to fear for her life. Munch depicted his forlorn friend in portraits called *Jealousy* and *Melancholy*. It was Jappe Nilssen, Munch's poster child for ruinous sexual obsession, who proposed to Munch that he woo Eva Mudocci away from Bella Edwards. This might well have given Munch pause, especially with his own personal life in shambles.

Edvard Munch was in a dreadful state of mind in 1902 as his volatile on-again, off-again affair with a striking Norwegian woman named Tulla Larsen reeled out of control. Born into the family of a wealthy wine merchant, Tulla was an independent, artistic young woman and a familiar figure in Kristiania's bohemian circle. Her relationship with Munch began in late 1898, when she was twenty-nine. From the start, there was turmoil. Tulla was eager to wed; Edvard resisted. He finally made a reluctant proposal in hopes of easing their misery, but the engagement had the opposite effect. Tulla begged him to make good on his promise and legalize the marriage. When Munch delayed, the drama escalated. Friends rushed to Munch with word that Tulla, in despair, had taken a dangerous morphine dose. Some accounts say that she feigned suicide, others that she made a half-hearted attempt. Shattered, Munch hurried to his fiancée's bedside to beg forgiveness, then became enraged when Tulla made a miraculous recovery. Munch later wrote to Nilssen that for three years he had been "bound to [Tulla]–I let myself feel compassionate and hurt until I was half dead."

In September 1902, the couple met at Munch's beach cottage in Åsgårdstrand to settle their future. An argument ensued and somehow Munch's revolver discharged, blowing off the top of his ring finger and leaving his left hand permanently disfigured. He rushed to the hospital, where surgery followed; Tulla did not go with him. Biographers disagree about the precise circumstances surrounding this event, but not about its lasting impact. As biographer Atle Næss has written, it would take Munch "the rest of his life to process the after-effects."

In Norway, a man breaking off an engagement could be called to account in the courts. Early in 1903, Munch wrote to his aunt that Tulla was suing for "blood money," adding that his finger was healing, "but it hurts all the time. It is not a pretty sight and it's not much use either, but it does what it can—it's short and stiff." This was Munch's state of mind as he planned his pursuit of Eva Mudocci. For Jappe Nilssen, the scheme clearly had special appeal. As it turned out, the prospect of insinuating himself between two women was irresistible for Munch as well.

Munch did not meet Eva during her and Bella's Scandinavian tour of late 1902, as Jappe Nilssen had suggested. He spent the winter of 1902-03 in Berlin, painting, preparing a catalogue of his prints, and fighting off influenza. By February 1903, he was well enough to travel and was making plans to show at France's annual Société des Indépendants exhibit. As he made arrangements to transport his paintings to Paris, his usual ambivalence about the city was tinged with dread. Friends had spotted Tulla Larsen there, keeping conspicuous company with a new fiancé—another painter. When Frederick Delius invited Munch to stop at his home in Grez-sur-Loing, some forty miles south of the capital, he accepted, adding, "I am afraid of a lady in Paris and expect new bad things—Write and tell me what you know—she herself has so many allies." On February 27, he wrote to his aunt that he was heading toward Paris, but would be staying outside the city and would keep himself "hidden for understandable reasons."

What worked against anxiety and alienation, as Munch packed his bag, was ambition. Despite personal disasters, his career was on the upswing. As he neared his fortieth birthday, Munch was on the verge of a breakthrough. A decade earlier, in 1892, an exhibit of his paintings in Berlin was deemed so shocking that it was quickly shut down. That made the enthusiastic reception given to his monumental *Frieze of Life* series at the 1902 Berlin Secession all the more gratifying. Fresh from that triumph, Munch was determined to make his mark in Paris. He was hopeful that the paintings he would show at the Indépendants exhibit—selected from the *Frieze of Life* series—would secure his reputation. He only planned to show eight paintings, but arranged to have all twenty-two of the *Frieze* canvases delivered to a studio he rented at 65 boulevard Arago. His plan was to find a venue where the entire series could be hung.

Edvard Munch had a great deal to manage in March 1903, but neither dread nor driving ambition distracted him from the project of meeting Eva Mudocci and Bella Edwards. He had prepared

Edvard Munch in 1902. Munch Museum, Oslo

by securing a letter of introduction from their Danish concert promoter, Rulle Jørgensen. By the time the Indépendants exhibit opened on March 20, Munch had left Delius's house and checked into the Hotel d'Alsace on the Left Bank. He arranged to meet Eva and Bella for supper at a café, very likely Le Dôme on boulevard Montparnasse, and brought along Norwegian impresario Rudolf Rasmussen to make it a foursome. They conversed in German, a language they could all navigate. Mudocci found Munch's conversation witty and lively, as she recalled in a letter nearly fifty years later. She described the "queer jerkiness" of his phrases and how his conversation "springs from one thing to another with little connection. To talk with him one had to be on the tips of the toes constantly to follow his thought, which nevertheless was always logical & deep with meaning. He never used many words but with very few he could say more than most people with many."

Munch soon appeared at Eva and Bella's small flat on rue las Cases carrying a large, ostentatious lupin, a plant distinguished by its erect, foot-long flower spikes, and announced in his practically non-existent English that he had come for "tea o'clock." He was the kind of intense, difficult man whose attentions can be especially rewarding, and Eva found him quirky and magnetic. Munch was fascinated by Eva and relieved to have found lively companions with no ties to Tulla Larsen. By this time, news of the broken engagement and the scandalous gunshot episode had spread, and Paris's Norwegian colony had closed ranks around Tulla. Munch had cut himself off from most of his old acquaintances.

Acutely aware of his "enemies," Munch nevertheless stayed on in Paris. He spent many hours with Mudocci, walking the city and visiting the church at Saint-Cloud, a town some six miles west of the city limits that Munch had known well since living and working there a dozen years earlier. They sometimes met at La Closerie des Lilas, a fashionable café at the intersection of boulevards Saint-Michel and Montparnasse named for the big potted plants that encircled it. Ernest Hemingway immortalized La Closerie and its waiters in his memoir *A Moveable Feast*, describing encounters there in the 1920s with the Left Bank's American and British expatriates. But in 1903, La Closerie was a favorite gathering place of the city's German and Scandinavian residents, and could be relied upon for good beer and wine, the comforting smoke of familiar cigars, and relief from what were, for many northern European intellectuals, the daily narcissistic injuries inflicted by speakers of French. Edvard Munch liked the place well enough to risk an encounter with Tulla. His usual table was close to the bar and offered an unobstructed view of the entrance—clear advantages for a hard-drinking man mindful of enemies and afraid of a run-in with his ex-fiancée.

In the weeks that followed, Eva was drawn to Edvard, but felt unprepared for a sexual encounter. She had been raised on Victorian stories of pure love. As she later explained to Edvard, her idealism and inexperience with men made everything tense and awkward:

> . . . I went for so many years without meeting a man whom I could touch with a thought. I lived like a nun for my beloved ideals and then at last you came and so finally, since I was so lacking in experience and so stupidly innocent, I didn't know what to do with the reality that was finally there. I didn't understand you—I didn't understand myself—I was like a sweet child who had dreamed for too long and had become blind in the sudden light—.

In the same letter, Eva conveyed, more telegraphically, that her love for Bella had also gotten in the way: "There were also other things involved that made it difficult and unnatural—you yourself wrote afterwards—('we have met each other under unfavorable circumstances')." And indeed, in the spring of 1903 she showed no signs of abandoning Bella. Eva was conflicted, Bella was wary, and Edvard—still traumatized by the gunshot and the ensuing scandal—was severely agitated. They tried socializing as a threesome but could not keep up the expected affability. Edvard complained that the tension was making him ill. He compared one evening spent together to "snow on spring flowers": "It was [one of] those evenings when we were at [la Closerie des] Lilas—and altogether you both, after this evening, were completely changed;—where does this come from? I think I know—I haven't changed—I became sick and very nervous, which is probably a mistake—but how can I help it?"

A few weeks at this emotional pitch was all Munch could tolerate. On April 5, he wrote to his German patron, Max Linde, that he had to get away from Paris because of a "private matter"—"a lady." The lady in question may have been Eva, given that the triangle was making him "sick and very nervous," but was more likely Tulla Larsen—still close by and surrounded by allies. "Here, sad to say, too many Norwegians now," he told Linde. "I must leave, otherwise I predict great disaster." In reply, Linde invited him to come to Lübeck to paint portraits of his family. On April 17, still in Paris, Munch wrote to his aunt that he would soon be leaving for Germany. Once the plan was set he made an abrupt departure, leaving behind Eva and Bella and a studio full of paintings.

Munch's sudden appearance in the spring of 1903 unnerved Bella, but she was distracted by another drama. Just as Edvard Munch was preparing to leave Paris, Edvard Grieg arrived for concerts and galas marking his sixtieth birthday. Since the 1890s, he had been the most frequently performed foreign composer in France; that April, Grieg fever raged in Paris. Seven years earlier, he had written to Bella that being in the same place without seeing her would be unbearable. Now they were in the same city.

On April 19, Eva and Bella joined an audience numbering more than three thousand at a concert that turned out to be unforgettable, and not just for the music. Anti-Dreyfusard hecklers were out in force to protest Grieg's outspoken criticism of the French government's role in the Dreyfus Affair. The composer, who was conducting, carried on valiantly. Even more momentous for Bella may have been the inclusion on the program of "The Swan"— the song she had sung to Grieg's piano accompaniment during their "three-day relationship with no regrets."

A week later, on April 26, a Grieg concert at the Salle Pleyel was completely sold out; on the day of the performance, the box office did not bother to open. Bella wrote to Grieg to ask for help with tickets, and, just hours before the concert, received a gracious, formal reply inviting "Miss Edwards" and "Miss Mudocci" to attend. He had not been given any complimentary tickets, he wrote, adding, "Can you believe it?" But he could offer them seats on the stage, behind a sheer curtain, in a section reserved for the composer's wife and special guests.

For Bella, this should have been a triumphant moment. At thirty-eight, she was successfully choreographing the duo's career, including tours in Scandinavia and Germany that significantly raised their profile. Bella's social skills were considerable, and she was becoming a central figure in Paris's Scandinavian colony, as Christian Krohg's portrait of her made plain.

Entitled *Bella Edwards*, the portrait would later be exhibited in Germany along with several paintings by Edvard Munch. It was full of exuberance. Bella lacked the classic features and delicacy that made Eva Mudocci so unforgettable. The portrait had no air of mystery—no inscrutable half-smile or downcast eyes. What Krohg caught—in the upswept hairstyle, the tilt of the piano lid, the flight of birds on the decorative screen—was Bella's natural buoyancy. Her dress, surprisingly low-cut, added to the sense that she had little to hide. In portraits and photographs, Eva always seemed to be gazing inward. Krohg showed Bella turning her head to look out at her audience. But he also conveyed the tension between the friendliness of her glance and the power of her muscular forearms and large hands. They seemed to have a life of their own.

As Eva and Bella took their seats on the stage at Edvard Grieg's concert, Edvard Munch was settling in at the home of Max Linde in Lübeck. Only a month had passed since his first encounter with Eva Mudocci. A letter from Eva soon arrived. "It is fate that brought us together," she wrote, sure that supernatural intervention had played a role. Munch did not reply that, in fact, fate had taken the form of Jappe Nilssen. He had good reason to conceal the unsavory proposition that had prompted their meeting.

But for Munch as well, the sense of familiarity was uncanny. "I have an *idée fixe*: that your experience has been the same as mine," he wrote to Eva. It did not escape his notice that Eva's appearance, especially her thick dark hair, bore a striking resemblance to the sensuous, irreverent *Madonna* portraits he had been creating for a decade. It was as if he had been painting Mudocci for years. Eva's devotion to Bella was a complication, to be sure, but in the spring of 1903, Munch was determined to capture Eva's affections—and her likeness.

Christian Krohg, *Bella Edwards,* c. 1903, oil on canvas, 24 x 18 in.
(61 x 46 cm). PRIVATE COLLECTION

Edvard Munch, *Madonna*, 1895, oil on canvas, 34-1/2 x 28 in. (90 x 71 cm).
KUNSTHALLE, HAMBURG. Some sources mistakenly identify Mudocci as the model;
in fact, Munch painted it eight years before meeting her. Munch's first known
attempt to paint Mudocci, in 1903, referenced his *Madonna* images by endowing
Eva with a red halo.

4

Enchantment

Art historians record that Edvard Munch created three portraits of Eva Mudocci, and that all three were black-and-white lithographs. But in 1903, he attempted at least one additional portrait—this one in oils.

Not long after meeting Munch, Mudocci sent her mother a newsy letter from Paris. "Teddie is going to be painted by Krohg," she wrote, using her affectionate name for Bella. "And I am being painted again by another Norwegian painter—and this is the best picture ever made [of me]." She wrote that it was "excellent as [a] portrait and then set in such a fantastic way that it has quite a bit of poetry—it is only the head and arms and violin." Mudocci's description leaves little doubt that the unnamed Norwegian painter was Edvard Munch, whose distinctive *Madonna* images of the 1890s had featured crimson halos: "I wear a blue silk blouse that he makes to look like some Saint Cecilia drapery and behind my head is a red halo—and on my breast my silver cross—and the whole against a black ground intensely black—don't you think it sounds beautiful?"

Late in life, Mudocci recalled that Munch was never satisfied with his efforts to paint her. The "silver cross" painting has not been found; it may have been destroyed or painted over. But a lithographic portrait of Mudocci wearing a striking piece of jewelry did survive and is widely considered among Munch's most beautiful works. Over time, this portrait, like its subject, became known by multiple names, including *Lady with a Brooch* (as Mudocci referred to it), *The Lady with Long Hair and Brooch*, and, confusingly, *Madonna*. Munch called it *The Brooch—Eva Mudocci*. It is often referred to simply as *The Brooch*.

Munch was especially invested in this portrait, judging by its sheer size (approximately twenty-four by eighteen inches). He repeatedly reworked the lithograph, each time transferring the image to a new stone, producing numerous states of the print. In a 1950 interview, Mudocci recalled sitting for the portrait at the Hotel Sans Souci in Berlin. ("When [Munch] arrived I had just washed my hair. It was not yet dry and was floating around my shoulders. Thus, *Lady with a Brooch*.") But Munch had clearly studied Eva's publicity photographs. He incorporated imagery reminiscent of earlier portraits of women, including flowing hair and downcast eyes; at the same time, Munch endowed Mudocci with more mystery and complexity.

The lithograph lacked the carnality of the *Madonna* images. It showed Eva clothed in a black garment that is primly fastened with a large brooch. This brooch did not spring entirely from Munch's imagination. Mudocci actually wore a Norwegian brooch as a pendant in the publicity photo that served as an inspiration for the portrait. It had been presented to her in 1901, during her first visit to Norway, by Jens Thiis, then conservator at the Museum of Arts and Crafts. According to Thiis, "I became acquainted with [Eva Mudocci and Bella Edwards] before Munch did, in Trondheim during a concert tour, when we had a little party for them in our home at Stavne. The brooch which Eva Mudocci is wearing is traditional Norwegian jewelry which I gave her on this occasion."

With the photograph as a starting point, Munch reimagined Mudocci. He captured the tilt of her head and the intensity of

Detail from 1901 publicity photo showing Eva Mudocci wearing a traditional Norwegian brooch.

Edvard Munch, *The Brooch—Eva Mudocci*, 1903.

her expression, but replaced her gauzy gown with the kind of cape typically worn over a traditional Norwegian dress and fastened with a brooch. Munch enlarged and simplified the brooch, making it the portrait's focal point, and drew attention to it in his title. Munch later made another lithographic portrait of Eva wearing a brooch, entitled *Salome.*

Scholars have naturally speculated about the meaning that brooches held for the artist. Some have connected it with the brooch that Munch's mother Laura wore at her neckline in a family photograph (with baby Edvard perched on her lap) taken just four years before her death. Other scholars perceived a primitive face on the brooch's surface and suggested that Munch slyly imprinted himself on Eva's breast. Both of these insights shed light on his process, but there is more to the story. The ornament highlighted by Munch was a wedding brooch.

In general, the brooch had special significance in Norwegian culture. Typically silver-gilt, it was thought to protect the wearer from evil by deflecting light rays, and was therefore called a *sølje* (from the Norwegian word for the sun). The *sølje* was a folk healer's indispensable tool and a family's prized possession, often handed down through generations.

Different types of traditional Norwegian brooches were associated with specific life events and relationships. Munch showed Mudocci wearing a *bolesølje,* a brooch meant to be worn at times of transition to ward off trolls and troubles. Small ones, typically no bigger than an inch across, were given as christening gifts; larger ones were traditionally presented to brides by their grooms. Over time, the *bolesølje* became a customary part of a bridal ensemble, to be worn after marriage on special occasions. Munch's mother would have worn her wedding brooch for celebrations and formal occasions (including sitting for a photographic portrait).

In his portrait of Mudocci, Munch simplified the wedding brooch, highlighting its typical symbolic elements: a circular center, signifying Christ, surrounded by filigree roundels (six larger and six

Laura Catharine Bjølstad Munch with her son Edvard, 1864. MUNCH MUSEUM, OSLO

Traditional *bolesølje*.
NORSK FOLKEMUSEUM, OSLO

smaller), representing the apostles. While incorporating Christian symbols, wedding brooches also harkened back to age-old folk beliefs. In Norwegian folktales, wedding brooches protected brides and grooms from *huldre-folk*—baleful forest creatures who were thought to inhabit a hidden world and cause havoc for ordinary people. In one tale, the *huldre-folk* stage a mock wedding, dressing an innocent dairymaid in bridal finery and shoving her toward a bogus groom. The evil plot is foiled when an old woman pins onto the bride's dress a large filigree brooch, cleverly fending off the evil spirits and preserving the maiden for her true love. In another tale, the *huldre-folk* whisk a wife away to their invisible realm. When she tries to communicate with her husband, he does not sense her presence until she presses into his hand the wedding brooch he had given her. In these tales, the brooch provides protection and well-being; in addition, it emblemizes the spiritual bond and mystical communication between soulmates.

The brooch in Munch's portrait carried these meanings—as Edvard suggested in a letter to Eva. In the summer of 1903, Munch wrote that the photograph she sent him "hangs over my bed." His draft continued, "You look as though you would protect me from evil spirits." Mentioning his placement of the photograph gave Munch's letter an intimate tone; at the same time, it conveyed his use of her likeness as a charm—the kind that, in Norwegian folk tradition, was hung over the bed to repel demons and prevent nightmares. Munch attributed to Eva curative as well as protective powers. "Sometime," he wrote, "I will bathe my sick soul in your music—it will do me good." In the aftermath of the Tulla Larsen affair, as enemies and internal demons closed in on him, Munch was sorely in need of solace and spiritual healing. "I get a little rest when I talk to you," he wrote to Eva.

Mudocci understood what Munch needed from her and sent promises, written over several years, to help and comfort him, to soothe his frayed nerves. One letter, sent in the summer of 1903, pledged to "follow you in my thoughts and keep all evil spirits far from you with both my hands." Another posted that summer promised to "put my hand on your forehead to quiet your thoughts when you cannot sleep. I can kiss you—once on each eye and once on the forehead . . . so you will drift into an enchanted sleep . . . I will sometimes do it in thought before I fall asleep—maybe the spell will work from afar."

In actuality, Mudocci's "spell" worked better from afar than in close proximity. The correspondence that began when Munch left for Germany in late April 1903 started out friendly but slightly formal: "Perhaps we shall be fortunate enough to meet again sometime," Eva wrote to Edvard. The tone quickly became more intimate as they acknowledged not only attraction, but also obstacles—perhaps insurmountable. "It is something unusual, something special that draws us to each other—something deep in both our natures and perhaps stronger than our wills," Eva wrote, "but I also know that, in a way, there is a gulf between us that we can never bridge." Munch drafted a seductive reply, holding out hope for a relationship: "It is a wonderful spring full of sunshine, longing and desires—We met in unfavorable circumstances—I truly believe this—we shall meet again when things are different." Reaching for metaphor, he added, "You are pure music."

In mid-May, Eva and Bella left Paris for Brighton to spend the summer with Eva's mother. The correspondence continued. Eva could match Edvard's earnest tone in one letter ("I go to Sainte Clotilde Church, which you loved, and with holy water make a sign of the cross on your letter"), then, in the next, sound more like the sardonic Bella. When Edvard complained about the friends who had turned on him, Eva retorted, "At least be proud of it. It would be nice if a man could be such an angel that everyone had to love him, but it's also good to be well hated. For my part, I don't love angels." Ending the same letter, she asked Edvard why he had said that she seemed like two people.

In one draft, Munch told Mudocci that she was like a sister to him; in another, erotic overtones were unmistakable: "(I wish that you were here—I would hold you in front of me—both your hands in mine and both your eyes in mine—in this way I would speak with you—)." Despite this longing, Munch kept his distance. "Do you think of me?" he asked in another seductive letter written during Eva's stay in England. "I kissed your little letter—and I see your white cliffs in the distance—I almost went to you but my work forces me."

The months passed uneventfully. When the changeable Brighton weather allowed, Eva and Bella swam, strolled, and enjoyed the sea air. As more letters arrived and Eva's infatuation deepened, she tried to reconcile Bella to the idea of her friendship with Edvard, but that was proving difficult. "Bella is with me of course," she wrote to Munch. "She is still angry with you because she thinks you made me unhappy in Paris. She is mistaken—you have brought me no unhappiness and never could."

As autumn approached, Eva and Bella traveled from England to Denmark to vacation with Bella's family on the coast, then returned with them to Copenhagen. From Copenhagen, Eva wrote to Edvard that she had dreamed she was in a boat with him: "You kissed me and in your kiss was all the beauty of life & our breath was a potion of Paradise that we took from each other."

In Denmark, Eva and Bella were preparing for a concert in Copenhagen scheduled for October, and Eva invited Edvard to attend. Then, abruptly, plans changed. "You should not hurry here for the concert," Mudocci wrote to Munch matter-of-factly in late September. "There is none. I told you that Mrs. Edwards was very sick, and thirteen days ago she died. But if you want to come to Copenhagen anyway, I will be happy to see you." Eva's brittle letter betrayed less feeling about Bella's bereavement than about Edvard's cancelled visit. Six months after Jappe Nilssen's plan was set into motion, Edvard had reason to believe that it was succeeding.

Eva and Edvard clearly found points of connection. Both had known early loss and suffering and were prone to dark thoughts. The biographical roots of Munch's pain are easier to trace, beginning with the deaths of his mother and older sister from tuberculosis and the confinement of a younger sister in a mental asylum. Munch would later write, "I inherited two of mankind's most frightful enemies—the heritage of consumption and insanity." More recently, the Tulla Larsen affair had been devastating. It was during this period, in 1903, that Munch gave form and color to his anguish in *Self-Portrait in Hell*. Mudocci was less forthcoming about her personal trials. She had been abandoned by her father and felt deeply the loss of Carl Schneider; she suffered when she played in public, even after decades of concertizing; and she could not forget the raw, unnamed trauma that, as she wrote to Edvard, caused her anguish whenever she spent time in England.

Neither was writing in a native tongue. Mudocci's written German was straightforward and serviceable, but by no means free of errors; Munch's reached for a more expressive register, but the syntax was awkward. Nevertheless, their poetic impulses surfaced frequently. Suffering was far from their only subject. In their correspondence, both wrote compelling accounts of their emotional states and spiritual longings. Both experienced awe in the presence of nature and sought out inspiring places.

Rooted in fin-de-siècle culture, both were trying to gain their footing on fast-changing cultural terrain. Mudocci was more at home with Felix Mendelssohn than with the growing number of modernist composers who, taking their cues from Gabriel Fauré and later from Igor Stravinsky, would rewrite the rules of melody, harmony, and rhythm. Munch felt more kinship with Vincent van Gogh and Paul Gauguin than with the rising generation of painters who, inspired by Paul Cézanne and later by Georges Braque and Pablo Picasso, would reinvent the rules of perspective.

They shared a sense of drama and a vulnerability that

sometimes veered toward paranoia. Edvard was always on guard against detractors of his work and other foes—Tulla's allies foremost among them. In January 1904, Eva told him "how much I wanted to help you against all your enemies if possible," and asked him to come to see her because she had intelligence to share with him. She wrote in a postscript, "Come, come, there is danger for you—I know what I'm saying." The nature of this danger remains unknown.

Eva and Edvard shared a mystical bent, taking to heart notions that the more pragmatic Bella Edwards would have made light of. Both were preoccupied with the life of the soul, aspiring to lives that could rise above the commonplace. Munch wrote that his journals recorded not ordinary life, but rather his spiritual experiences; Mudocci wrote that she feared losing all that truly matters "behind the non-essentials of the non-heroic life." Working in different media, both explored the artistic possibilities of the unseen—of tension and vibration, of waves and rays. Each was immersed in the spiritual dimensions of sound: the violinist in her daily practice, the creator of *The Scream* as the world's most celebrated painter of pulsating, unheard sound—the vibrational force that comes from nature.

Both were interested in Theosophy, a religious movement that drew many musicians, artists, and writers by teaching that every individual has access to God through personal inspiration. In particular, Theosophists valued music as this world's most direct bridge to the unseen realm, and thought the violin possessed especially powerful spiritual potential. The ideas of Theosophy saturated Mudocci's thinking throughout her adult life. In her seventies, she wrote that the very term artist "has less a social than a spiritual origin," and that the making of an artist cannot be fully explained by education, environment, or even talent, but comes from an "indelible characteristic with which a child enters the world. Each is a direct cosmic ray." Theosophists associated the cosmic ray with cosmic love or wisdom.

Munch understood this vocabulary. In the new century's first years, the languages of science, art, and the occult were merging. Newly discovered waves and rays (wireless radio-telegraphic waves, X-rays, cosmic rays) were transforming scientific understanding and artistic imagination, and Munch was intrigued. He was not alone. On Paris boulevards, crowds of pedestrians would gather to watch X-ray demonstrations.

Munch's interest in waves and rays was especially intense at the start of the new century. Deeply impressed by the X-ray of his hand made in 1902 to assess his gunshot wound, he was struck by the implications for penetrating not only the human body, but also the mind and the soul. At the same time, he was captivated by the way light waves could be transformed into photographic images, and bought his first Kodak camera. Looking back on these years, Munch later recalled that fascination with "enigmatic rays and ethereal undulations and waves" was among the contemporary trends that influenced his work on the *Frieze of Life* series.

Munch claimed to see auras around people. He would not have scoffed at Mudocci's fascination with séances or her conviction that consciousness outlives the body. Both believed that there are phenomena around us whose actuality we doubt only because we lack the perceptual equipment to experience them directly. In a 1908 sketchbook, Munch made this entry under the heading "Are there any spirits?"

We see what we see because we have eyes that are made just so . . . Had we different stronger eyes—we would—like X-rays— see . . . the skeletal system . . . And if we had still different eyes. . . . we would surely see different forms.—In other words why should—other beings with lighter—insubstantial Molecules—not exist among us—The Souls of our dear ones—for example? Spirits.

There was, in short, a spiritual and intellectual bond between Eva and Edvard—a dense cluster of shared interests and beliefs. But that alone could not sustain a relationship. Neither was well equipped for a casual flirtation, particularly one conducted at a distance. The testing and teasing in their early correspondence sometimes verged on adolescent. Three months after meeting Edvard, Eva asked the artist for his photograph, complained when it did not arrive promptly, and then, when she finally received it, wrote that she was not fond of the likeness. He in turn complained that her photograph, while beautiful, gave no sense of her character. He nonetheless wrote that he had hung it over his bed.

Eva needled him when he wrote on grubby notepaper or when his handwriting was hard to decipher. "You say that men and women don't understand one another. Is that why you write so illegibly?" she asked, attempting wit. Munch's feelings were hurt. "Another snowfall," he wrote in a letter that took him a half-dozen drafts to get right. Mudocci replied, "Can't I have a little joke with you any more, that's how I am, I have to joke so as not to quake in my boots at the sheer horror of life. Apart from which I am your friend, which gives me the right to tease you." This was Mudocci's chemistry—an amalgam of the "sheer horror of life" and lighthearted teasing in a single message. Munch was fascinated and constantly off balance.

Eva assured Edvard that she was not asking anything of him, but she did seem to want the trappings of a proper romance, or, at the very least, respectable stationery and suitable phrases. And she wanted him to appreciate Bella. The perversely ill-mannered Munch, drawn to Eva, made an effort but could not keep it up— especially as daylight dimmed and the effects of alcohol took hold. "I am ill and very nervous of making a slip, but what can I do?" he wrote. "So I shall no longer write to you in the evening, I shall write on good paper and if possible more clearly. You see, I just want to fit in with you." He was like an Ibsen character trying to romance a Jane Austen heroine. Injuries were bound to happen—and they did.

Edvard, Eva, and Bella all came together again in the fall of 1903. The two women arrived in Berlin in mid-October and checked into the Sans Souci, a large hotel at 37 Linkstrasse that was just steps from the offices of the Wolff agency and from Bechstein Hall, the important concert venue where they would soon be performing. It was a setting Eva and Bella knew well, not far from Potzdamer Platz, close to the old Hochschule für Musik (which had moved to a new building the previous year).

It was a gratifying return. The duo was scheduled to give high-profile concerts on November 4th and 13th, to be followed by a tour with the celebrated lieder singer Raimund von Zur-Mühlen that had been arranged by HermannWolff's agency. When that tour ended, Eva and Bella did not go directly home to Paris. Instead, they made an extended stop in Berlin, where Munch was spending the winter.

The tension was thick. It was dawning on Munch that his flirtation with Mudocci could lead to more upheaval. The letter he drafted to the recently married Delius reflected his ambivalence: "So you've gotten hitched and I am still a free man. But I always have feelings toward the enemy—Woman. I think you know Eva Mudocci and her friend B. Edvards—they are here—Fraulein Mudocci is wonderfully beautiful and I almost fear I have taken a fancy—(one of thousands). What do you think? After the last affair with T[ulla] I am madly apprehensive."

At first, their time together went well. Eva gladly went with Munch to the winter 1903/04 Berlin Secession exhibit of works on paper, where he was showing forty-seven prints. Edvard once again promised to paint Eva—this time with Bella. He had rented space at 121 Kurfürstendamm, but his studios were always cluttered and uninviting. With no place to sit, visitors often had to stay on their feet, and so it was agreed that Edvard would work at the Sans Souci. He filled Eva and Bella's hotel room with paint tubes, brushes, bottles, and blank canvases, but the double portrait did not materialize. They would arrange to pose for Munch, only to be stood up. One or

Edvard Munch, *The Violin Concert,* 1903, lithograph 18-1/2 x 21-1/4 in. (47 x 54 cm). EPSTEIN FAMILY COLLECTION

another of the trio would refuse to meet, or would set conditions for meeting and then reconsider. Icy notes were exchanged. Finally, Eva demanded that Edvard retrieve his equipment. He obliged and then, according to recollections shared by Eva late in life, sent to their room the heavy lithographic stone for *The Brooch* with a note that read, "Here is the stone that fell from my heart." Eva recalled that the stone was so heavy, it took two workmen to carry it up to their hotel room.

Munch never completed a painting of Eva and Bella—or if he did, the painting has not surfaced. But in 1903, he did produce a

Eva Mudocci and Bella Edwards, 1901. PHOTOGRAPH BY HARRY PAETZ, MUNCH MUSEUM, OSLO

Edvard Munch's *The Violin Concert* reversed, as Munch would have drawn it on the lithographic stone. This view suggests a connection to Pierre-Auguste Renoir's *Woman at the Piano*, 1875-76, oil on canvas, 36-9/16 × 29-1/8 in (93 × 74 cm). THE ART INSTITUTE OF CHICAGO

lithograph called *The Violin Concert* that depicted the two musicians on stage. It is loosely based on a publicity photograph, but Munch portrays both women as more sensual. Bella's low-cut dress, upswept hair, and posture recall Christian Krohg's painting of her. Munch may also have had in mind another model for his image of Bella, a painting called *Woman at the Piano*, painted three decades earlier by an artist Munch claimed had little influence on him—Pierre-Auguste Renoir.

In *The Violin Concert*, Eva wears no brooch, but once again there is a primitive face—the kind that, in Norwegian folk tradition, was thought to ward off danger. This time it appears on the surface of Eva's violin: the two f-holes take on the look of eyes, and a highlighted portion of the fingerboard resembles a nose. The face has the shape of a skull, as does the train of Mudocci's long dress. Mudocci owned an early state of *The Violin Concert*, and kept it at her mother's Loschwitz house.

Late in 1903, Munch produced a third lithographic portrait of Eva Mudocci, calling it *Salome*. The contours of her face and the shading suggest that he once again found inspiration in a publicity photo. Munch depicted Eva wearing another brooch, but this one contained a shape that suggested a fetus—an image sometimes used by Munch to evoke both birth and death. Once again, Mudocci had an enigmatic look, but now there was also a hint of lechery. Munch showed her with a strange, self-satisfied smile; he placed his own gaunt, detached head where one would expect to find Eva's violin.

Mudocci understood that Munch's portraits expressed his own conflicted emotions and were as likely to provoke as please, but this time he had gone too far. She was furious. In particular, she was appalled by the title *Salome*—a reference to the Jewish woman in the New Testament who kissed the lips of John the Baptist's decapitated head. The very name had become synonymous with debauchery, scandal, and, some critics say, with the lurid sensuality often attributed to Jewish women in this era.

The connotations would not have been lost on viewers. At

Edvard Munch, *Salome*, 1903, lithograph,
15-1/2 x 12 in. (39.4 x 30.5 cm). MUSEUM DE REEDE,
ANTWERP

precisely the moment when Munch created the print, Oscar Wilde's
1891 tragedy *Salome* was playing in repertory at Max Reinhardt's
Neues Theater in Berlin, with a staging that emphasized the title
character's blend of childlike naïveté and sensuous depravity. Given
the notoriety of its author, many viewers associated the play and its
title character with homosexuality, a link that sparked scandal in
later stagings.

Mudocci was incensed. "I thought you were my friend," she
wrote to Edvard. She said she had never believed the unflattering
stories she had heard about him from all directions. "I only thought
the best, but I'm beginning to think that your ill manners can
actually be put down to bad character." Tulla Larsen had insisted

Eva Mudocci, undated. The contours and shading of Mudocci's face suggest that Munch had studied this photograph before creating *Salome*. MUNCH MUSEUM, OSLO

upon marriage; Mudocci now made a demand that proved to be equally impossible. "Recently you said you wanted to respect my wishes," she wrote to him. "I wish you could be just a little polite." They fought and then they reached an uneasy truce. A month later, on January 13, 1904, Munch wrote to Jappe Nilssen from Berlin, reporting: "I am painting and drawing—and am together with Eva M." Munch seemed to be signaling that his friend's request was at last being carried out. He was again attempting to paint Eva, this time without Bella.

When Munch wrote to Jappe Nilssen, it appears that he had not yet explicitly broached with Mudocci the nature of her relationship with Bella Edwards. That conversation soon followed. It is not known exactly what was said, but the exchange was heated. Seared in Eva's memory were Edvard's words—"not normal."

5

"Not Normal"

For more than a year after Munch wounded Mudocci with the words "not normal," from early 1904 to late 1905, there was no direct contact between them. The relationship that began with a dare could easily have ended there, but it did not. Early in February 1905, Munch added a postscript to a letter to Frederick Delius: "Please tell me how Fräulein Eva Mudocci is getting on—have you run into her?" Delius replied, "Fräulein Eva Mudocci is in Paris, I know, but I have not seen her for a long time. She is charming." A month later, Munch wrote to Delius again, asking him to "give my regards to Fräulein Mudocci" and asking whether Delius knew her address. Eva and Bella had moved to a new flat at 11 rue Malbranche, on a picturesque block that Woody Allen featured a century later in his film, *Midnight in Paris*. They loved the building—especially the lush pergola that separated the entryway from the rear living quarters.

Eva Mudocci had a hold on Munch. Scholars have considered her beauty sufficient explanation, but Munch was drawn to Eva before ever setting eyes on her, based solely on Jappe Nilssen's letter. And she was hardly the only attractive, gifted woman in Kristiania, Paris, or Berlin. If Mudocci was indeed "one of thousands" who appealed to Munch, as he wrote to Delius, why did he pursue her with such deliberation and persistence?

It is, of course, possible that he was fascinated by the prospect of romancing a widely admired violinist, but Munch was never a keen concert-goer. He appreciated music less for the artistry of performance or brilliance of construction than for its purely vibrational qualities and the colors he associated with various kinds of sound. Mudocci recalled that "he was fond of good music, but I do not think he had special skills or interests in that direction." Nevertheless, she added, he "often came to our concerts."

Or perhaps, as some biographers say, Mudocci appealed to Munch because she was unthreatening. Her attachment to Bella and her dedication to her own work would have been reassuring, they reason, given Munch's resolve to avoid the pleas for marriage that had proved so corrosive in his relationship with Tulla Larsen. Munch did indeed fear that commitment to a woman could sap his creative energies, and Mudocci, over time, proved to be as allergic to conventional family life as Munch. But for a man hoping to avoid distraction, Eva Mudocci was hardly a safe choice. If Munch succeeded in coming between Eva and Bella, feelings could be expected to run high. And Munch was hardly resolved about his own affair with Tulla Larsen. The contemplated liaison with Mudocci would create not one, but two anguished triangles that could easily shatter whatever peace of mind Munch could manage.

Still, Munch was not deterred. Why Mudocci? Looking at all the evidence, it is hard to escape the conclusion that Munch pursued her not despite the fact that she was presumed to be a lesbian, but—at least in part—because of it. Her relationship with Bella did not discourage Edvard. It stirred him.

It might be presumptuous to conclude that Munch imagined insinuating himself into a lesbian relationship if not for the fact that he recorded such fantasies in his journal. Munch's entries often combined reminiscence and invention, without distinguishing between them. In one extended fantasy excerpted here from Munch's

1908 notebook, he imagined a large dinner party and placed the narrator—an alter-ego named Brandt who appeared frequently in the journals—between two women:

> Brandt was aroused by the Champagne and more Wine was
> brought in—
> —Come let us go upstairs says Miss L—
> —They were in the Ladies' Dressing Room
> —Isn't Madame H graceful—says Miss L—You can bet she
> has a pretty Chemise—
> —Would you like to see—Come, take off your Bodice— says
> Miss L.—and she unbuttoned the little plump Madame—
> —the plump naked Arm appeared—and the golden
> Breast lay there hidden in the white
> Silk shift—

As the erotic adventure continues, Munch's intoxicated alter-ego finds himself on a sofa, wedged between the two women. He kisses first one, then the other.

In Munch's paintings, the appeal of this kind of entanglement is evident. As in his journal entry, Munch inserted himself into intimate scenes when he painted pairs of women in bedroom settings. He took up this theme early in his career, returning to it in 1902-04, when he first became aware of, and then acquainted with, Eva Mudocci and Bella Edwards, and again in 1917-19. There are numerous such canvases. Biographers have tended to overlook these paintings, to characterize the subjects as sisterly, or to view them as puzzling aberrations; one insists that lesbian subject matter was "hardly relevant to Munch." His journal entries and his premeditated pursuit of Eva Mudocci suggest otherwise.

To be sure, an artist did not need to have his own, personal romantic triangle to explore the theme of intimacy between women. There were many two-dimensional models to draw upon. Gustave Courbet, Edgar Degas, Henri de Toulouse-Lautrec, and Pierre-

Left: Edvard Munch, *Two Nudes*, c. 1903, oil on canvas, 43-3/8 x 63-3/8 in. (110 x 161 cm). NATIONAL GALLERY, OSLO. *Right:* Edvard Munch, *Two Nudes Standing by a Chest of Drawers*, 1902-03, oil on canvas, 33-2/3 x 27-1/3 in. (85.5 x 69.5 cm). WESTPHALIAN STATE MUSEUM OF ART AND CULTURAL HISTORY, MÜNSTER

Auguste Renoir were among the many artists depicting lesbian themes, sometimes as serious works of art (as in the case of Courbet's *Sleepers*), but more often as popular erotica. In rejecting the mores of their parents' generation, many Europeans who came of age at the nineteenth century's end developed an intense curiosity about unconventional relationships. Well aware of increasing demand, publishers accommodated with a great variety of offerings. The tourist industry also responded. Visitors to Paris could rely on popular guides to point them in the direction of lesbian and gay haunts, and to let them in on prevailing codes (for example, advising close attention to the breed of pet dog perched on a lady's lap).

At the same time, bohemian Europe was devouring the works of a new generation of researchers and scholars who were writing about homoerotic relationships and speculating about the impact of political and social emancipation on women's choice of intimate partners. Recently published works by Sigmund Freud, Richard Krafft-Ebing, and Havelock Ellis were read and discussed. Munch's library did not contain books by those authors, though he was no doubt familiar with their theories. He did, however, own a copy of *Sex and Character*, a book published by Otto Weininger in 1903 and recommended to Munch by playwright August Strindberg.

Weininger, a gay man and a Jew who converted to Christianity, took despicable positions with respect to women and Jews; at the same time, he wrote more nuanced accounts of homosexuality. In an era when most sexologists treated gay men and lesbians as pitiable "inverts," Weininger asserted that humans are naturally bisexual, with traits associated with both genders. He viewed homosexuals as having a greater proportion of traits associated with the opposite sex than heterosexuals. He saw genius as, simply, "perfectly developed, universally conscious maleness." Weininger wrote, "A woman's demand for emancipation and her qualification for it are in direct proportion to the amount of maleness in her." He believed that those few women capable of genius were necessarily more masculine, and therefore more likely to be drawn to other women. These were ideas that Gertrude Stein, for one, found praiseworthy.

Late in October 1903, soon after the book's publication, Weininger committed suicide, at age twenty-three, by shooting himself through the heart. His book became an instant sensation among Europe's German-reading intelligentsia. In mid-1904, soon after Munch's "not normal" charge caused a rift with Eva Mudocci, he was reading Weininger. Munch's friend Johan Roede recalled seeing *Sex and Character* on a table at Munch's beach house in Åsgårdstrand that summer. What caught the friend's attention was the object Munch was using as a bookmark as he read about varieties of sexuality—his revolver.

Always obliging, Frederick Delius made sure to carry out Munch's request—"give my regards to Fräulein Mudocci"—though he had not seen Eva and Bella for some time. He visited with them at least twice in 1905. During one autumn visit, they played one of his pieces for him. "It was stressful for us because it was very boring," Eva recalled, "but we had to act as if we liked it." She preferred, among contemporaries, the impressionist composer Claude Debussy, whose evocative, sensual works spoke to her more directly. Eva nevertheless enjoyed Delius's company and valued his close relationship with Edvard Munch. She admired his wife, painter Jelka Rosen, and considered her wise. The couple were in close touch with Munch during this period, and in 1905 may have helped to reconnect him with Eva.

In time, Eva reached out to Edvard. In the fall of 1905, she wrote from Paris, "As you don't write, I'm not sure you've received [my letter]. It would have been good to know that you are still my friend, that you don't believe lies about me, just as I don't believe any ill of you. Please do write, I consider you my friend, write to me please." Judging by the letter's content, the rumors she was eager to refute related to her social contacts with Tulla Larsen's circle. She received no reply.

She made another try a few weeks after her thirty-second birthday. Childlessness was much on her mind. Her preoccupation with parenthood may have been prompted by her birthday or perhaps by the frequent presence in their home, at this time, of a friend's young son. The previous year, Oda Nielsen had written from Copenhagen asking Eva and Bella to look after her talented eighteen-year-old son Kay, who was coming to Paris to study art. Kay rented a room near their flat and, over the next several years, frequently took meals with them. They regarded him as a "foster son."

Whatever the cause of her regrets, Eva did not conceal them from Edvard:

> It is a long time since we have corresponded, and I have longed and longed for a letter from you—With each year, a childless person has less pleasure in life; people who have children see in their children the return of their own lost hopes—they have joy enough—but those who are on their own, who little by little must abandon dying hopes and dreams and powers, do

not easily relinquish all they have once held dear—you once took pleasure from my letters and I from yours—write to me one more time, I'd love to know something of you—to again read at least a word from you.

Her mood was bleak. She and Bella had called off their 1905 Scandinavian tour. Eva was not well, and doctors had cautioned her not to perform for six months. She wrote to Edvard that she had been diagnosed with "heart disease." Judging by Eva's own description of her state, the ailment may actually have been a nervous condition.

Edvard, in the meantime, continued to drink heavily and remained preoccupied with Tulla Larsen and her allies. Late in the fall, he finally wrote back asking Eva whether she had been socializing with the "enemy camp." On December 4, she replied that she had indeed ventured into the Norwegian colony, but emerged unscathed and had heard nothing malicious about Munch. "I do not think anyone would dare speak ill of you to me—at least not twice," she wrote. Eva told Edvard that during the year that they were out of touch, she had been thinking a great deal about him. "I've made a long study—do you know what of—mostly you—you—you—your work—your art—your self—everything I did not understand has become so clear now—your picture & your photograph hang on the wall & every time I look at them I tell myself—I understand—I understand and with this understanding I'm growing too."

At the same time, she let him know that Bella was never far from her thoughts. "[B]ut Bella plays—beautiful, fantastic music, even as I write—& it runs through my thoughts." Eva then turned abruptly to another subject, responding to a question Munch had apparently asked: "Am I engaged!—no—to whom would I get engaged?"

Eva and Bella spent Christmas 1905 in Frederiksberg with Bella's sister and brother-in-law. They had plans to resume performing, and had scheduled a concert in Copenhagen for the second week of January. Munch, meanwhile, was in Germany's northern woods in Thuringia, seeking relief from his own ailments. He wrote to his aunt that he wanted to test the effect "of country air on my nerves."

Once their concert was over, Eva and Bella would be returning to Paris. Each of them had taken on private students and had lessons scheduled, but they could spare a few days. The return trip would take them through Germany, and Eva proposed a detour to visit Edvard. On December 24, she wrote to him, "I want to see you! Bella wants to come, I just do not know yet how it can be made possible." She added that Bella wanted to stop to see friends in the northern German town of Rostock. "I'm going to see how far it is from Rostock to Elgersburg—but arrange it I will," she promised. As in the plaintive "dying hopes" letter written two months earlier, she sounded more like a woman in her waning years than one with nearly half a century yet to live:

—[T]he years pass by so fast & life is all so meaningless if one cannot here & there make a beautiful moment happen for oneself—in the end, with the last thoughts, only some wonderful memories—like jewels that one has worn secretly and sees again with life's last glance—yes—I see you smile at me like you always do when I go too high up in the clouds, but think of it—to sit together once again & chat like old, old friends—& we are truly old friends now!

She signed off, sending greetings from Bella.

When Edvard did not answer immediately, Eva shot off another letter, saying, "I only hope you're not sick!" She asked where he was spending Christmas. Munch would have understood that "sick" meant, in effect, "the worse for drink." (The previous year, she had written to him, "Are you really sick? Or just hung over?") Eva got half of the story right. Munch, drinking heavily, spent Christmas Eve 1905 in a brothel.

Over the next two weeks, Eva sent Edvard a half-dozen letters, and a number of telegrams as well, announcing plans and then abruptly changing them. Her initial plan was to leave Copenhagen on Saturday, January 13, the day after the concert, and arrive in Elgersburg the next day: "Please reserve a small room for two days." But the departure kept getting pushed back. Eva wrote apologetically that she would not arrive until Monday, and then Monday became Tuesday. "I'll explain why later," she wrote, "but I want to see you—if you are not so impatient now that you do not want to see me! No, you are not—I will come even if it is just for one day." Fearing that her letter had not arrived in time and that Munch had already traveled to meet her, Eva dashed off another note, setting a new date. The plan was finally in place, but by this time, the visit was fraught. "You will understand that I myself have become so nervous about all of this—if only you will not be nervous—I am so anxious about making you nervous."

Finally, on Tuesday, January 16, Edvard met Eva's train in Elgersburg. The day was calm, unseasonably mild. He was agitated; she was unnerved, practically mute, unable to hold back tears. The encounter lasted just a few hours. It did not go well.

Boarding a train at Elgersburg, Mudocci parted from Munch, unsure when—or whether—they would meet again. On the long ride to Paris, she wrote to him, apologizing for weeping and blaming her tears on fatigue. Three days later she wrote again from Paris, sounding frantic: "I think about you all the time, I think you know what I mean when I say that I must make myself free, free to think only of you, all I can think of is you, whether we meet again or not, I live for you, I want to help you, do not be afraid!" She seemed to grow calmer as she wrote, managing to end on a more composed, reassuring note: "If this meeting was not successful, if perhaps I made you even more nervous, it would go differently another time.

It is strange that in your presence I become mute, something in my soul trembles before you, like something shaken before a storm. But I will work to overcome myself and to be strong so that I can help you."

The letters that went back and forth in the weeks that followed contained confessions, misunderstandings, recriminations. With nothing to lose, Mudocci was openhearted and full of regret. On February 6, she wrote:

In your first letter from E[lgersburg] you asked me if I was engaged and I answered no, which was and remains the truth. That of which I had told you was already long past. It was only for a very short time, not more than a few days, and I couldn't do it any longer because I didn't love and I felt it to be like a big horrible sin, what I had done. I broke it off, I just lack[ed] the courage to tell the man that it was over forever since I felt so bad about hurting him too much. That perhaps is the greatest sin, I don't know. But now I could do it because I felt it was the only right thing if I wanted to continue to write to you. Do you understand now?

The next part of the letter showed that motherhood was very much on Eva's mind and that, once again, she was not afraid to let Edvard know it. She wrote that she was born with two ideals, "the one was to be a great artist, the other was to meet a great artist before whom I could kneel down, love him and have a child with him so that our two natures could be perpetuated in one life stream." The letter suggests that Eva and Edvard had discussed the possibility of her conceiving a child, and that a misunderstanding had ensued. Eva referred here to her recuperation from her health crisis of the previous year:

I was also then very weak—nervous—you think I said that I couldn't conceive a child—I could never have said that—why would I have wanted to have said that?—it was only that I was afraid of the reality—I thought for the first time that if I should have a child I could die. Now that I am strong and healthy, it makes me regret so my own weakness from then, which spoiled everything.

Mudocci had reason to fear childbirth, which was far from safe at the turn of the twentieth century. But there may have been a more immediate source for her sudden realization "that if I should have a child I could die." Eva and Bella may well have heard the story of a young Danish woman named Birgitte Marie Andersen, who had died alone in Dresden a year earlier, a few days after giving birth to a son. The father of Birgitte's baby was their friend, the Danish writer Louis Levy, who was married to someone else.

As for Munch, it is hard to know how he got the impression that Eva was infertile. Perhaps he simply misconstrued something she said. Or perhaps he was influenced by the popular notion that lesbians and gay men were sterile—as Havelock Ellis had written in 1901, "by instinct and congenital diathesis non-procreative."

Finally, Mudocci returned to the subject of her sexual reticence and to the accusation that seems to have inspired an ill-fated affair with a man she did not love—a drastic attempt to prove to herself that she was indeed "normal":

> After you left Paris, I still could never free myself of the shyness—I couldn't answer your letters one single time the way I wanted to—often at the beginning I felt sorry for you because I, out of complete shyness, wrote somewhat mockingly instead of [expressing] the passion of my whole soul which longed for you infinitely, and so things went on

and then came the time in Berlin where I became stupider and still stupider, and then afterwards I was haunted by what you'd said—that I was not normal—and because I wanted to know, I did what I told you about—and now that everything is over, you wonder why I am writing all this and telling you all this. I am writing it because I want to be free of it—never think about it again   I have the feeling that having once said it, I would be free of it, calm, cool, and contented, better able to be a friend who could really be a help to you—just remain my friend—you must do that—write—let us meet—as friends.

Eva's anguished February 1906 letter to Munch ended on a surprisingly pedestrian note—given her conviction that "everything is over." In Paris, she had met the American writer Vance Thompson and had spent an evening speaking with him about Munch. Nearly a decade earlier, Thompson's magazine, *M'lle New York*, had introduced Munch for the first time to American readers in a brief, provocative article that offered a compact account of the painter's work: "at once spermatozoidal and spiritual." Eva wrote that she found Thompson to be intelligent and believed he could popularize Edvard's work in America.

Here the letters between Eva and Edvard become sparse. In 1906, each was agitated to the point of illness. Munch, drunk much of the time, moved restlessly from one mountain spa to the next in search of composure. Despite his woeful condition, he found admirers in Weimar and was offered a number of commissions.

Mudocci, meanwhile, struggled to regain her balance. In mid-1906, she suffered another collapse. She wrote to Edvard in July that she hoped to see him in Weimar, since she and Bella would not be coming to Norway in the autumn as she had hoped. She described a relapse of the "heart disease" that had kept her off the concert stage in late 1905; now she again needed rest and only wished, "like you, to have complete peace of mind."

Peace of mind, for Eva, meant being once again anchored in her relationship with Bella and negotiating a truce between Bella and Edvard. She wrote to Edvard: "& Bella—she's so good to me & she would so like to see you too—she loves and admires you more and more because she now understands you better." There was no more talk of making herself free to be with Edvard. Instead, Eva imagined having a quiet visit with him somewhere, "like two old invalids" who offer each other "peace and tranquility."

Eva and Bella postponed their Scandinavian tour until the fall of 1907, when they did indeed have a quiet visit with Edvard Munch at his beach house in Åsgårdstrand. Afterwards, Eva wrote from Copenhagen that she was very happy to receive Edvard's picture of "the little house." She added, "I only wish we could have a picture of the garden below & the lovely small beach—how beautifully you captured it—so quiet and peaceful and filled with ever new colors for your painter's eyes. I'm glad that I've seen it." In another follow-up letter, written in what she called "Scandinavian," Eva said how much she had enjoyed the "amusing little food," and regretted that Edvard had taken ill. She was hoping to hear that he had recovered and would come from Åsgårdstrand to Kristiania for her birthday on October 9. "I will have something delightful for you," she promised, "for my sick child who never need be afraid of me."

Edvard declined, saying that the Norwegian capital was filled with his enemies. Soon thereafter, he left for Germany. He remained there through early 1908, working, drinking, and continuing his downward spiral. Eva and Bella, meanwhile, returned to Paris, where Bella gave piano lessons and coached singers each afternoon until five. Eva had fewer students. They still lived at 11 rue Malbranche, but after hearing complaints about their incessant music-making, they rented, in addition, a rehearsal studio at nearby 139 boulevard

Saint-Michel. While Bella met students at their studio, Eva now spent afternoons apart from her. By this time, they had developed a wide circle of friends and acquaintances, including many Americans and Scandinavians.

If Munch and Mudocci corresponded in 1908, their letters have gone missing. If they met during this period, they left no documentary footprints. But they certainly had opportunities to meet. In early March, Munch traveled to Paris in advance of the 1908 Indépendants exhibit. He checked into the Hotel du Sénat at the edge of the Luxembourg Gardens, a five-minute walk from Eva and Bella's studio.

Writing to Delius about Mudocci four years earlier, Munch had said, "But I always have feelings toward the enemy—Woman." In March 1908, soon before the exhibit opened, he wrote to his cousin with mock bravado that "the mighty commander appeared in Paris plumb in the middle of the Enemy camp. Of such stuff heroes are made." In a subsequent letter, the mighty commander promised to report later on "the battles at the Pantheon, Boulevard [Saint-] Michel, at [La Closerie des] Lilas, rue de Seine, and my fortress, Hotel du Sénat." This list is full of places associated with Mudocci, but there are no letters indicating that Eva and Edvard met during this stay.

By March 9, Munch was back in his studio in Warnemünde, Germany. The exhibit in Paris was set to open on March 20. He wrote to Delius, "Dear friend, I was in Paris for a few days and would have liked to visit you but had to get away again after a short time." He added, "I shall probably make another little trip soon."

6

Two Clinics

For a virtuoso, keeping time is second nature. The downbeats punctuate your breathing. You know where you are. An amateur may lose count, but not Eva Mudocci. In 1908, Mudocci fell behind. Two days late. Five. Eleven. It was spring, the season she had come to love best, when the horse-chestnuts bloom along the Seine and the treble tones of children's play in the Luxembourg Gardens start their annual crescendo.

It was during the same season of anticipation, five years earlier, that Edvard Munch first met the British violinist. Munch thought Eva "wonderfully beautiful," as he later wrote to Frederick Delius. Eva and Edvard had seen each other often in April 1903, sometimes with Bella, sometimes alone. In the intervening years, they had lived in different countries, meeting periodically for a day or two. The city grated on Munch's nerves, he told her. "As much as I would like to see Paris again," he once replied when Eva suggested a visit, "I can't—I have to stay here [in Thuringia]." He added, "I think often of the chestnuts in Paris."

As the days passed, Eva may have counted alone, or perhaps Bella was keeping time with her. Did they draw out their daily practice to modulate the suspense, or quit early to find distraction in cafés or shops? Once the pregnancy was confirmed, were there tears? Quarrels? Did they plan? Did they pack their bags, quietly talking over whether this dress or that coat might be altered to suit the circumstances? Did they consult bankbooks? Write to Eva's mother?

Staying on in Paris was unthinkable. Once Mudocci's situation became visible, there would be no way forward. Female performers who married—and certainly those who had children—were expected to retire. Camilla Urso, a violinist who came into prominence in the late nineteenth century, warned female colleagues that children were incompatible with a career. Mudocci would have known of such violinists as Leonora Jackson and Teresa Milanollo who left the concert stage to marry. Front-page headlines had reported the fate of American virtuoso Arma Senkrah, who abandoned her brief, extraordinary violin career at the insistence of the man she married, gave birth to a son in 1895, then five years later shot herself when her husband took up with another woman. There were isolated exceptions: women like violinist Wilma Norman-Neruda and pianist Clara Schumann had the wealth and stamina to combine marriage, children, and career. But in the classical music world, a performer who gave birth outside of marriage and lacked independent means could expect barriers to a career to be too high to scale.

There were, to be sure, some women musicians in the twentieth century's early decades who did not marry but drew support from longtime female companions. Nadia Boulanger leaned on Annette Dieudonné; Ethel Leginska had Lucille Oliver. Eva had come to rely on Bella Edwards's good sense and high spirits. Although born in Denmark to British parents, Bella loved, above all places on earth, the Left Bank of Paris. Leaving her adopted city and her friends and students, and interrupting her performance career, would have been heartbreaking under any circumstances; doing so because Eva was pregnant must have been especially galling.

There would have come a time when delay was perilous. By summer, when the pregnancy would have become apparent, capacious shawls or bulky coats would only have drawn attention. *Before*, with its familiar assumptions and priorities, had given way to an unknowable *after*. It was as if Eva and Bella had turned the page of an unfamiliar score and found the next bars missing. They would have to improvise.

In 1908, abortion was illegal in Paris, but widely available. Since the introduction of the curette some twenty years earlier, abortions had become commonplace, causing French policymakers to sound alarms about the country's unnaturally slow population growth. Terminating a pregnancy presented risks, of course, but the death rate from abortions was not much higher than that associated with childbirth.

Some women of Mudocci's class and artistic inclinations, especially those who advocated free love and women's rights, chose this route. Mudocci did not. It may not have occurred to her. She had an independent streak, and she lived in a way that led others to speculate about her sexuality, but she did not think of herself as part of Europe's feminist avant-garde. For Eva, aesthetic commitments carried more weight than social movements. She saw herself first and foremost as an artist with classical training and romanticist instincts; a violinist who had internalized the sensibilities of her grandfather's generation; an émigrée from a musical realm whose native language was Mendelssohn. She was more drawn, throughout her life, to spiritual than to political ideals, and the notion of sustaining the life force held strong appeal.

Terminating the pregnancy was not a possibility, but an alternative path was not clear. As a thirty-something, spiritually inclined, unmarried expectant mother with a public image to protect,

Eva Mudocci had no one to emulate, no one to learn from, no one, that is, except perhaps the American dancer Isadora Duncan.

Duncan had settled in Europe, founding a dance school in Berlin. Not only her organic, modern dance idiom, but also her edgy aesthetic and daring costumes, made her one of the twentieth century's first international celebrities, and the girls in her school became known as the Isadorables. Eva and Bella had seen an early Duncan performance in Berlin, and in the years that followed became friendly with Raymond Duncan, Isadora's brother, and Gordon Craig, the theatrical director and set designer who fathered Isadora's daughter. In 1908, Eva and Bella had not yet met Isadora herself (that meeting would come later), but they would have heard her story—and it was a cautionary tale.

When she became pregnant in 1906, the dancer quickly found that even those who admired her bohemian image distanced themselves. As she wrote in her autobiography, the wealthy patrons of her dance school sent her a long letter, "couched in majestic terms of reproach," saying they could not support a woman of such loose morals. Duncan saw that "the creed of these ladies was that anything is right if you don't talk about it!" She took the lesson to heart, going into seclusion in a Dutch seaside town and shutting her door to nearly all visitors. "I grew to dread any society," she wrote of this period. "People said such banalities. How little is appreciated the sanctity of the pregnant mother." When her daughter Deirdre was born, she took her back to Berlin but did not claim her publicly as her own. Deirdre was eventually introduced as the school's new enrollee, the littlest Isadorable.

Like Isadora Duncan, Mudocci relied on the largesse of patrons whose salons and *heures de musique* were the settings of many performances. And like Duncan, she concluded that a woman survives unwed motherhood by not talking about it—ever. She would not have to relinquish rights to her children, nor would she be able to claim them as her own. She understood that acknowledging a child would make her a pariah in polite society; on the concert circuit, she would be, quite simply, finished.

That was unthinkable. Since early childhood, Eva had devoted herself to music. In a tumultuous life, practice was the constant. Protecting her career meant preserving her image—and that image was all about ethereal beauty. With her slender figure and thick tresses, Eva embodied the pre-Raphaelite looks that were in vogue during the Belle Époque. She conveyed to fans and friends alike not only intelligence and determination, but also spiritual longing and fragility. Mudocci may have idealized motherhood, but public pregnancy did not figure in the image she wanted to project.

As for Isadora Duncan, she did eventually acknowledge her small daughter, as well as a son born two years later—but only after they died tragically in a freakish car accident in 1913. *The New York Times* carried the story on page one:

> PARIS, April 19.—A pathetic tragedy, which has cast gloom over all classes in Paris, took place in the suburb of Neuilly-sur-Seine this afternoon, when the two beautiful children of Isadora Duncan, the American dancer, were, with their Scottish governess, carried by an automobile, running wild, into the Seine River and drowned.

The public was willing to embrace an unwed mother once her children had been taken from her and she was considered duly punished.

By the summer of 1908, Mudocci needed to leave Paris. Where to hide was the immediate question. She was reluctant to return to England. Bella's homeland made the most sense, not only because it was familiar, but also because Denmark was gaining a reputation for progressive childbirth practices. But Copenhagen, where they had so many acquaintances, was out of the question. The Danish coastal town of Nykøbing, on the island of Falster, seemed a perfect spot for concealment. One could avoid meeting acquaintances en route by taking a train to Warnemünde, a port town on Germany's northern coast, then crossing to Nykøbing on the ferry.

Nykøbing had been established in the Middle Ages expressly to fend off intruders. In the twelfth century, ramparts were built on the headlands along Guldborg Sound, a narrow waterway that cut deeply into the land from the Baltic Sea and offered natural protection from pirates or invaders. In time, the fortifications gave way to a medieval castle and then a town. Over several centuries, Nykøbing offered seclusion to Danish dowagers. Much later, during World War II, it gave shelter to many Jews until they could be ferried to safety in Sweden.

In 1908, Nykøbing was a town of fishermen, farmers, and shopkeepers that had only recently begun to grow as the islands of Falster and nearby Lolland absorbed workers for new factories that processed sugar beets. When Mudocci arrived, sensible, modern buildings with red tiled roofs were springing up in and around the tangle of narrow, cobblestone streets that defined the market district, alongside thatch-roof cottages and ancient half-timbered houses. In the warm months, deep awnings shaded the shop windows that lined the streets. On Sunday afternoons, a dozen local men in top hats played brass instruments on an open-air bandstand.

The town had a handsome church, several respectable hotels, and a reassuring, three-story brick clinic staffed by nuns who made their home on the top floor. The clinic's ground floor now houses Thor's Bingo and Game Parlor; above is a large, private apartment occupied since the 1950s by a gracious woman named Mrs. Pederson. She recalled that when she and her husband moved in, the kitchen pantry held large white metal pans left behind by the nuns. When the Pedersons stripped off the wallpaper in their front room, which had served as the clinic's waiting area, they found dark, greasy stains left by the leaning heads of family members who spent anxious hours in the chairs that lined the room.

In Nykøbing, Mudocci improved her Danish and no doubt practiced her violin, but it was a backwater town, and living there would have been a disorienting if not dismal prospect for someone attuned to Europe's great capitals. And Danes were not free of bias about unwed mothers. The simple mention of such women was so distasteful that in 1905, the founders of the Danish Organization to Aid Mothers in Unfortunate Circumstances had to settle on that euphemistic name.

In August 1908, Edvard Munch boarded a steamer in Warnemünde. He had spent the spring and summer in the seaside resort town, painting virile bathers on its nude beach, capturing street scenes from unexpected vantage points, and conveying desolation and helplessness in a canvas he called *Drowned Boy*. As autumn approached, he packed his bags, telling a friend that he had grown tired of Warnemünde's bourgeois self-satisfaction.

He booked passage on the *Prince Christian*, a modern train-ferry that in a matter of hours crossed the Baltic to the Gjedser port on the southern tip of the Danish island of Falster. There, train cars were rolled from the boat deck onto tracks that led to the station at Nykøbing, some ten miles away. In late summer, the boat would have been met by multitudes of birds. Tens of thousands of common scoters and migratory geese passed the port each day, often in great flocks that darkened the sky. Always prone to fantasies of persecution, and never more powerfully than in mid-1908, Munch would have been especially alert to the birds of prey—low-flying red kites and rough-legged buzzards—that prowled the short stretch of coastline between the port and the pink-streaked rocky moraine at Denmark's southernmost point. Munch later wrote that on the trip from the port, a menacing bird-man, winged and cloaked, with the eyes of a falcon, had swooped into the train car.

Munch was forty-five years old. The last decade had produced a powerful body of work. He had made a series of recent sales that markedly improved his finances, and he had begun to secure his reputation—not only in Germany, where his genius had been acknowledged for some time, but also in Norway, where his radical commitment to depicting inner turbulence had met frequent resistance. At this point in his life, Munch might have been gathering his energies for an intense stretch of painting in Berlin, where he often wintered. Instead, he was falling apart.

The train passed through Nykøbing, where Eva Mudocci was spending her confinement, but it is not known whether Munch got off there. By the end of August he was in Copenhagen. It was a disorienting, frigid fall. Not long after his arrival in Denmark, the temperature dropped nearly to the freezing point, as if some malevolent force had sucked up all the warmth. The fifth was the coldest September day in Denmark's recorded history. Munch wandered around Copenhagen and nearby towns, drinking, brawling with strangers, imagining or provoking hostility from every direction. Restless, he remained on the move throughout September.

He complained of numbness in his hands and legs. The gloom and anxiety were not new, nor were the binges, but up to this point, Munch had always managed to focus on work and to approximate respectability. Unlike some bohemian friends, he had dressed with care even when his pockets were empty. A contemporary described him as "a striking beauty in rags buttoned up to the chin, with the air of a nobleman." Now, as he stumbled into a polite restaurant, he was taken for a vagabond and turned away. His purchase on reality was slipping. In desperation, he summoned his longtime friend Emanuel Goldstein and asked for a revolver. Goldstein promised to find him a doctor.

On Saturday, the third of October, Munch checked himself into a Danish *nerveklinik* run by Daniel Jacobson, a clinician and professor of neurology. If the place had been more forbidding, Munch might have bolted, as he had from the consulting rooms of other physicians. But this was a small, private establishment

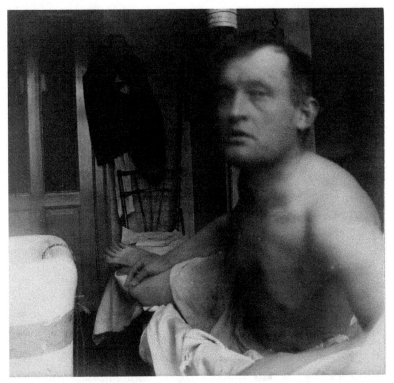

Edvard Munch, "Self-Portrait 'à la Marat,' beside a Bathtub at Dr. Jacobson's Clinic," 1908-09. MUNCH MUSEUM, OSLO

operating unobtrusively in a residential area of Frederiksberg. The clinic occupied a four-story brick row house that had been built a decade earlier, and was set back from the street, with shallow gardens in front and back. An ordinary front door led to a pleasant, square foyer and an unremarkable staircase, as in a private house. The walls were white, everything was white, too white for Munch's liking, but etched windows on the landings softened the light. Professor Jacobson's demeanor was soothing.

Jacobson diagnosed Munch as suffering from "dementia paralytica" associated with alcoholism, and prescribed a regimen of sleep, massage, and prolonged treatment baths containing pine needles and a variety of odd ingredients. "Electrification"—mild currents run through the body using a specially designed generator—was administered. Sunbaths in the leafy rear garden were prescribed.

Bed rest was basic to Professor Jacobson's approach. Through Munch's early days in the *nerveklinik*, he was given sleeping drops, probably chloral. He slept virtually round the clock, his long body framed by a white iron bed, a nurse in a starched apron looking on. As winter approached, he stayed awake more of the time, but was ordered to remain horizontal. In a letter to a friend in late 1908, Munch wrote that in the clinic, at any given time, "up to fifteen people, ladies and gentlemen, are lying in bed."

"I have proposed to the Professor," he added, "that this lying be utilized by placing half a dozen eggs in each bed to get chicks hatched." This fantasy played out vividly in his mind. "It would be noisy," he wrote.

For Mudocci, waiting for little ones to be "hatched" was no fantasy. In late 1908, as Edvard Munch imagined himself in a surreal lying-in establishment, thirty-six-year-old Eva Mudocci was seventy miles to the south, coping with her own confinement.

Mudocci surely knew of Munch's hospitalization. Bella's sister would have passed along the news. Professor Jacobson's clinic was less than a ten-minute walk from the large apartment house at 44 Frederiksberg Alle where she and her husband lived, and where Eva and Bella often stayed when visiting Copenhagen. And in any case, both Danish and Norwegian newspapers were reporting Munch's confinement. His allies' efforts at spin—their assurances that Norway's "most handsome man" remained vital—did not fool the press, nor did their allusions to fatigue and vague physical ailments. The day after Munch checked into the clinic, the Norwegian daily *Aftenbladet* reported the event, noting that it had been apparent for some time that the painter "was heading for a nervous breakdown."

A more intriguing question is what Munch knew of

Mudocci's situation. The massive archives in the Munch Museum offer no evidence that he knew of her pregnancy, and the known correspondence between Mudocci and Munch, begun in 1903, has a troubling gap from mid-1907 until late 1909.

Biographers do not wonder why Munch traveled to Denmark in August 1908; they explain that he sought to escape from imagined enemies lurking in Germany. Munch himself found it more difficult to explain what drove him across the Baltic, acknowledging that he had just as many enemies in Denmark. Did Mudocci figure in his thinking? In August, Eva was midway through her pregnancy and was no doubt already in seclusion in Nykøbing. Was it mere coincidence that Munch passed through Nykøbing at that time, or that some of his most vivid hallucinations were recollected from that train ride? Had she revealed her situation to him? Did Munch stop to see her when the train from the port paused in the town?

Did Mudocci's pregnancy contribute to Munch's breakdown? Munch was fascinated by procreation and incorporated images of spermatozoa and embryos into some of his most celebrated paintings and prints. He was said to see transcendent hope in this imagery, and to find cosmic significance in the procreative act and the birth process. The journal he kept at Professor Jacobson's clinic shows that these themes were very much on his mind in late 1908, but the journal was no less articulate about the impossibility of fatherhood for a man afflicted with what he considered to be a hereditary nervous disease. Whether or not he was the father, news of Mudocci's pregnancy could have unleashed a flood of emotion, ranging from awe to devastation. Perhaps he was the limp, drowned boy in the painting he had completed shortly before traveling to Denmark.

Munch's weeks of enforced bed rest drew to a close and the painter, still confined to the clinic, resumed work. Jacobson understood his need to draw, paint, take photographs, keep a journal, and write letters. Munch also managed arrangements for exhibits in multiple cities. Friends came to see him. He had been lonely in

Warnemünde. "I am puttering about on my own, which is enough to make anyone feel depressed," he had written to a correspondent. At the clinic, a regular routine and unavoidable companionship contributed to a growing sense of well-being.

On December 18, Munch wrote to his cousin Ludvig Ravensberg that he was beginning to go out into the world by himself and that, like a boy, he rejoiced at his freedom. But his plans for the future had not come together, and he was not yet ready to leave the Professor.

On the same day, Bella Edwards was equally uncertain about what the future held. She could not have been sanguine about the pregnancy, or the liaison that was its cause, but if she wanted a life with Eva, she had little choice. Like Eva, Bella had disappeared from the music scene in mid-1908, and it seems likely that she too spent the latter half of the year in Nykøbing. She was no doubt in the clinic's second-floor waiting room the next day, on December 19, 1908, when Eva Mudocci gave birth to twins.

Mudocci named the boy Edvard and the girl Isabella. For the rest of her life, she refused to name the father. According to Eva's granddaughter, it was Bella Edwards who disclosed, when the twins were grown, that their father was Edvard Munch.

The babies' names were entered into the two thick registries of the Nykøbing parish. The register for girls listed Isabella Estella Ellson Muddock; the register for boys—Edvard Ludvig Kay Ellson Muddock. The name Ellson, which the twins would later use as a surname, was associated with Eva's maternal grandmother. The names that Eva gave to her son included Edvard and Ludvig—the Germanic form of Louis. The choice of Ludvig may have honored violinist Ludwig Straus, or Danish writer Louis Levy, or Eva's cousin Lewis Hann, or her teacher and benefactor Carl (Charles Louis Eduard) Schneider, or perhaps all of them. The boy was to be called Kay (rhymes with "my"), perhaps in honor of Carl (Karl) Schneider. Kay was also the name of Oda Nielsen's son, the young artist of whom Eva and Bella were very fond. One more name appeared in the birth register, but was crossed out: Frank. Perhaps there was a momentary impulse to honor Bella's brother Frank Edwards or Eva's cousin Frank Hann.

The mother, "Evangeline Hope Muddock (Eva Mudocci)," was listed in both books as "unwed" and the births were recorded as "illegitimate." Unlike the other babies registered in the parish that month, Mudocci's twins were not baptized as newborns. By the time the babies were four months old, Eva and Bella were back in Paris. In late April, they performed together, and in early May, a solo appearance by Mudocci won praise from a reviewer who called her "the Botticellesque violinist, as delicious to look at as to hear." Eva was probably accustomed to lascivious winks in descriptions of her stage presence. Indeed, she may have been relieved by the reference to her slender figure. No one was to know that she had given birth just a few months earlier.

Munch, meanwhile, remained an in-patient at Professor Jacobson's clinic. Had he known about Eva's pregnancy? Was he informed of the twins' birth? A clue may be hidden in a series of graphics and accompanying text that he produced during his clinic stay, when Dr. Jacobson allowed him to spend time at the nearby zoo. One image in particular includes a face resembling Mudocci's and was captioned with this explanation at a 2013 Munch Musem exhibit:

Alpha and Omega: alternative Adam and Eve narrative. The story begins when the man, Alpha, and the woman, Omega, become a couple. As time passes Omega begins to have sexual relations with the animals on the island and in the end abandons the island riding on the back of the deer. In the meantime, her bastard children approach Alpha calling him father. When Omega returns, Alpha kills her in vengeance. Omega's children then slay him and take over the island.

This story and its illustrations have not been linked with Mudocci and her twins, but given the timeline, the possibility is intriguing.

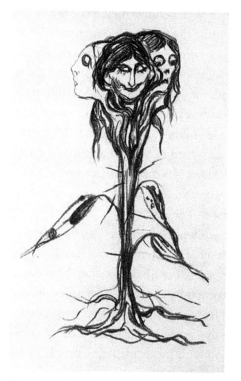

Edvard Munch, *Vignette: Amaryllis* from the *Alpha and Omega* series, 1908-09, lithograph on wove paper. Image: 11-3/4 x 7-3/8 in. (30 x 18.8 cm) THE ART INSTITUTE OF CHICAGO

When he left Jacobson's clinic in the spring of 1909, Munch settled in Kragerø, a seaport town on Norway's southern coast. That summer, Eva and Bella set out on another Scandinavian tour that included an August concert in Kragerø. They stopped by Munch's house for a visit. Two months later, Eva sent Edvard a breezy thank-you note, telling him how much they had enjoyed eating cherries and drinking wine in his garden. She said she hoped to be in Kragerø again the following year.

It is hard to imagine this seemingly casual get-together. Since their last meeting, all of their lives had changed drastically. Could Eva and Bella have sat, admiring the garden and sipping wine, without mentioning the babies, now seven months old? If so, how did they account for their whereabouts during the previous year?

In the same month that Munch received Eva's thank-you note, he received another—this one from his doctor. Professor Jacobson wrote to say how much he was enjoying Munch's parting gift—the "etching of Bella E. and Eva M." He added, "I never tire of looking at it."

The journals Munch kept in the clinic did not mention the two women by name, but the print he chose to present to his doctor, and Jacobson's familiar reference to "Bella E. and Eva M.," suggest that they loomed large in his thoughts and, most probably, in the conversations between patient and doctor that were central to Munch's recovery.

The twins' early years coincided with the frenetic cultural activity that preceded the First World War. Despite artistic experimentation, dresses were still long, as were the lists of social strictures that guided women's lives. Living openly as the unwed mother of twins would have exposed Mudocci to scorn. Eva and Bella could not simpy turn up in Paris with two infants.

For women musicians, supporting oneself was challenging; supporting a family would have been a daunting prospect. Performances produced some earnings, of course, but then as now, making ends meet as a soloist or chamber musician was immensely difficult—especially for women, who were disqualified from orchestra positions. Even a woman as successful as the American violinist Maud Powell, who was living in Europe, told a *Strad* interviewer that earning a living as a performer was "uphill work." The rewards were not large, she explained, once railway and hotel expenses and commissions to managers were paid. Powell added, "of course, when the musical season is over, one earns little or nothing."

Managers helped musicians secure concert dates, but typically expected performers to underwrite a variety of expenses, such as advertising and printing costs for tickets and programs. All but a handful of celebrated virtuosos risked spending more than they earned. Performers like Mudocci and Edwards could add to their earnings by playing at receptions in the drawing rooms of wealthy patrons or by filling out programs of dramatic recitation or vocal performances. They each had students. Was that enough?

In the years before the First World War, Eva and Bella traveled across Europe frequently. They no doubt relied, to some extent, on Carl Schneider's bequest. When his will was executed in 1899, Eva's mother Lucy had inherited £15,000—a considerable sum. The bequest (not including the value of Linden Villa) was equivalent in buying power to about $1.5 million today. When Schneider died, Lucy Muddock could well afford to pay for Eva's tuition at the Hochschule and to help her launch her career. Ten years later, when the twins were born, there was, presumably, enough money left to help support them.

And yet Eva lived apart from her children. At least two powerful forces were at work. The first was Eva's abstract, elevated notion of procreation—as she had written to Munch in 1906, "two natures perpetuated in one life stream." That stream was apparently meant to burble along on its own. In her interactions with her children (and later, with her grandchildren), Eva's maternal instincts were not often in evidence.

The second force was at least as strong—the desire for respectability. Bringing the children to Paris was impossible if Eva and Bella were to continue attracting concert audiences or playing for polite Parisians at evening parties in the Faubourg. In Paris, as in other European capitals, the circumstances of one's birth were vastly important, and not only to the titled. Isadora Duncan had carried off a sleight of hand by introducing her illegitimate children as young pupils in her school. Eva had no such cover.

Paris was not their only option, of course. They could have lived in Loschwitz, which, as the summer retreat of the famed Russian teacher Leopold Auer, was attracting Europe's most gifted violinists, including young Jascha Heifetz. They could have stayed in Denmark, where they had a wide following and Bella's family close at hand. Or, they could have allowed the children to be adopted by a family in any of these places. They did none of these things. Instead, they resumed their lives in Paris. Eva spent summer holidays with the twins in Loschwitz or Brighton, returning to Paris as the days shortened and leaving the children in the care of others.

When Eva and Bella returned to Paris in 1909, they found a new flat at 37 avenue Denfert-Rochereau, close to La Closerie des Lilas. Socially, they picked up where they had left off before Eva's pregnancy. They moved in several circles, taking part in gatherings of Paris's Scandinavian colony; mixing with the city's growing crowd of lesbian writers and artists at the Montparnasse home of Gertrude Stein's close friend, American sculptor Janet Scudder; and entertaining music lovers from several countries, including the United States. In April 1910, Eva and Bella gave a concert in the home of the American Ambassador to France—an event that was covered in the *New York Times*.

SCANDINAVIAN MUSIC
IN
ANTIQUE PEASANT COSTUMES

For all engagements

apply to

James Campbell

15, Rue du Cherche-Midi

EVA MUDOCCI

BELLA EDVARDS

Promotional handbill. PRIVATE COLLECTION

Musically, Eva and Bella were in their prime, but they could not support themselves solely with tours and concerts, given all of the associated expenses. They continued to play at the receptions of wealthy Parisians and to take on private students. And like many performers, they found an angle. They appeared in antique peasant costumes, adding folk dances to their programs and in the process solidifying the notion that both women were Scandinavian. One American student remembered Eva as "a pleasant, wan Danish woman." Even longtime acquaintances Janet Scudder and Malvina Hoffman were was under this impression, referring to Eva and Bella in their memoirs as "Danish friends" and the "Great Danes."

Eva and Bella's "at-homes"—now held on Thursday evenings—combined music and dance with spiritualist activities. To one such gathering, held on June 7, 1910, Janet Scudder brought along Malvina Hoffman—a 25-year-old American who had come to Paris, accompanied by her mother, determined to make contact with the celebrated sculptor Auguste Rodin and convince him to take her on as a student. Over time, her own work earned Hoffman a reputation as the "American Rodin."

The daughter of a pianist, Hoffman had grown up listening to chamber music and was passionate and knowledgeable about music. Her travel journal reported on one of Eva and Bella's gatherings under the heading "An Evening of Spirits!!"

Act I
This appalling creature Mlle Mudocci plays with power and steady free bowing—a good tone and confidence— Her figure is grace personified, in the most unexpected exciting lines of repose or action. The pianist is a real artist & they gave me that strange angry sensation which half crazes me.
     I hear just this sort of music!
     Fire kindled in the heart of Hell. Ssh!

Act II
After Borodin's the Steppes by Mlle E[dwards] & Paganini's [W]aterfall by Eva M & splendid Norwegian dances by both, we call the spirits to our aid and concentrate on a remarkable séance of "Writings."
     "The peasants of Toscana are caring for her but you better go and find her—"
     We are indignant with our ghost and at 11:30 bid goodnight to two of the most unique & talented creatures that I have ever come across in my short life.

Malvina Hoffman would remain friends with these "unique & talented creatures" for decades.

     Eva and Bella continued to travel. In 1912, they visited London and once again toured Scandinavia. That year, they were invited to the Pink Palazzo in Venice, holiday home of sewing-machine heiress Winnaretta Singer, also known by the title and name she had acquired through marriage—La Princesse de Polignac. Singer's primary home was a Paris mansion where she presided over a prestigious musical salon, championing the work

Eva and Bella on the balcony of Linden Villa.
SHATTUCK FAMILY COLLECTION

of innovative composers Igor Stravinsky, Erik Satie, and others, commissioning new works, and entertaining such literary celebrities as Marcel Proust and Colette.

Singer was known to have female lovers. A fashion icon of her day, she defied popular stereotypes of lesbians. Virginia Woolf once wrote, "To look at Winnie Singer, you'd never think she had ravished half the virgins in Paris." At the Pink Palazzo, she famously entertained the most fascinating women of her day. Some accounts say that more than one husband stormed the Palazzo in pursuit of wayward wives. One is said to have shouted to the Princess from outside the Palazzo, "If you're half the man I think you are, you'll come out and fight me."

Late in 1913, Eva and Bella traveled to London, accompanying their friend Georg Brandes on his Shakespeare lecture tour. As

Brandes prepared for the tour, Mudocci had helped him with his English pronunciation. She had not performed in the country of her birth since her Rose Lynton days. On December 14, Eva and Bella gave a concert in posh Upper Phillimore Gardens, Kensington. An announcement noted that the afternoon concert by the Misses Mudocci and Edwards was "under the patronage of Dr. George (*sic*) Brandes, who has promised to be present."

There is little doubt that Eva's pregnancy and the birth of her children had provoked a crisis in her relationship with Bella, but they came through it and seemed to be closer than ever. In the years leading up to the First World War, the two women became inextricably linked in the minds of friends and acquaintances as well as audiences and critics. "Dearest Bella, Darling Eva," close friend Arthur Shattuck would begin his letters to them. The composer Christian Sinding referred to the pair playfully as "Beva and Ella." Over time, the musical duo of Mudocci and Edwards became known to the concert-going public in France and Scandinavia simply as "Eva & Bella." One well-known critic wrote: "It is a fact that one cannot imagine the one without the other. Music has made these two human beings into one."

Some represented the two women as sisterly. Artist Clement John Heaton portrayed them as Martha and Mary of Bethany, the sisters of Lazarus, in a stained-glass window destined for the Strasbourg Cathedral. He had convinced them to serve as models despite Eva's protestation that, as she wrote to Edvard Munch, "sitting eternally in a cathedral window" would be exceedingly boring.

In April 1913, Georg Brandes made available to an English-language wire service a profile about Eva and Bella—a puff piece that may have been his way of thanking Eva for English lessons. The article began, "There is a little home in Paris known to a good many Scandinavians, visited by many foreigners, especially Americans of both sexes, a home with a certain tinge of poetry." The article described them as "sisterly without being sisters"—a

Clement John Heaton, Stained-glass window, 1908, (dimensions unavailable). Eva and Bella were Heaton's models for the sisters of Lazarus. WEBER FAMILY COLLECTION

characterization that some readers of the day would have had no trouble decoding.

Brandes's profile offered some background on the two women, with several factual errors, and offered this startling description of Eva's heritage: "The blood of her German mother is so mixed, that it is impossible to determine her nationality, for of the grandparents of the mother, the one was a rabbi and the other descended, as an old family escutcheon shows, from the illegitimate love affair between an English King and a French lady."

For the second time in her career, Mudocci was identified in the press as Jewish. Brandes's account does not square with available genealogical evidence, but it does seem likely that the source was Mudocci herself. As she had during her first Scandinavian tour a decade earlier, Mudocci seemed to be allying herself with her Jewish friends and acquaintances. At about this time, according to her granddaughter, Eva was entering into an arrangement with writer Louis Levy to lend his surname to her son. That plan was soon abandoned, and the boy was thereafter known as Kay Ellson.

In their first years, the twins moved from one home to another. From the start, Eva's Danish doctor had taken a special interest in the twins he delivered in 1908. Photographs taken in their early years show them in Nykøbing with Dr. Lemvigh-Müller and his wife Alice, who had no children of their own and brought the twins to live in their large, ivy-covered corner house. In one photo, the twins are in the care of a nurse (possibly a fondly remembered nanny they called Didi). They were also looked after in Loschwitz by their grandmother, Lucy Muddock. When they were no longer babies, Lucy took them from Loschwitz to London, and a visit to Linden Villa suggests why. Pushing toddlers up and down the steep

A nurse holding the twins, 1909. Weber family collection

cobblestone path that led to the house would have been arduous in good weather, perilous in bad. Moreover, renovations were underway at Linden Villa to install central heating and hot water and expand the top floor.

British census records show that in April 1911, Lucy Mudock (*sic*) headed a London household consisting of her sister, Emily Hann, and two-year-old "Danish" twins who were listed as Edvard and Estelle Francke. Edvard was Kay's legal name, and Estelle was a variation of Estella, Isabella's middle name. Lucy may have avoided recording a name she associated with Bella. But where did the surname "Francke" come from? Why had Lucy discarded Muddock and Ellson—the two surnames that appear in the 1908 Nykøbing birth registers—in favor of one that had been crossed out in the boy's entry (Frank)? Perhaps she had in mind the composer, César Franck. What is certain is that Lucy Muddock, in her dealings with public officials, was eager to blur family history and was endlessly inventive.

In 1913, as the twins neared their fifth birthday, Lucy Muddock was approaching her seventieth. Eva needed to think about the future, and the children's education had to be considered. She took them to Denmark. The same parish registers that recorded their births show that on August 12, 1913, the twins were baptized in Nykøbing's Danish Church. Dr. Carl Lemvigh-Müller was listed as the godfather of Isabella Estella, but (for reasons that remain unknown) not of Edvard Ludvig Kay.

In the summer of 1914, the children were back in Loschwitz, vacationing with their mother. That is where they found themselves in August when war broke out.

Dr. Carl Johan Lemvigh-Müller with one of Mudocci's twins, 1909. WEBER FAMILY COLLECTION

Dr. Lemvigh-Müller with Isabella and Kay, c. 1913. WEBER FAMILY COLLECTION

7

Stranded

In the summer of 1914, Bella vacationed with friends in England while Eva spent time at Linden Villa with her mother, Aunt Emily, and the children. Eva and her family were in Loschwitz on the first of August, the day that Germany and Russia declared war on each other and France issued a general mobilization. Eva captured the events that followed in a volume of poetry called *For Them: Poems and Anecdotes of the War*, published in London a dozen years after armistice under the pseudonym Harry Brander—a name she took from family lore about her grandmother's one-time royal suitor.

In "How the News Came to Dresden," Mudocci recalled that the dreaded declaration of war came in the form of paper leaflets dropped from the post-house window to the crowd that had gathered in the square:

> Then a hand out-reaching—casting down
> Tatters from bands of the Death unchained—
> Fluttering, cursed white tokens rained
> To the clutching hands of Dresden town.

There was little time for deliberation. Within days, Britain would enter the war, and the residents of Linden Villa would become enemy aliens. The German borders would soon be closing. If they were going to leave, there was no time to lose.

When war broke out, there were some 18,000 British residents in Germany. By its end, many had been expelled, and more than 4,000 men had been interned, in part to retaliate against British internment of German civilians. On that August day, Eva and her family could not know how enemy aliens would be treated during the initial mobilization or beyond.

Nevertheless, Lucy Muddock, now age seventy-one, and her sister Emily, two years older, were determined to stay put. Less than a year had passed since they had completed major renovations on the house. If they abandoned Linden Villa in the midst of war, there was no telling what would happen to it. Over twenty years, they had developed warm relationships with the neighbors. They would not leave.

Eva panicked. Leaving her mother and aunt behind was unthinkable, but remaining in Germany would mean a long separation from Bella, and there were the five-year-old twins to consider. Mudocci's poem, "How the News Came to a Little Town on the Edge," repeats the refrain: "With the children, unknowing, asleep on the bed." It describes how she roused the children, dressed them, threw together their things, and joined the crowds of frightened people, both Germans and foreigners, who were rushing to Dresden's train stations. Eva planned to take the children to neutral Denmark, but arriving at the chaotic Stettiner Bahnhof in Berlin, she was not sure there would be any way to get there. In the end, they barely managed to leave Germany before the borders closed. Decades later, Eva recalled that she had set off from Loschwitz in such an anxious state that she left her documents behind. Before 1914, this would not have caused major difficulty; Europe's intelligentsia crossed borders frequently and easily, often without showing documents, and stayed as long as they pleased. But suddenly the world had changed. At the port in Warnemünde, Eva had to be rescued by a sympathetic fellow traveler who claimed her and the twins as his family.

In ideal circumstances, the trip from Loschwitz to Denmark by train and ferry would have taken some sixteen hours; in the confusion following the outbreak of war, it was more arduous. Eva reached Denmark in such a frantic state that she was admitted to a Copenhagen clinic. The children were left with Dr. Lemvigh-Müller and his wife.

Bella Edwards, in the meantime, spent the first weeks of the war on the Isle of Wight, off the English coast, at the home of music-loving friends F. Fleming Baxter, a British sculptor, and his American wife, Molly. She was desperate for news from Eva and her family. In the early chaotic days of the war, arranging passage to Denmark was a virtual impossibility.

As Eva rushed with the twins to the Dresden railway station and Bella anxiously followed the news from England, Edvard Munch was among the throng of Norwegians gathered outside the Kristiania offices of *Morgenbladet*, straining to read dispatches posted in the newspaper's window. The outbreak of war left him distraught and disoriented. His political sympathies lay with France, but for decades, the artists, patrons, dealers, and critics who best understood him had been Germans. His own countrymen continued to undervalue his work. The emerging generation of Norwegian artists, inspired by Henri Matisse, were filling galleries with paintings that Munch called "enlarged Christmas cards." It was the German expressionists associated with groups called Die Brücke and Der Blaue Reiter—artists who would later be called "degenerate" by the Nazis—who understood and extended Munch's efforts to give dimension and color to the complex life of the soul.

The surviving Munch-Mudocci correspondence includes no wartime letters, but Eva and Edvard may have met in Scandinavia in 1914 or early 1915. Based on conversations with Mudocci's daughter, art historian John Boulton Smith wrote, "She, her twin brother and their mother met Munch together somewhere around 1914-16, either in Copenhagen or Germany. Mrs. Weber claims that Munch later made a portrait from memory of her and her brother, but I have been unable to trace this." Such a portrait has not surfaced.

After initial delay, Bella sailed to Denmark. The Knupffer manuscript, drawing on Eva and Bella's written recollections, coyly hints that an extravagant romantic gesture inspired Bella to rush to Copenhagen at a moment when Eva could not be without her:

> Music was the best consolation for Bella [on the Isle of Wight], and often there were musical soirées at neighboring houses. When once, after playing at the home of a charming American, she was presented with a bouquet of roses, she found a lovely diamond ring hidden in a bloom. Anxious to join Eva and make plans for their future, she left for Copenhagen at the first opportunity.

This was a courageous decision, given that a sea voyage was the only possibility and German warships patrolled the waters between England and Denmark. Passengers had reason to fear mines. Nevertheless, in the anxious autumn of 1914, Eva and Bella reunited in Denmark, where they intently followed news of Germany's siege of Paris, France's staunch defense of the capital, and the immense losses suffered in the battles that kept the enemy at bay. They could have safely spent the war years in Denmark while performing for enthusiastic audiences, but for the two musicians, Scandinavia had become a place to tour. Paris was home, and within months, they were making plans to return.

They first made a detour to Norway, completing on its west coast what turned out to be their last Scandinavian tour. With the outbreak of war, questions about Mudocci's nationality became more pointed. When interviewers inquired about her origins, Eva could be slippery, as Christian Krohg discovered when he interviewed her before a concert in Norway. He reported the interview this way:

> "You're Italian," I said to Mudocci in French.
> "No, I'm not," she replied in Norwegian.
> "But your name is?"
> "No, it's just Italianized. It is Spanish actually. I was born in England, but have no wish to be English. I've spent just as long in Germany."
> "So you're German?"
> "No, I certainly don't want to be that! I'd prefer to be Scandinavian. Perhaps because Grieg and Ibsen are, or because my grandmother loved the exiled Gustav Vasa the Fourth of Sweden."
> "So you have royal blood in your veins?"
> "I didn't mean that."

Over the course of Mudocci's career, writers identified her birthplace as Denmark, Scotland, and Poland. In 1917, the journal *Musical America* identified her as an English and Italian violinist, then three years later called her a Spanish violinist. Eva did little to clear up the confusion.

In mid-February 1915, an article in the local Trondheim newspaper announced that the famous duo would be giving a concert there on the second of March, before bravely returning to France (via England) to play for wounded troops. In March 1915, Eva and Bella celebrated Bella's fiftieth birthday, then sailed from Bergen across the North Sea to Hull, England. It is hard to overstate the risks. The British Wilson Line that operated this route lost so many ships to torpedoes or capture in the early years of the war that in 1916 it was forced to sell out to another company. But Eva and Bella reached Hull safely. They joined grim British soldiers on a troop ship headed for Le Havre, then made their way by train to Paris.

Records in the Dresden City Archives show that Eva's mother and aunt spent the entire war in Loschwitz. Once war broke out, Linden Villa was considered a British holding. As an enemy alien, Lucy Muddock had to submit to administrative supervision of her property by a local court official and put up with frequent searches of the house.

The twins remained in Nykøbing with Carl and Alice Lemvigh-Müller. They loved the doctor who had become, in effect, their foster father, and called him "HmHm." It would be years before they would see their mother or grandmother again.

Arriving in Paris in the spring of 1915, Eva and Bella found their flat intact, but this was not the same city they had left the previous summer. Everywhere they looked, they saw young men on their way to the front and women dressed in black or blue, whether or not they had yet suffered a loss. "The gaiety of Paris is gone as if it never existed," their friend Arthur Shattuck wrote in his diary after a brief visit to Paris early in the war. "The theaters are all closed. There is no music in the restaurants. There are no concerts, no amusements of any kind, not even a moving picture show. Very few shops are open and little business is being done. Everywhere one turns it seems as if the word WAR was written in letters reaching to the very sky." As an American art critic wrote, New York City had suddenly become the world's cultural center because "Paris, London, Berlin and Petrograd had simply gone 'out of business' as far as the arts were concerned."

This Paris was a sadder, more solemn city than the one they had known. The front lines had moved north, away from the capital, but seemingly random bombardments unnerved Parisians. Many of Eva and Bella's old haunts were shuttered or deserted. Many of the musicians and artists they knew had gone elsewhere or were "with the colors" and heading for the front. There were exceptions—

including the thirty-year-old American sculptor Malvina Hoffman, who was at work on her monumental sculpture of the prima ballerina Anna Pavlova. Hoffman wrote that toward the end of 1915, Paris recovered some of its energy, but it was a nervous, palpitating energy. "Concerts, exhibits, benefits, stranded artists, troubles in every shape & form, crowd one upon the other—days pass, I meet old friends that look older." The friends who looked older included Eva and Bella. The pair did their best to adjust to the new realities, continuing to perform and socializing with the few friends who remained in Paris. Among the people who sought out Mudocci was Henri Matisse, painter and amateur violinist. They had an acquaintance in common—Norwegian painter Christian Krohg, who had spent years in Paris and arranged for his son to study in Matisse's atelier.

Matisse was three years younger than Mudocci, and like her, had moved to Paris in his twenties. At that time, Matisse was relatively unknown and was struggling to support a wife and three children. He had allied himself with a group of artists who sparked the fauve ("wild beast") movement that rejected the sentimental charm of impressionism and post-impressionism. The fauves painted with ferocious brush strokes and fierce colors. Public response was ambivalent, and recognition came to Matisse in fits and starts. At the 1904 and 1905 Salon d'Automne exhibits in Paris, his paintings and those of other fauve painters scandalized many viewers—including Mudocci and Edwards. Matisse managed to sell a painting, his first major sale, at the 1904 Salon d'Automne, but the following year, a painting that had taken months to complete was initially rejected.

"And now," wrote Matisse's friend Gertrude Stein in *The Autobiography of Alice B. Toklas*, "Matisse's serious troubles began, his daughter was very ill, he was in an agonizing mental struggle concerning his work, and he had lost all possibility of showing his pictures." He continued to paint, sculpt, draw, and, Stein added, "he played his violin."

Matisse's work ethic sustained him, and his reputation grew steadily in the decade that followed. Acceptance in his own country came gradually, but he had begun to establish a solid following abroad. By 1915, Matisse's international reputation was sealed with a one-man show at New York's Montross Gallery, prompting the American art critic Frederick James Gregg to write in *Vanity Fair*, "There has been more quarreling about Henri Matisse than about any other individualist of our epoch." He added, "But this solid artist, who looks more like a professor of biology than a painter, is quite undisturbed by such popular clamor."

Matisse was indeed demonstrating genius, but he was seldom "undisturbed." Friends knew him to be chronically nervous and frequently on edge. One acquaintance described him as "Matisse the anxious, the madly anxious!" And during periods of stress, as Gertrude Stein had observed, Matisse craved violin practice. He played long and hard, determined to improve, acutely aware of the time he had lost by dodging lessons in his youth. Some biographers say that in music he sought solace and mental balance. Others believe that he needed release from the physical and emotional rigors of painting. His wife said that he counted on the violin as a way to earn a living should his eyesight fail. Whatever the reason, draining bouts of obsessive practice seemed to come at times of distress or dislocation.

If Matisse was high strung in the early years of the century, he was—along with much of Europe—wound almost to the breaking point as the war colored virtually every aspect of daily life. As the news worsened and his country's plight seemed increasingly precarious, the painter dreamed of joining the war effort. A quarter century earlier, Matisse had joined the other youths of his town in signing up for compulsory military service, but had been rejected due to medical problems. Now, as a rheumatic forty-five-year old, he again tried to enlist, and again he was turned down.

And so, in the winter of 1915-16, Matisse was in Paris, hard at work in his longtime studio on quai Saint-Michel. He was struggling with the ideas of cubism, which intrigued him but could not satisfy his sensual impulses and ultimately left him cold. He was also deeply invested in the violin. He had bought an important instrument and hired an eminent Belgian violinist, Armand Parent, to teach him and his son Pierre, sometimes paying for lessons with artwork. During the war's darkest periods, he repeatedly painted scenes with violins or violin cases, including *Interior with Violin, Interior with Violin Case, The Moorish Screen, The Violinist,* and *Music Lesson.*

Matisse's preoccupation was personal; at the same time, it reflected a passion for violin playing that overtook Europe and the United States during the war years, when public cultural life was sharply curtailed. Sales of violins were brisk. The recording industry, still in its infancy, was making phonographs and records more widely available. Virtuosos Franz Kreisler and Eugène Ysaÿe were early recording stars, and by 1915, were as popular as the most admired singers. These great violinists became the rock stars of their day. Eva Mudocci never approached their prominence, but she and Bella Edwards were never in greater demand or more deeply appreciated by European audiences than in the anxious days of 1915-16.

Avid concertgoers, Matisse and his son were among those who saw the duo play. Pierre later commented that his father captured, in portraits of Mudocci, the dreamy, soul-searching look that was characteristic of the violinist when she performed. Mudocci would have been an especially welcome guest during this period. Matisse enjoyed spending time with violinists and playing duets. He and his son were studying the piece violinists call "The Double"—J. S. Bach's *Concerto in D minor for Two Violins.*

During the winter of 1915-16, Matisse created several portraits of Mudocci, including a series of action poses of the violinist (an etching and two drypoints) and three drawings. The drawings are now seen as masterpieces, sometimes grouped by art historians with his "grand experimental portraits of outsider women." They are large, bold portraits, executed in charcoal and graphite. The best known is a severe charcoal-and-graphite drawing that Mudocci thought hideous. It is valued by historians, in part, as evidence of the artist's brief foray into cubist territory. Matisse exhaustively reworked the portrait, and in the process, he captured two sides of Mudocci. If you look carefully, you can see a half-erased, spectral rendering of Eva's face that is more sensuous than the austere, foreground portrait, with curved eyelid, full lips, and suggestions of wavy hair.

The Morgan Library and Museum in New York City owns another of Matisse's portraits of Eva Mudocci. Reproductions fail to convey the portrait's size and power, and they obscure its sly allusion to a fellow artist. Matisse showed Mudocci dressed in a V-neck blouse; at the bottom of the "V" he drew the fanciful suggestion of a brooch. Its faint, playful lines contrast with the long, bold strokes used for the rest of the portrait. Here is Matisse tipping his hat to Edvard Munch.

There is nothing playful about a companion drawing that depicts Mudocci in a similar pose. Matisse used denser lines and darker shading to add weight and drama to the portrait, emphasizing Eva's long neck, broad mouth, and resolutely closed, wide-set eyes. Late in her life, Mudocci said that the shock and revulsion she experienced during the First World War had never left her. This portrait conveys the pall it cast, especially when set next to the portraits Munch had created a dozen years earlier.

Henri Matisse, *Eva Mudocci*, 1916, graphite on jointed paper mounted on canvas, 36-1/2 x 28 in. (92.7 x 71.1 cm). THE METROPOLITAN MUSEUM OF ART, NEW YORK, PIERRE AND MARIA-GAETANA MATISSE COLLECTION

Henri Matisse, *Eva Mudocci*, 1916, charcoal and graphite on wove paper, 14-3/4 x 11-1/16 in. (37.6 x 28.2 mm) *Below:* detail, Henri Matisse, *Eva.* MORGAN LIBRARY AND MUSEUM, NEW YORK, THAW COLLECTION

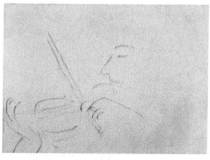

Henri Matisse, *Eva Mudocci*, 1915, drypoint on paper, 2-9/16 x 3-5/8 in. (6.5 x 8.9 cm). PHOTO: ARCHIVES HENRI MATISSE, PARIS

Henri Matisse, *Eva Mudocci*, 1915, charcoal on paper, 15 x 8-1/4 in. (38.1 x 21 cm). PHOTO: ARCHIVES HENRI MATISSE, PARIS

Eva and Bella endured the difficult middle war years (spring 1915 through winter 1917) in Paris. Eva began writing the poems that would later be collected in her book, *For Them*. In the preface, she explained that the poems, written during and after the war, "were direct impressions at the moment, many of them—anecdotes and reminiscences—set down to relieve strain, and with no thought at that time of publication." She added, "These are now offered as a token, to those who suffered and endured, and to those who so long after are still suffering and enduring."

The collection began with "Premonition," a collage of sights and sounds that presage death. Its use of light and color to tell the story pointed directly toward Edvard Munch. The opening stanza evoked *The Scream*, with its darkly flowing waters and crimson sky.

> We walked beside the river, he and I—
> The darkly flowing river—and he said,
> "There is a light out there, across the sky
> Which troubles me . . . It is as if the dead
> Stooped down to us—trailing crimson nets thereby."

The next poem, "1914/The Days Before," described an eerie silence. It depicted not only the calm before the cataclysmic storm of war, but also Mudocci's inner landscape. For her, keeping quiet was a desperate, ultimately futile attempt to ward off danger.

> Where we walk in silence nor dare to lift
> So much as a muted whisper's sound
> Lest over the sick world's gaping rift
> It might waken the dark Gods stirring round.

These rhythmic poems put ordinary human experience and emotion—what Mudocci in a letter to Munch once called the "non-heroic life"—side by side with the horrors of war. They told of daily life in Paris, of suffering and friendship in the trenches, of political battles, of atrocities. In a poem called "Cold," Mudocci evoked Paris during the frigid winter of 1916-17: "With the big guns hard at the gate/And frost beneath and death above." The poem vividly recalled the life she and Bella led at a time when the city's coal supplies were scarce and their flat was unheated.

> But some there are, in the freezing day
> Who cover themselves in bed;
> With belts strapped tight and beads in hand,
> And mufflers over their head.
> —And mumbling prayers for the dead.

Mudocci's poetry reflected a keen awareness of the war's impact on children. She showed them playing at war in the Luxembourg Gardens ("In the garden the babes play 'die'"); orphaned and lost near the front ("a little forgotten child/Alone in ruin's wake"); executed by German soldiers ("There were ten lay there—young, old, men, women and a child"); impaled by a bayonet that pierced both mother and child ("Her arms held the body of the child, and there was no trace/Of other than surprise upon her face").

While Mudocci agonized over the fates of children in wartime, her own young son and daughter were growing up without her, some seven hundred miles to the north. Between them lay Germany.

Eva and Bella joined the Parisians queuing up on frozen streets to buy a loaf of bread or a pound of coal in a paper bag. With no access to the resources in Germany left to the family by Carl Schneider, they sold some of their possessions and memorabilia to pay for necessities. Most if not all of their performances were charity events, so they relied on erratic earnings from teaching. Few Parisians could pay for lessons, but Americans still had means, and Eva took on

Paul Scott Mowrer, a ukulele-playing *Chicago Tribune* reporter who wanted to try his hand at the violin. Bella continued her teaching as well.

In 1917, they left Paris. Like Henri Matisse, they longed for respite from the cold and headed south to the Mediterranean coast. For a stretch of time, they played nightly at a resort on the Riviera, often for wounded troops. The arrangement was a godsend that was likely financed by their American friend Arthur Shattuck, who had inherited a fortune from his father, Kimberly-Clark founder F.C. Shattuck. He had recently donated $60,000 for war relief (about $1.3 million today), with special attention to European musicians affected by the conflict.

In the summer of 1918, financial necessity separated Eva and Bella. A wealthy Vichy family invited Bella to live in their home, teach their daughters, and play for their friends. In early November, she wrote to her Danish friend Ferdinand Prior (whom she affectionately called simply Prior) that she was giving concerts for "elegant audiences." Bella's optimism had seemed limitless; music had always sustained her. But the circumstances weighed on her, and there were days when even music could not buoy her spirits. "When you have to survive by using your ten fingers, the times tempt you to sell your soul," she wrote. "If you could choose to always play as you feel, then it would all be wonderful. You wrote that all pianists pretend, and you were so certain—No, Prior, I NEVER pretend. But I don't always play from my soul, unfortunately."

The war was winding down. Bella joined Eva in Nice, where together they celebrated the armistice of November 11, 1918. Reluctant to return to Paris, given the bleak wartime winters they had spent there, they stayed on, giving charity concerts in Monte Carlo, accepting private engagements, and playing for the American doughboys who waited for ships to take them home, including regiments of African-American soldiers. Eva spent time painting. They met old friends, such as Emma Calvé and Raymond Duncan, and visited Isadora Duncan in her villa perched high above

Nice. Eva went to séances organized by a friend whose son had been killed on one of the war's last days, Bella to the baccarat tables in Monte Carlo's casinos, now once again brilliantly lit.

In February 1919, Eva and Bella returned to Paris. They found a city neither at war nor completely at peace. More than 1.5 million French lives had been sacrificed, the greatest wartime loss by a single country up to that time. Across the city, women waited with trepidation for sons and husbands to return from the front or mourned those who would not come back. Foreign soldiers filled the streets.

Life was easier, but not much easier. Most flats remained unheated, and many Parisians tried to stay warm by rubbing themselves with cat-fur mittens bought at local drug stores. The cost of living had skyrocketed during the war. Parisian price tags, always staggering, were impossibly high; morale was low. Conversation in trams and shops revolved around *"la vie chère."* While rent, food, and clothing prices were exorbitant, concert tickets remained cheap and musicians were hard pressed to make ends meet.

Eva and Bella soon realized that their Paris, the effervescent Paris of the century's first decade, was no more. In the immediate aftermath of the war, they met old friends. American sculptor Janet Scudder had sailed to France toward the end of the war, celebrated the armistice in Paris, and stayed on for a time. In 1919, Arthur Shattuck came for an extended visit, and Malvina Hoffman arrived to oversee the installation of her sculpture, *Bacchanale Russe*, in the Luxembourg Gardens. But their get-togethers were flat, heavyhearted. As Janet Scudder recalled in her memoir, everyone seemed stunned:

> The moment of exaltation that followed on victory left an appalling void; the object of life appeared suddenly to have vanished. Where were we! What were we going to do! How under the sun could we go back and pick up the threads dropped four years before? Like everyone else who had been

through that horrible upheaval, I was bewildered, not only as to the future but also as to the immediate present.

Bella was finding her bearings. But as the armistice receded in time, Eva remained among the bewildered, slow to pick up the threads. Months would pass before she would visit her children. Armies no longer stood between them, but the massive demobilization made travel across Europe chaotic and complicated. And in any case, the reunion would be emotionally fraught. Eva and her eleven-year-old twins would meet again as virtual strangers.

8

Starting Over

Eva and Bella welcomed the year 1920 at a New Year's party in Paris with their American friend, Arthur Shattuck, who had sailed to Europe soon after the armistice. The journal *Musical America* reported on the gathering and published a grainy photograph of the participants. Shattuck was the focus of the article. In the years leading up to the war, his celebrity had grown, meriting an invitation to the White House by President William Howard Taft in 1912. His philanthropy during the war further raised his visibility. The caption highlighted Shattuck and the host, Norwegian sculptor Stephan Sinding (brother of composer Christian). Other members of the party were named incidentally and mostly inaccurately, including the "Danish pianist Bella Evard" and the "Spanish violinist Eva Murducci."

The decision to return to besieged France in 1915 had proved to be life-changing, fracturing their families during a frightening stretch of years and exposing Eva and Bella to considerable misery. Once they reached Paris, any thought of resuming familiar routines had been quickly dashed. For Eva, time would dull memories of food and coal shortages, but not recollections of heartbroken neighbors

New Year's Eve, December 31, 1919. *Bottom row:* Stephan Sinding and his wife, Anna. *Middle row:* Eva Mudocci, Bella Edwards, Arthur Shattuck, and an unidentified woman. *Standing:* two unidentified males.

and maimed soldiers, not accounts of atrocities she had heard from those who had witnessed them firsthand.

Early in 1920, Eva and Bella traveled to Denmark. In the five years that had passed since Eva left them in Nykøbing, the British violinist's children had transformed into thoroughly Danish schoolchildren. As the visit drew to an end, it was decided that Kay would return with his mother to Paris. Isabella remained in the care of Dr. Lemvigh-Müller, whom she adored. There was talk of formal adoption, first by the Lemvigh-Müllers and later by some of their relatives, with whom Isabella sometimes spent vacations, but Eva would not hear of it. She would neither give up the children nor acknowledge them. Once back in Paris, Eva introduced her son to friends and acquaintances simply as "Kay Ellson." How she accounted for him is not known, but both Eva and Bella were known to have students, and the presence of young people in their home was not unprecedented. A decade earlier, young Kay Nielsen had taken many meals with them while attending art school. And after Bella's stint of private teaching in Vichy, she had brought one of her young students with her to Nice. Onlookers could draw their

Above: Isabella
and Kay Ellson, c.
1914

Below: Kay and
Isabella, c. 1919.

BOTH: WEBER
FAMILY COLLECTION

own conclusions about Kay—and in the post-war years, there were fewer onlookers.

The early 1920s brought practical concerns. Traveling to Linden Villa, Eva found the house to be run-down. Relationships with once cordial neighbors were strained. Life in postwar Germany was difficult, at best. Retreat to Loschwitz was not an option, but survival in Paris had become emotionally and financially draining. Money was scarce. Carl Schneider's bequest had dwindled and could no longer buy peace of mind.

A sudden paucity of concert dates added to Eva's disorientation and anxiety. Wartime had opened up opportunities for Eva and Bella to play for audiences large and small—often at charity events. On the Riviera, they had performed frequently, both as a duo and, with an American cellist, in a trio. When they returned to Paris soon after the armistice, they had resumed their featured role at Janet Scudder's at-home musical events—now with many disabled veterans in attendance. But as the months passed, demand for the duo's emotionally evocative repertoire evaporated. As one composer put it, "We did not want Mendelssohn at that time." What struck a chord with post-war audiences was the mechanical sound of Erik Satie's music or the ferocious energy of Igor Stravinsky's. At the same time, American ragtime arrived in Paris, and salon culture gave way to music hall fare. Jazz seemed to be everywhere.

Eva and Bella had differing responses to changing tastes and musical idioms. Eva remained committed to the music of romanticism; Bella was intrigued by experimental compositions. In 1912, Satie had set to music a poem called *The Puppets Dance*, blending classical and popular art forms. Working in the same vein, Bella Edwards explored the musical possibilities of stylized movement and syncopation, creating her own score and choreography for a one-act pantomime entitled *Pauvre Pierrot*.

After the war, she reworked and orchestrated the score, traveling to Copenhagen to oversee production of the ballet, which premiered at the Royal Theatre on September 11, 1923. She later published two waltzes from the score.

Eva, in the meantime, was devouring the writings of poets and mystics, continuing to work on verse she had begun during the war, and immersing herself in spiritualist activities. She gave solo performances in the hall of the Paris Theosophical Center, and offered unaccompanied musical selections at readings by the Danish writer Karen Bramson.

By 1923, Eva and Bella's old friends were visiting less frequently. A new generation of artists was coming to Paris. This was the start of the *années folles*, when Paris became the epicenter of artistic experimentation. In its cafés and bistros, artists and writers from many countries were drinking, arguing, and imagining new ways of seeing and representing the world. They were resolutely young. Gertrude Stein would call the 1920s "the period of being twenty-six"; for Eva Mudocci, it was the period of being fifty-six. She was oriented to the passing generation, not the rising one.

London was the obvious solution. In more staid England, the passing generation remained a cultural force. London's "bright young people," as they were called, were just as interested in strong drink and lively conversation as those filling Paris cafés, but on the whole they were less focused on upending convention. And for aging artists, life in London was more convenient and compact than in Paris, and better upholstered. In London, Eva could be closer to Lucy Muddock, who had rented out the Loschwitz house and was based in England. And she could reunite her family. In time, Bella agreed.

By the time Bella returned from the Copenhagen premier of *Pauvre Pierrot* in late 1923, Eva had arranged the move and was already in England. For Bella, relocating could not have been easy. She adored Paris. Although born to British parents, she had never actually lived in England. Her English was fluent, but not native, and she spoke with a strong Danish accent. But Eva needed to be home, and post-war dissonance was taking a toll on both of them, so together they started over.

They continued playing together. Eva had held onto the Stradivarius, and the Mudocci-Edwards repertoire was still appreciated by English music lovers and their American houseguests. Despite their diminished circumstances, there were remnants of the refinement and gentility that for Bella were a source of comfort and for Eva, a necessity. They reconnected with English friends they had gotten to know in Paris, and made new acquaintances. Friends from their Paris days occasionally appeared on their doorstep. In this way, years passed.

London's musical fare was for the most part unexciting, but its theatrical life was vibrant, and that is where they set their sights. Eva renewed her acquaintance with popular stage actor Leon M. Lion, whom she remembered as a velvet-clad prodigy declaiming in the same Victorian parlors where she had concertized as Miss Rose Lynton. Through Lion, she made the acquaintance of writer John Galsworthy, with whom she shared an interest in Theosophy. Eva and Bella became music directors for a Garrick Theatre production of Galsworthy's play *Escape*, which featured Lion. They were also musical directors for the Garrick production of *The Bear Dances*, a Soviet play about a Russian-Jewish émigrée named Vera Levine who returns to the Soviet Union.

A play about dislocation—about returning home to a place both familiar and alien—no doubt had emotional resonance for them. The adjustment was not easy for Eva and Bella, or for the children. For a brief period, in the late 1920s, they all lived in the same country, but years of separation and disavowal had taken their toll, and the relationships were brittle. The twins continued to be burdened by the haphazardness of their lives and by the weight of family secrets.

As entries in Isabella's 1922-24 autograph book show, she had spent her secondary school years in Nykøbing with the Lemvigh-Müllers, traveling to Loschwitz for holidays. By 1927, when the twins were eighteen, both were living in Brighton with their grandmother. Up to this time, Isabella had been known to close family and friends by the affectionate Danish nickname "Dukke" ("Doll"). Once in England, she answered to the British version of her name—Isobel. Her brother adopted the British spelling of his name as well—Kai.

In England, Isobel enrolled at the Trinity College of Music, where she studied piano. She was an accomplished player, and on the evening of May 11, 1927, she gave a recital at St. James Hall that featured Beethoven's *Sonata in F major* ("Spring Sonata"), with Dora Gibson on violin. A photograph taken during this period shows Isobel wearing a polite string of pearls.

Kai, in the meantime, was drawing and painting, at times taking courses at the Brighton Art School. His gift was recognized, and he was taken on as a student by the eminent painter Augustus John. For a time Kai had a steady girlfriend, but he had always been emotionally fragile, and in 1927, when both twins suffered a long, debilitating bout of rheumatic fever, Kai's relationship fell apart. It was then that his serious psychological problems surfaced. Perhaps the difficulties predated his illness; perhaps they were potentiated or worsened by the neurological changes that can occasionally accompany rheumatic fever. Whatever the cause, Kai became unbalanced and prone to hallucinations. By 1930, when he was twenty-one, he was back in Nykøbing, living with Dr. Lemvigh-Müller. The following year, Kai was admitted to the state mental hospital at Vordingborg. He would spend the rest of his life there.

Isobel's life took a more predictable course. In 1931, she married Geofrey T. Weber, a thirty-one-year-old Swiss bank clerk whom she had met through mutual friends. On the marriage certificate, the bride's name was listed as Isabella Estella Muddock Ellson. The blank reserved for the bride's father was occupied by the late, fictitious "Louis Ellson, author (deceased)."

Within a few years of their return to London, Eva and Bella were mixing with the crème of London's musical crème. In the late 1920s they were often invited to perform at the homes of prominent admirers. At the same time, they continued the tradition of Thursday at-home concerts that they had inaugurated in Paris. Among the guests were new friends, including Gertrude Norman, Marcia Van Dresser, and Lady Maud Warrender.

Gertrude Norman would become Eva and Bella's confidante and most devoted friend. She was a British theatrical journalist and one-time stage actress, accomplished in her own right, but identified by the archivists who organized her papers as companion and secretary to American lyric soprano Marcia Van Dresser. A fascinating picture of their lives and friendships emerges from the 3.2 linear feet of documents in the Norman-Van Dresser collection archived at the New York Public Library.

Norman and Van Dresser met in America in 1898, as ingénues. Gertrude was eighteen and Marcia was twenty. Both had been cast in a stage adaptation of Thomas Hardy's *Tess of the d'Urbervilles*, starring the formidable Minnie Maddern Fiske in the title role. Norman was a diminutive young woman with a boyish figure, and in *Tess*, she played the heroine's younger brother, Abraham. Van Dresser, stunning and a head taller, was cast in a more conventional role. Boyishness was a quality that Gertrude Norman cultivated. She called herself "Tommy," which was later abbreviated to "Toto"—the name by which she was, for the rest of her life, known to family and friends. And there were scores of friends, both inside and outside the theatrical world. As one correspondent wrote, Toto had "a genius for friendship."

Toto and Marcie (as Marcia was known to friends) soon became inseparable. They continued appearing with the acting company led by Mrs. Fiske, who counseled young actors to trust their own instincts. "You must not allow yourself to be advised, cautioned, influenced, persuaded," she said. Her motto was, "Above all, ignore the audience." In their personal lives, as in their work, Toto and Marcie took these principles to heart.

In 1900, Toto and Marcie were again cast together as supporting players in a costume drama called *In the Palace of the King*. One review passed over Van Dresser, but praised Gertrude Norman's "artistic acting." Their names were soon linked in the press. In 1901 the *Omaha Bee* told readers of its "Amusements" section that "Marcia Van Dresser and Gertrude Norman have returned from London. They will both be members of Otis Skinner's company." Later that year, they appeared in the play *Francesca da Rimini*, with Van Dresser in the title role.

While both continued to appear on the stage, and Van Dresser was singled out as a beauty, neither was riveting in dramatic roles, and by the middle of the decade they had made a new plan. Van Dresser went to Europe for intensive voice training. Norman accompanied her and never looked back. She turned to writing, contributing long, lively profiles of European theater figures to an American monthly, *The Theatre Magazine*. Their plan paid off. In 1907, Marcia Van Dresser made her opera debut in Dresden, singing Elisabeth in *Tannhäuser*, and then went on to roles in London and Frankfurt before re-crossing the Atlantic to sing for two seasons in Chicago. Although relatively brief, spanning a single decade, her operatic career was distinguished.

When the two couples met in the 1920s, Eva and Bella had much in common with Toto and Marcie in background, experience, and temperament. They all came from middle-class families. Both couples had shared their lives for decades, performing together and supporting each other. They valued artistic and personal freedom, as well as social respectability and propriety. They shared musical passions and friends. In the late 1930s, during a visit to London by Norwegian composer Christian Sinding, Eva and Bella arranged for Van Dresser to perform his music.

It was not surprising that Bella and Eva would befriend Toto and Marcie; their friendship with larger-than-life Lady

Maud Warrender was less predictable. Born Ethel Maud Ashley-Cooper in 1870, Lady Maud was the daughter of the eighth Earl of Shaftesbury. In her twenties, she married Vice-Admiral Sir George Warrender, with whom she had three children. The Warrenders' estate, known as Leasam, was situated in Rye, a seaside town some fifty miles east of Brighton. As a young wife with an independent streak, Lady Warrender was introduced to society-page readers as one of Britain's first and most exotically dressed female motorists. "No one more thoroughly enjoys automobilism in all of its forms," declared a 1902 publication. A 1903 magazine reported that Lady Maud had been seen at the wheel wearing "a beautiful cloak of the skins of reindeer's feet and the Japanese blue-fox."

But to the extent that those reports paint a life of total frivolity, they are misleading. Lady Warrender was an amateur singer whose contralto voice was applauded at the charity concerts that she organized and often headlined. She actively supported women's suffrage and advocated for women's access to contraception. She was a staunch supporter of the Girl Guides, and the local Rye troop was known as "Lady Maud's Own." During the First World War, she organized benefit concerts and toured with Lady Randolph Churchill, Winston's mother. She was a persuasive voice in the movement to make concerts and other cultural events accessible and affordable for those with limited means. In Rye, she took a public stand against the widely accepted policy of reserving ambulance service for those who could pay for it.

In middle age, Lady Warrender continued singing in public, but whenever she extended a toe across the boundary from amateur to professional performance, the critics were ready to pounce. When she performed Ethel Smyth's songs for mezzo voice and chamber ensemble in a 1920 concert, a reviewer wrote, "Lady Maud Warrender appeared as the vocalist of the evening, but we could find no adequate reason for her doing so." Nevertheless, she left her mark on London's musical world. Over time, she became to Edwardian London what another amateur musician, Winnaretta Singer, had been to Belle Époque Paris: a hostess of high-minded musical salons; a patron of sterling composers; a cultural force. Like Singer, she was an elegant widow with impeccable aristocratic credentials who saw herself as a paragon of respectability. And like Singer, she was discreetly but unapologetically a lover of women.

Warrender counted among her friends such cultural icons as composer Edward Elgar and writer Henry James (just as Winnaretta Singer mixed with the likes of Igor Stravinsky and Marcel Proust), but she also claimed as friends Britain's most gifted and conspicuous lesbians, including Radclyffe Hall, Una Thurbridge, Edith Craig, Clare Atwood, and Christabel Marshall. Her circle overlapped with Singer's. She was, for example, a close friend of composer Ethel Smyth, Singer's one-time lover.

Numerous sources say that after the death of her husband in 1917, and perhaps before, Maud Warrender had an intimate relationship with Marcia Van Dresser and brought her to live at Leasam. However, there is no evidence of a breach between Marcie and Toto. They shared a flat at 14 Ladbroke Square in Notting Hill Gate, a short walk from Lady Maud's London house at 2 Holland Park. Gertrude, Marcie, and Maud spent considerable time together at Leasam. In the mid-1930s, during Van Dresser's final illness, the three women lived there together. After Marcie's death, Toto and Lady Maud remained close and Toto continued her extended stay at Leasam. She later moved into Lady Maud's Holland Park house in London. In a note written late in their lives, Bella referred to Marcie and Maud as Toto's "two angels."

Beginning in the late 1920s, Toto, Marcie, and Lady Maud were close to Eva and Bella, spending time with them in Rye as well as London. Beginning in the early 1930s, they all became neighbors. Eva and Bella moved to Notting Hill Gate, first to 1 Hanover Terrace, Ladbroke Square (now 1 Lansdowne Walk), and later to 10 Ladbroke Square, just steps from Toto and Marcie's flat. The Norman-Van Dresser archive includes Norman's explanatory notes, which briefly describe Bella and Eva's musical career, adding:

"There are many letters from these two sweet & great women. I have treasured their letters & love."

But where are the many letters? The collection includes just two letters and three brief notes from Eva and Bella, all sent soon after Marcia Van Dresser's death and stashed among the dozens of condolence messages in a folder of tributes. Nearly all of the accounts of Eva and Bella come from other correspondents' letters. Perusal of the archive explains why. Toto was unwilling either to disavow her relationship with Van Dresser or to display it publicly. The collection contains no letters between Toto and Marcie, nor does it include correspondence with the woman who became indispensable to both of them—Lady Maud Warrender. There are no folders devoted to the "treasured" letters from Eva or Bella.

There was good reason for discretion. They had all lived through the November 1928 obscenity trial that followed publication of Radclyffe Hall's lesbian-themed novel *The Well of Loneliness*. They had seen the many newspaper accounts depicting Hall and her kind as freaks of nature, determined to corrupt the young. Within months of the trial, a conservative member of Parliament had proposed adding to the *Criminal Law Amendment Act*, under which Oscar Wilde had been indicted, a clause on "Acts of Gross Indecency by Females."

To escape the publicity, Hall and her lover, Una Thurbridge, relocated to Rye, taking up residence at 4 High Street in an ancient brick house with handsome leaded windows. Over several decades, Rye had been home to many writers, notably the American, Henry James, who wrote novels in the garden cottage next to his large house. The locale was also home to a fascinating community of women. In Rye, Una and John (as Radclyffe Hall was known to friends) socialized with Lady Maud, Toto, and Marcie, and they no doubt knew Eva and Bella as well. They shared Eva and Toto's interest in the spirit world. There is little documentary evidence of these friendships, however. As she prepared her papers to be archived, Toto Norman carefully minimized the presence of all of these women. They appear primarily in the one folder Toto would not censor—the one devoted to tributes to Marcie received in the weeks after her death. Eva and Bella had sent condolence letters expressing great affection for Toto, and horror at Marcie's loss. They were among the list of close friends—including several pairs of women—who sent flower arrangements. (Eva and Bella sent a wreath of lilies; Una and John, an arrangement of yellow and white lilies, yellow roses, and bulrushes). While most condolence messages assured Toto that the writer grieved with her, those written by Una and Eva added that they "understand" her. They truly knew the depth of her loss.

With few letters from Eva or Bella, and none addressed to them, the Norman-Van Dresser archive should not yield significant insight into their biographies, but that is not the case. Warehoused in cardboard boxes are decades of their lives. Here they are in the late 1920s playing Grieg and Corelli for American musicians in a sun-filled Chelsea flat, charming their guests at their at-home musicales, playing at an elegant dinner party. Here they are in the 1930s dealing with financial reversals, coping with health problems, mourning the death of Marcia Van Dresser. And in the 1940s weathering another war. That Eva and Bella come to life in these boxes reflects the unceasing presence of a Greek chorus.

Among the musicians who found their way to Eva and Bella's "at-homes" in London were three American pianists: Arthur Shattuck, their old friend from Paris days who had made New York City his home; Henri Deering, another Manhattan dweller; and a Californian named Lyell Barbour. The three were well acquainted. All were younger than Eva: Shattuck by one decade, and Deering and Barbour by two. They had established themselves with different repertoires. Shattuck was known for cerebral interpretations of Bach; Deering for performances of what was called "the modern school," in particular Sergei Rachmaninoff; and Barbour for adventurous programs that often combined works by composers as varied as Mozart, Robert Schumann, and Claude Debussy. They shared a lasting affection for their London friends, and they all corresponded regularly with Toto Norman.

Their archived letters respond in detail to Toto's reports of Eva and Bella. Their commentaries leave three strong impressions. First, the correspondents thought Eva charming, but seemed to have a limited view of her reality. They were keenly aware of her dedication to Bella and her impulse to deny herself in order to provide for Bella. They saw her as fascinated with the occult and tenuously connected to the necessities of daily life, such as eating and budgeting. Mudocci's poetry was not mentioned. Her association with Matisse never came up. And it is uncertain that in the interwar period, the name Edvard Munch would have meant much to Eva's friends. Eva's children and grandchildren were never discussed until Isobel made a late cameo appearance in letters that mention an illness and financial struggles.

Second, there was unflagging admiration for Bella. Barbour, Deering, and Shattuck invariably referred to the pair as "Bella and Eva," not the reverse, and it was Bella who shone in their letters. Of course, they shared with her a dedication to the piano and its repertoire, but their admiration went beyond her music. From the correspondence of Mudocci, Munch, and some acquaintances, it is possible to see Bella as domineering, a bit heavy-handed, and, in comparison with Eva, unlovely. But for the three pianists, it was Bella who was the more appealing, vibrant presence. Lyell Barbour wrote to Toto that in her younger days, Bella must have been a "brilliant and arresting woman." In an artistic circle that valued reflected glory, it was Bella who had cachet by virtue of her acquaintance with Edvard Grieg and performances that were seen to convey Grieg's own intentions and temperament.

And third, accompanying the drama that the three pianists chronicled was the banal, melancholy melody of advancing years.

Eva and Bella came of age at a time when a prodigy feared reaching fifteen, and a woman of thirty was considered past her prime. In her early thirties, at a particularly self-indulgent moment, Eva had written mournfully to Munch about her diminishing powers and narrowing hopes. She resented the insulting accumulation of years, and had long felt entitled to discount her age by a decade, as the birth date on her passport showed. Now her dread of old age had given way to its daily indignities. For their younger friends, it was heart-rending to watch. As Eva and Bella grew older, more fragile, and less solvent, the pianists' letters expressed increasing dismay. Attitudes toward Eva gradually changed. Along with abiding affection, there was also unmistakable exasperation. Much of it revolved around a string of pearls.

9

A String of Pearls

London's musically inclined high society admired Eva and Bella and felt affection for them, but never fully embraced them. A discreet same-sex bond was no hindrance to full membership; penury was. By the mid-1920s, Carl Schneider's bequest no longer protected them. Hyperinflation in post-war Germany would have wiped out whatever funds were left in German banks and shrunk the family's rental income from Linden Villa. There were tuition expenses for the twins and, increasingly, bills for the care of Eva's ailing mother.

In the 1930s, Eva entered her sixties, and Bella her seventies. These years brought distinct satisfactions—deepening friendships and the publication of Eva's book of poetry—but also new reversals. In Britain's Great Depression years, social safety nets were flimsy. An old-age pension, for those who qualified, was counted in shillings, not pounds, and scarcely covered groceries. The country's medical insurance scheme was no match for serious illness. By 1931, Eva's treasured Emiliani was sold to a London dealership, William E. Hill & Sons. For any violinist, the loss of a treasured instrument is difficult; for one so identified with her violin, it would have been crushing. Mudocci continued to play for friends on a less precious violin, but her golden age was over.

Today, selling a Stradivarius would make the owner a multimillionaire, but at the time Mudocci sold the Emiliani, violins by Antonio Stradivari were going at auction for about £1,500 (about $90,000 today). This was certainly a lot of money in that era—enough to support an older couple for several years, but not for two decades, especially once health problems multiplied and medical bills mounted.

Proceeds from the sale eased their situation and in the early 1930s financed travel. In 1931, Bella crossed the Atlantic and spent six weeks with friends in Vermont. Mudocci's passport recorded multiple trips to France and Italy. Eva also made three visits to Denmark to see her son at the psychiatric facility where he was an in-patient.

But by the late 1930s, their savings had dwindled and their health was declining. Bella developed heart problems; she took a serious fall. Their friends

Eva Mudocci, c. 1930.
WEBER FAMILY COLLECTION

were concerned, but had worries of their own. Lady Maud and Toto Norman were preoccupied with the care of Marcia Van Dresser, who was gravely ill at Leasam and died in July 1937.

In August 1938, it was Eva who was facing a serious health crisis. She was hospitalized and underwent surgery (seemingly abdominal); a second operation followed in early 1939. Lady Maud and Toto provided substantial emotional and financial help, and the three pianists contributed as well.

The letters exchanged by these friends dealt primarily with practical concerns, but they also conveyed alarm about political developments in Europe. Arthur Shattuck, in particular, expressed horror at Adolf Hitler's grip on power. As for Eva and Bella, they had reason to worry that the outbreak of war could separate them—as it had in August 1914. In late September 1938, Shattuck wrote to Toto that Count Ove Scheel, a leader of the Danish émigré community in London, had come to see him. "He tells me that he plans to take Bella away from London at the first sign of danger—Eva, of course, cannot be moved for some time to come—She is progressing, however, and is looking much better—They are feeding her, a thing she has neglected to do for herself."

Eva and Bella continued to inspire affection and loyalty from their better-off friends, but also an unmistakable condescension. Barbour and Shattuck repeatedly assured Toto that she and Lady Maud had been "saintly" in their concern for the "pathetic" Bella and Eva, and there were explicit suggestions that the two musicians were in part to blame for their own circumstances. Eva was faulted for wanting to buy things for Bella, Bella for being too proud to consult "insurance doctors" or ask for help from her Danish relatives.

Such attitudes were most pointed in the letters of Kimberly-Clark heir Arthur Shattuck. Just before sailing to New York, Shattuck wrote to Toto, stressing "how unwise it is to hand out any more at one time than is necessary for daily expenses—Even last week, Bella was the recipient of a 'collier de perles'! Why? Because 'pearls are more becoming to darling Bella than anything else she can wear'—so, my dear Toto, I am enclosing a little cheque to you, to make use of as you see their needs." He later reprised the same theme, outraged that Eva, out of an "insane desire to do something to please Bella," would save a few shillings each month "that should have been spent on food" in order to buy "a wretched [string of pearls] which Bella doesn't want."

By all accounts, Bella made her way through hard times with cheerful resignation and an eye to the future. As for Eva, there were dark moods, to be sure, but she was less focused on daily deprivations or physical ailments than her friends imagined. Eva's deepest distress was metaphysical, and lodged more in the past than the present. Wartime experiences had left her traumatized, as her poetry showed. Always intrigued by Eastern mysticism, she had in recent years taken a deeper dive into spiritualist texts and activities, searching for ways to live with a piercing awareness of human suffering. All of this she poured out in a dense, nine-page letter to her close friend Toto Norman written in 1937, two months after the death of Marcia Van Dresser. The letter to Toto was intended to offer comfort and hope. Instead, it pulsated with psychic pain. It was Eva Mudocci's scream.

"Yes I understand you—in everything," Eva wrote to Toto in September 1937, desperate to console her friend, "& I know too that so long as one is in the flesh one must grieve for the loss of those one has loved in the flesh—."

This passage came at the beginning of a long handwritten letter preserved in the Norman-Van Dresser archive, midway through a thick file of condolence messages. The letter was signed "Eva," and Toto had penciled an M on the top right corner of the letter, presumably to help with alphabetizing, but the author remained unidentified. There is no doubt that it was written by Mudocci, judging by the content. Her close handwriting, with its hasty dashes and emphatically crossed t's, looked much as it did in her letters to Edvard Munch and conveyed the same sense of urgency.

Eva continued, "I know it, dear, I have lost loved ones, & the years that have passed since they went have not softened the loss & the ache of longing for them—But, I know that I shall find them again—that we shall be drawn together again in life after life—both in spiritual life & in manifested life—by the magnet of affinity—of love & association."

This was the consolation Eva wanted to offer: Toto and Marcie would meet again, she had written, and not only in the spirit world, but also in this one, in new incarnations. The language came straight out of Theosophical texts, and in some passages gave the letter a preachy, impersonal feel. It could easily have been off-putting, but Eva trusted that Toto Norman would understand her. Toto either shared her spiritualist inclinations or, in the years after Marcie's death, became very receptive to Eva's influence. One acquaintance, the son of a dedicated spiritualist, recalled a visit from Toto Norman during this period. He said that Toto was, like his father, "a believer in reincarnation," and that she "hoped that she and her deceased American girlfriend—an opera singer in this life—would be reunited in the next."

Eva's letter urged Toto not to dwell on the memory of Marcie's suffering. "For one thing you are keeping it in her memory, when she should be allowed to forget—our thoughts are so much more powerful than we realize & especially touching the other side where communion is telepathic." She added that one must not exaggerate the importance of physical suffering, which must have meaning that we cannot fathom. "This life is so full of it that if it were what it seems to be the world could not contain it—human existence would perish utterly under the burden."

What followed was a crescendo of feeling, a reverberating anguish, colored by an acute consciousness of human pain—physical, psychological, spiritual. Eva wrote that she was tormented by thoughts of wartime suffering—"people dragged from their homes—mangled—mutilated—without limbs." Here she summoned an image startling in its resemblance to Munch's most famous canvas, "screaming blindly against a horror they cannot understand—Do not they all cry 'why? Why?—what have we done to deserve this?'"

In her poem "Premonition," Eva had associated Munch's *Scream* with the cataclysm of war. The scream in this letter suggests another premonition. As Eva wrote to Toto on September 15, 1937, the radio and newspapers were saturated with news of the previous week's Nazi Party Congress at Nuremberg, where Hitler reviewed 600,000 troops at a massive, choreographed rally.

Eva's letter turned to the "cruel lingering" suffering and death of people she loved—her mother, her grandmother, her nurse. She recalled losing her beloved uncle, and recounted the martyrdom of Bella's brother, a civil engineer who was gravely injured while trying to save workers at the site of a construction disaster. Finally, Eva poured out her heart about her deepest anguish, the suffering of her twenty-nine-year-old son. Even now, writing to her dear friend, she did not claim him as her son.

> In Denmark today, in an asylum for the hopelessly insane, lives one I love. From his birth he was loving, unselfish, generous—a great soul—brain & heart—& a genius—not his body but his great mind is lingeringly disintegrating—& the cruelest is that in his still sometimes recurring lucid moments, he understands that he is kept a prisoner, & in letters scarcely readable, cries to me—'Why do they keep me shut up?—why cannot I have my freedom?—tell them they must let me come to you.'

"Toto, darling," Eva continued, ". . . to see the very personality of one we love apparently rot away before our eyes—so that we cannot find the being we knew any more—that is a horror one must thank God for having been spared it.—I have not been spared that—& for long I asked myself what I had done to merit that? & yet more—what had he done?"

What had Eva done? Was she making a point about the suffering of the innocent? Or perhaps she was thinking about the conception of her children and the moral injunctions she had defied. Perhaps she had in mind the havoc she had created in other people's lives—Bella's, of course, and no doubt her mother's. Was she thinking of her remoteness from her children, the wall of silence that separated her from them? That remoteness can be felt in Eva's letter, which made no mention of her daughter or young grandchildren.

"And now," she lamented, "I have only my darling Bella—and life has brought us to this that I see her growing old & weak with age, & with need of all the comforts & necessities that I can no longer give her, because even money has been taken from us."

"Even money has been taken from us," Eva wrote in 1937. She and Bella had certainly come upon hard times, but how, exactly, had it happened? Their medical expenses were steep and their savings were depleted. Bella was said to be too proud to turn to her Danish family for help, and Eva had no family resources to speak of. When her estranged father, J.E.P. Muddock, died in 1934, he left a meager estate of seventy-two pounds to his wife Eleanor, and nothing to the family he had abandoned. Then, when Lucy Muddock died in 1936, there was no will or probate, suggesting that her resources were exhausted or perhaps held jointly with her daughter. But Linden Villa had been sold the previous year. What happened to the proceeds of that sale? Was this the money that was "taken from us"?

The troubling answer can be found in decades of documents buried in public and private files in Germany. In the 1920s, Lucy held onto Linden Villa, renting it out when she returned to England. Once Adolf Hitler came to power in the early 1930s, ownership of the house became more problematic. Dresden authorities sent Lucy Muddock a series of notices about newly discovered code violations, including demands that she tear down a shed used to house the cart needed to get supplies up and down the steep path. The shed was finally allowed to stand—but only in 1936, after the house was acquired by a retired German schoolmaster named Fritz. The new owner wrote to local officials that he had recently purchased the house from Frau Muddock and wished to make use of the shed. He ended his request with the words "Heil Hitler!" The new owner's request was quickly approved. When magnified, a photograph of the house taken soon after its sale to the retired schoolmaster shows a Nazi flag hanging from the veranda.

Fritz and his descendants held the deed to Linden Villa for the next sixty-five years. They had the distinct impression that Frau Muddock was Jewish, and they passed along this impression to the couple who bought the property from them in 1996. Documents kept by Fritz's descendants explain how they reached this conclusion. The purchase contract shows that on the day of the closing, in May 1935, Fritz paid 25,000 Reichmarks in cash to Lucy Muddock—equivalent in purchasing power to about $150,000 today. Given the depressed German housing market of that time and the shabby state of the house, long neglected by its absentee owner, the price was not unreasonable. Lucy Muddock died the following year. Proceeds from the sale should have eased Eva and Bella's situation considerably.

But records show that the money did not go directly to Lucy Muddock in 1935, nor did it go, after Lucy's death, to her daughter. Rather, the funds were deposited in a blocked account at the Deutsche Bank in Berlin. Eva's inheritance was mired in regulations designed to fleece Jewish emigrants. To address its currency shortage, the Third Reich required residents transferring funds abroad to deposit them first into a blocked account at a subsidiary of the Reichsbank. Such accounts were ostensibly set up to guarantee that various taxes and impositions would be paid; in reality, huge deductions were made in the form of a "flight tax." In 1934, the deduction amounted to 20 percent of the total sum; it increased to 68 percent in June 1935, to 81 percent in October 1936, and to 90 percent in June 1938. The seller was also responsible for taxes, fees, and legal costs. In the time that it would have taken for Eva to bury her mother and lay claim to her assets, there would have been little left, and even that paltry amount may have been out of reach. Eva was right—their money had been taken from them.

Above left: The path leading to Linden Villa, c. 1900 (foliage obscures the house).
Above right: Linden Villa, 2016.
Below: Linden Villa under new ownership, 1935.

The story does not end there. Fritz's sons owned the house through the Second World War. In its aftermath, Dresden and its suburbs became part of East Germany. The family fled to West Germany in the early 1950s, and Linden Villa was seized by the East German authorities. Over the years, Fritz's grandsons tried unsuccessfully to assert their rights to the property. Then, after reunification, they again petitioned for its return. This was granted in 1996, but only after years of intensive examination to ensure that the family's acquisition of the house during the Nazi era had been legitimate.

It may well have been banking records of the blocked account that prompted the intervention of the International Conference on Jewish Material Claims against Germany in the 1990s, when Fritz's grandsons were trying to reclaim their property. The work of the Conference was to seek compensation on behalf of Jews who sustained material losses during the Third Reich, and it made a claim on behalf of Lucy Muddock's descendants, apparently without their knowledge. The claim delayed the restoration of the property to its owners by several years, but the German court eventually ruled against the Conference, pointing to a lack of evidence that Lucy Muddock was part of Dresden's Jewish community or had suffered persecution based on racial identity. It was the intervention of the Jewish Conference that left Fritz's grandsons with the impression that the Muddocks were Jewish, and they conveyed this notion to the current owner. Eva Mudocci's puzzling claims of Jewish heritage, made decades earlier, unaccountably anticipated this episode.

Mudocci's life had moved into chapters of history that the sensitive young prodigy from Brixton could not have envisioned in her wildest imagination. From a practical standpoint, Eva could not have foreseen that when Lucy Muddock rented out Linden Villa and returned to England in the 1920s, it would later prove difficult, if not perilous, to return for the belongings that had been left behind. And so, when the new owner took possession of Linden Villa in 1935, he discovered in the attic a yellowed scroll of paper.

Unrolling it, he found a depiction of a violinist and pianist, bearing the signature of Edvard Munch. For the next eighty years, his family took it to be a drawing by the Norwegian artist. In fact, what he had found was a rare early-state print of *The Violin Concert*, Munch's double portrait of Eva and Bella in performance. When Fritz's heirs fled East Germany in the 1950s, they carried the print with them. It was in poor condition, and eventually they had it restored and framed. Today, the lithograph hangs on the wall of Fritz's grandson.

Early state of Edvard Munch's *The Violin Concert*, found in the attic by the buyers of Linden Villa in 1935. Private collection

10

Last Glance

On a muggy Sunday in early September 1939, the telephone rang in the flat at Notting Hill Gate where Eva Mudocci and Bella Edwards usually slept late. On this morning, like millions of other Londoners, they were trying to come to grips with the realities of another war. For those who had been traumatized by the events of 1914, the premonitions were especially vivid.

Preparations had been underway for some time. Gas masks packed in square cardboard boxes, like fruitcakes, were being distributed to civilians. At eleven fifteen that morning, Prime Minister Neville Chamberlain broke into regular BBC programming to announce that the country was at war with Germany. Almost at once, air raid sirens began to wail. It was a practice drill, but like their neighbors, Eva and Bella understood that the time for rehearsal was drawing to a close. Chamberlain's somber speech was followed by a series of announcements. For the next three days, major arteries in and out of London would become one-way thoroughfares to accommodate the anticipated exodus from the city.

No longer young, Eva and Bella were leading a more cramped existence, spending much of their time together in their flat. Their

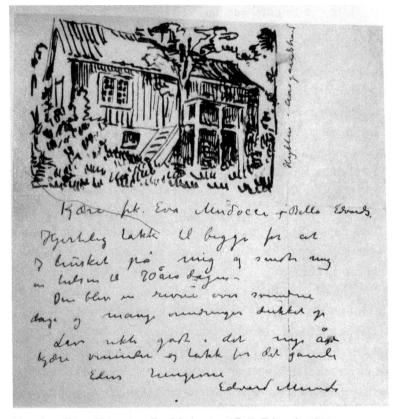

Note from Edvard Munch to Eva Mudocci and Bella Edwards, 1933.
MUNCH MUSEUM, OSLO

remaining friends and acquaintances had scattered. Some, like Louis
Levy and Henri Nathansen, were in Denmark; others, like Janet
Scudder and Malvina Hoffman, were in the United States, as were
the three American pianists whom they counted among their close
friends. It had been years since they had last received a card from
Edvard Munch—a nostalgic response to the seventieth-birthday
greeting Bella had written from the two of them in 1933. Depicted
on the note was the house at Åsgårdstrand where the they had all
spent time together.

Life had thinned out, but visitors could be counted on to appear. Isobel Weber was a dutiful daughter, although preoccupied with the care of two small sons and soon to give birth to a daughter—Janet. A small band of acquaintances popped in from time to time, taking tea, admiring mementos, and enjoying accounts of fascinating people and places. Spending time with young people was agreeable, but Mudocci and Edwards felt most at home with their contemporaries, who understood their turn of mind and did not see them as relics. They were delighted and relieved, on the first day of the war, to receive a call from Lady Maud Warrender. They must leave London right away and come to Rye, Lady Maud said. And so it was in Rye, on England's southern coast, that Eva and Bella took refuge with Lady Maud and Toto on the eve of the Blitz. They spent the next year there.

The flat that Eva and Bella rented in the 1930s was modest, but the corner building that contained it was very handsome—the showplace of the nineteenth-century architect who had designed and then occupied it. It had a sculptural, multi-level profile, geometric windows, and, from multiple angles, a lovely view of the gardens across the road. Eva craved privacy and would have appreciated that the building had the bearing of a diminutive fortress. Its wide, wooden front door encircled the address—ONE HANOVER TERRACE— with an inlaid design. The mail slot bore the inscription, in capital letters: DO NOT RING UNLESS AN ANSWER IS REQUIRED.

One Hanover Terrace was a fine house, but humble in comparison with Lady Maud's stately home. Leasam House stood alone atop a vast grassy hill, with commanding views of the sea. In 1902, it had been advertised in *Country Life* this way: "FOR SALE, with from six to 20 acres, an Elizabethan Residence of great attraction . . . The gardens are exceedingly well timbered and encircle the house; . . . known as Leasam, comprising a small mansion, containing 24 rooms."

When Eva and Bella left London for Rye in September 1939, they brought with them memories of the aerial bombardment of

Paris in 1915. They could imagine all too well what lay ahead. And removing to Leasam House did not free them from anxiety. Rye residents were soon warned that their port was likely marked on Hitler's map as a strategic point of invasion. Instructions for "what to do and how to do it" in case of a German invasion were distributed to residents. Months earlier, Arthur Shattuck had written to Toto Norman that he wished she and Lady Maud would "move inland," but they felt secure on the estate, and they were sure Eva and Bella would be safer with them than on their own in central London.

When Eva and Bella arrived, they found another guest in residence—author and mystic Alice Dew-Smith. A close friend of Lady Maud, Mrs. Dew-Smith had lived in Rye for decades, but at eighty, was thought to be better off at Leasam House than on her own. Looking after the five women was a large staff, including a secretary, two housekeepers, lady's maid, parlor maid, two housemaids, cook, kitchen maid, and hall boy. All were registered as residents of Leasam House in September 1939, when Britain conducted an emergency census and issued national identity cards.

Eva and Bella no doubt found Alice Dew-Smith to be an engaging, witty companion. It was she who was credited with a limerick describing their host:

> There is an enchantress called Maud,
> Her voice!—let me hereby record
> That the angels who hear it
> Turn pale, for they fear it
> May rival their singing to Gawd.

As a young woman, Alice had shocked Victorian contemporaries by smoking cigarettes and mixing with other freethinking women. She became an ardent feminist. After the death of her husband, she moved to Rye. There, she hosted women's suffrage meetings to which her American friend Henry James would bring his housekeeper. James once told a mutual friend that Mrs. Dew-Smith had joined a local rifle club "& lies for hours on her stomach in the Marsh (awaiting her prey)."

Over four decades, Alice Dew-Smith contributed to several British periodicals and published six books, including fiction reflecting her mystical inclinations, eccentric accounts of gardening and husbandry, and two spiritual guides that were described as "agreeably dotty." In one of these guides, she illuminated the workings of spiritual gravity, which she considered an essential corollary of the law of physical gravity. This conviction apparently resonated with Eva, whose 1937 letter to Toto Norman had assured her that the souls of people who have loved each other in this world literally gravitate to each other in the next.

The five friends spent the war's first year talking, reading, following news bulletins, and strolling among the statuary of Leasam's formal gardens. Looking out to sea and listening to the screeches of Rye's voluble gulls, they could follow the proliferation of blimp-like baffle balloons, set aloft to fend off low-flying planes. They entertained friends and patronized the town's shops and tearooms. They dined on the fish caught by local anglers when commercial trawlers were banished from Rye's harbor. Many hours were spent in the mansion's paneled, ornately decorated music room, where a carved inscription taken from Alfred Lord Tennyson decorated the fireplace:

> Let there be music here that softer falls
> Than petals from blown roses on the grass
> Music that gentler on the spirit lies
> Than tired eyelids upon tired eyes.

For a full year, Leasam proved to be a safe haven. But on the afternoon of August 18, 1940, as many residents were enjoying Sunday dinner, the Luftwaffe scattered bombs across the ancient town and its environs, causing Rye's first casualties and destroying the garden cottage where, decades earlier, Henry James had worked.

Leasam House, Lady Maud Warrender's residence in Rye, 1906. Francis Frith Collection

More bombardments were anticipated. It was time to move inland. Before Eva and Bella took their leave, Lady Maud wrote in Bella's autograph book: "Lady Maud Warrender, September 1939-August 1940: 'War and Peace' at Leasam—happy days of music and laughter."

When Eva and Bella left Leasam House, the danger in London had not lifted; indeed, the worst days of the Blitz lay ahead. They resumed their lives in their parlor flat at 10 Ladbroke Square, which family members referred to as "No. 10." Like other Londoners, they carried on. They struck up friendships with their downstairs neighbors, corresponded with friends, kept up with Toto and Lady Maud, and entertained the occasional visitor. Bella had little energy and wrote to a friend that she stayed in bed until noon. The last Christmas of the war was spent at the home of Danish acquaintances, a rare occasion to dress up and go out. Another followed soon thereafter, in the spring of 1945, when Toto and Lady Maud hosted a dinner in honor of Bella's eightieth birthday at the posh Claridge Hotel.

During the war years, Eva and Bella took refuge in their past, spending countless hours organizing letters, programs, and scrapbooks, and recording myriad details of their adventures for their Russian friend Lucy Knupffer, who signed her letters to them "Lucy K." Two decades earlier, in the wake of the Bolshevik Revolution, Knupffer and her family had fled St. Petersburg and joined a community of monarchist exiles in London.

According to her grandson, Lucy K.'s life revolved around the Russian Orthodox Church and all things Russian. She moved in different circles from Eva and Bella, but they likely shared at least one acquaintance: Princess Kapitolina Mestchersky, described in Lucy Knupffer's manuscript as "a very gifted Russian . . . who was enormously rich and lived a luxurious but eccentric life . . . Under the pseudonym 'Tola Dorian' she wrote novels and essays and even a short history of France." The Princess lived near Paris, and "so much enjoyed the company of the two artists that she tried to persuade them to come and live with her." Mudocci and Edwards were said to be occasional houseguests of the Princess, but did not move in.

To be sure, Eva and Bella were often in need of patronage; nevertheless, this was a surprising link for a violinist who once claimed Jewish roots and counted Jews among her close friends. Princess Kapitolina Mestchersky, aka Tola Dorian, the author of mediocre French poetry and prose, was a notorious anti-Semite. It is not certain whether the Knupffers knew the Parisian Princess Mestchersky, but they certainly were acquainted with her first cousin by marriage, Princess Alexandra Mestchersky, a central figure in London's White Russian colony.

"My beloved friends," Lucy K. began a letter to Eva and Bella in early 1944. She reassured them that her inflamed appendix could probably be resolved without surgery, and that this would require rest. "*Please* don't speak to *anyone* about it," she added, with emphasis, "as I believe so much in the power of thought and therefore avoid thinking by other people about myself." She clearly shared Eva's belief in the power of thought, as well as her penchant for secrecy. The remainder of her letter outlined many requests: would Eva and Bella write down "missing links" about family history and about Bella's early career? She asked for "the required facts with as much as possible of detail and color," and signed off, "Fondest love from your devoted friend." Eva and Bella kept up with Lucy K's requests, and by the war's end, the account was finished (no doubt with much correction and polishing by Eva, judging by the wobbly syntax of Lucy K's letter and the Victorian flourishes of her manuscript). Its final line reads: "If now hate and suffering darken the horizon, the two musicians remain confident of the final victory of good over evil."

Victory did come. Eva and Bella had come through the war. They were increasingly frail, but counted themselves among the fortunate. There had been more than one hundred fatalities in Notting Hill Gate attributable to German attacks, about half in one devastating bombardment in January 1941. Several homes on Ladbroke Square had been leveled. Their generation was dwindling, and many of their old friends and acquaintances did not live to see the war's end. Louis Levy died in 1940, as did Janet Scudder. Christian Sinding died in 1941, Winnaretta Singer in 1943, and Edvard Munch in 1944. Lady Maud Warrender died in December 1945, just months after the Allied victory in Europe.

On Thursday, May 18, 1950, at a quarter past nine in the morning, a car pulled up at the Meadow Nursing Home at 49 Mulgrave Road in Sutton, some thirteen miles south of central London. Today, the square brick semi-detached house is configured as a four-bedroom townhouse; then, it was a small nursing home with an open ward, and though her friends thought it a cheerful, compassionate facility, Eva hated it.

Eva and Bella had grown accustomed to their flat at 10 Ladbroke Square, close to the house that Maud Warrender left to Toto Norman. In their own flat, they could continue performing for guests. Poul Rée, son of old Danish friends, visited along with his wife in 1947, and wrote that "they played quite enchanting music for us." In addition, Eva and Bella enjoyed the company of their neighbor, an accomplished painter of miniatures named Grace Rosher. Rosher shared Eva's spiritualist inclinations and had recounted to her friends her extraordinary experiences with automatic writing—the method that her deceased fiancé used to communicate with her from the other side. Eva and Bella lived just above Grace, her sister Frieda, and their mother, and were sorry to part with them. They had reluctantly agreed to the move when they could no longer manage on their own. Bella was frail and needed more help than Eva could manage. Eva no doubt needed looking after as well. But once settled in the nursing home, she could not get used to the lack of privacy.

The car made its way through London traffic to the BBC studio where Eva was scheduled to record recollections of Edvard Munch for the Norwegian Service. She had asked her daughter Isobel, now forty-one and the mother of three, to accompany her. Did they talk about Munch? Would this have been an opportunity for Isobel to ask questions that had clouded her childhood? And if not, did they chat about something else? Avoid speaking? Eva had never revealed to Isobel the name of her father, but Bella had told her that it was Edvard Munch. It could not have been lost on Isobel that her mother was about to broadcast to thousands her recollections of a man who was the subject of a vast silence between them.

Once at the studio, Eva sat in front of a BBC microphone the size of a brick. A photograph taken that day shows that she had

Eva Mudocci in May 1950, recording for the BBC Norwegian Service. WEBER FAMILY COLLECTION

dressed carefully, completing her outfit with a cardigan, flowered scarf, and dark beads. She wore a thin band, perhaps a watchband, on her right wrist. Her health had recently improved, and she looked every bit the well-preserved star. She rested a smart handbag on her lap, and seemed to be going over the script that lay on the table in front of her. She would be speaking in Norwegian, but there was no hint of nervousness; she had the instincts of an experienced performer. For once, Eva Mudocci gazed directly at the camera. Nearly fifty years had passed since her first meeting with Munch, and now, for the first time, she would be speaking publicly about their friendship. The program began with a musical selection, noted on the script as "Bach D major"—very likely the evocative *Air* from J.S. Bach's *Orchestral Suite No. 3*.

The half-hour program was broadcast in Norway on June 26, 1950. At that time, London had not yet come to appreciate Munch. The artist had visited England only once, in 1913. Not until 1936 was his work thought to merit a one-man show. In that year, the London Gallery had hung an array of his paintings, drawings, and prints. A catalogue essay by Herbert Read, "The Significance of Edvard Munch," told British visitors: "Munch is an artist whose work is little known in this country, but there is no doubt that he has been one of the most important influences of the last fifty years. He occupies, in relation to the modern German movement, a position comparable to Cézanne's in French painting." Newspapers mocked these claims. Those that covered the exhibit ran such headlines as "Unapproachable Artist" and "An Artist Recluse," characterizing Munch as a misanthropic eccentric with a grudge against the English. They did not bother to discuss the work.

One reviewer did take the exhibit seriously, but he too derided the notion of Munch's significance. Thomas Wade Earp, a leading art critic of the day, told readers of the *Daily Telegraph* that an 1892 show of Munch's work in Berlin had stirred so much controversy that the exhibit had been abruptly closed. "To-day the loud colour and cavalier brushwork of 'Woman Reclining,' 'The Sick Child,' or 'Waterside' create no shock. Their violence seems superficial and not to have worn so well as the rather weak academicism it overlies." The comparison of Munch to Cézanne may have irked Earp, who had written reverently about the French artist, while diminishing Munch, in a book published a year earlier called *The Modern Movement in Painting*. "Munch deserves the honour due to a pioneer," he wrote, "but beside Cézanne and Renoir he does not rank as a leader."

This was the second article about the Munch exhibit to appear in the *Daily Telegraph*. A fortnight earlier, a particularly snide, unsigned article in the same newspaper, entitled "Edvard Munch's Goloshes," had reported on a preview of the show. It reported that Munch's "sensitive soul has been much worried by the exhibition. He had, he wrote to a friend, a dream in which he was selling galoshes—worn-out ones—for vast prices, and everyone called him a swindler." The reviewer added, "As far as I could judge there was no direct connection between Mr. Munch's pictures and his pedicultural nightmare." Seven months later, Adolf Hitler would open the Nazis' Degenerate Art Exhibit in Berlin with a speech that called artists like Munch "art swindlers," attacking them in cruder but not unsimilar terms.

Munch dispatched no more works to London. He remained virtually unknown in England. Then, six years after the artist's death, England discovered him, thanks in no small measure to Sir Kenneth Clark, Director of Britain's National Gallery of Art, whose archived papers include a typescript appreciation written by Clark when Munch died in 1944. He called Munch "one of the greatest figures in contemporary art" and added: "The almost total neglect in this country of an artist roughly equivalent to Strindberg in literature or Sibelius in music reflects the influence of the theory of 'pure' painting." Clark concluded with the hope that after the war, "a representative collection of Munch's work will be shown in this country, for there is much in it which could be of value to English painters."

Accordingly, in 1950, the Tate Gallery began preparing for a month-long exhibit of Munch's paintings, etchings, and lithographs scheduled for November of the following year. As plans for the exhibit unfolded, an enterprising Norwegian painter and art critic remembered the striking Englishwoman in *The Brooch*. Waldemar Stabell, who was then living in London, tracked down Eva Mudocci and asked her to write out reminiscences of Munch. He would turn her recollections into a script to be recorded for broadcast by the BBC's Norwegian service.

Stabell suggested that she focus on Munch's ambivalent relationship to Norwegians in Paris during the century's early years, and about their gatherings at such haunts as Le Dôme, but Eva demurred. Munch had often avoided his countrymen, and "it could so easily be misinterpreted, nor would it serve his popularity in Norway to spread the fact of his dislike of the Norwegian Colony in Paris." Eva recalled Edvard's cautioning her against getting "too caught up in that 'bummeln' [loafing] as he called it, which had, certainly, its fascination. He need not have feared for me as what he said was true—that we had the same faculty of sitting beside oneself, criticizing oneself and judging—a sure guard against being 'caught' up."

In another letter to Stabell, Mudocci wrote: "As with so much else in Munch's life, as in his character, there was the blending of tragedy & comedy, which to anyone knowing him for what he truly was, a great & gallant soul, was heartbreaking, knowing its cause."

The recollections she sent to Stabell contained several anecdotes that have become standard fare in Munch biographies, including an account of how Munch sent the weighty lithographic stone from *The Brooch* to Eva and Bella's Berlin hotel room, with the note, "Here is the stone that fell from my heart."

Eva recalled that in one of the letters lost during the war, Edvard had spoken of her "two thousand year old eyes." Writing to Stabell, she wondered: "Would he recognize these eyes now? If they no longer seem two thousand years old, but only the eyes of a very tired old woman? I think he would because he never looked merely at the surface of anything but always beyond—therefore his drawings. I think I understood that from the first."

Mudocci offered an account of the last time she and Bella saw Munch. "We went—in time for his beloved tea-o'clock, & found him looking ill, but greatly moved at seeing us again after so long." Mudocci did not put dates to events, but this meeting may have occurred when Eva and Bella returned to Scandinavia after the armistice. They found Munch suffering from a severe bout of influenza.

She wrote to Stabell:

The following day we received [a message] early, that we were to come to him. We found him in bed, surrounded by medicine bottles. He believed that he had influenza, which was likely, as he often suffered from that mysterious malady, but on that account he did not want us to stay—since the whole of Åsgårdstrand was—he was sure—now full of microbes—so to satisfy him we left—being refused the hotel bill, as 'Mr Munch had settled that,' and carrying with us the sad last sight of him we were ever to have—except in memory where to this day I keep it holy—Holy because through all the vagueries (*sic*) masking it at times, nothing could keep the holiness of a character noble and pure and great from shining out.

In a postscript, Eva wrote to Stabell: "I do not know at all if anything I have sent you is what you want but I have done my best. I could say much more in praise of him but do not think it necessary."

The decades had not diminished Eva's partiality for epistolary tidiness. She told Stabell, "I apologize sincerely for sending you such ill written copy, but there is no time to improve upon it, & in any case, my hand being rather shaky, from neuritis—I fear I could not make a better one." She went on, "I do hope at least that in what I have been able to give you will find a few useful notes—though nothing can give the character of a man who out of a sort of shyness would feign hardness to hide the warm, generous great heart beneath the mask." Eva added, "It is also difficult to write in an open ward like this, with no privacy or convenience for writing."

When Eva's friends learned of her BBC broadcast, they were astonished. On May 20, 1950, Lyell Barbour responded to Toto Norman's news: "It is miraculous about the Munck (*sic*) revival, and that Eva is to broadcast . . . I do hope that this will lead to better times for them; the fact that she is so much better shows that either that is the result of the Munck situation or perhaps that her 'star' is slightly rising."

Three weeks later, he told Toto that he had received "a most touching letter from Eva," describing her broadcast "regarding the Munch Affair." Barbour wrote: "How extraordinary it is the way an artist or composer may suddenly come into posthumous fame!

I think it is most romantic about her long correspondence with him, etc."

That the "Munch affair" so astounded Lyell Barbour suggests that Eva and Bella kept this chapter of their history from the close friends who came to think of them as gifted and charming but nonetheless pathetic. For Eva, the recollections had been held close. As she had foreseen when she wrote to Edvard Munch nearly a half century earlier, "in the end, with the last thoughts, only some wonderful memories—like jewels that one has worn secretly and sees again with life's last glance."

Eva's friends were stunned to learn that she owned two "pictures" by Munch. "Couldn't they be sold?" Lyell Barbour asked. In the months that followed the Munch revival and the BBC recording, Eva's star did not rise. Her son Kai remained in a long-term care facility operated by Denmark's Vordingborg Mental Hospital. In July 1950, friends heard the news that Eva's daughter Isobel was being treated for cancer. Eva reacted by losing herself in astrology magazines. A year later, she broke her wrist.

Friends continued to send occasional checks (usually through Toto or the Musicians' Benevolent Association). Tension over financial support for Eva and Bella strained longstanding friendships. Henri Deering lived around the corner from Arthur Shattuck on the upper east side of Manhattan, and the two pianists sometimes lunched together. In 1950, the two men fell out when Henri's letters, asking whether Arthur might be able to do more for Eva and Bella, went unanswered.

Henri Deering and Arthur Shattuck never spoke again. On October 16, 1951, Shattuck, age seventy, was found dead in the bathtub of his Park Avenue apartment. Deering assured Toto that he had broken the news to Eva and Bella, "so they may now cease to hope ever to hear from him." He added, "I can only feel that with him avarice was a veritable malady." He was disgusted to hear that Shattuck had left $20,000 to one of "two young morons" who had lunched with Arthur every day for his last two years. As Deering supposed, there was indeed a malady, but it was more lethal than avarice. It was later revealed by Arthur's brother that he had become addicted first to sleeping pills and later to other narcotics.

Despite losses and setbacks, Eva and Bella continued to take pleasure in each other's company. On January 4, 1952, Lyell Barbour wrote to Toto, "I was so happy Bella and Eva had a lovely Xmas and their being together still is terribly touching."

The "being together" came to an end two months later. On February 25, 1952, Eva died at age seventy-nine at Dulwich Hospital in London, where she had been taken due to an intestinal blockage resulting from scarring from past surgery. A cremation at Honor Oak Crematorium in London was arranged by Frank Thistleton, a violinist who served as president of the Musicians' Benevolent Association. This organization, whose board long included Maud Warrender and Gertrude Norman, had for years contributed to Eva and Bella's support.

Bella Edwards and Eva Mudocci, c. 1950.
WEBER FAMILY COLLECTION

When he learned of her passing, Henri Deering wrote to Toto, "You are right, she has gone on to a happier place where she will find the answers to all the things that so fascinated and interested her on this planet. Also, to have had her wish not to be separated from Bella right up to the end."

Bella was eighty-seven and was, for the first time in a half-century, on her own. She lived for two years after Eva's death, and friends remarked that she seemed to be taking life "philosophically." They marveled that for a time, she seemed to have renewed optimism and energy. Toto wrote to Lyell Barbour that, contrary to what some acquaintances believed, Eva had dominated Bella, and that perhaps Bella now felt some sense of release.

Barbour replied, "I of course realized always Eva's fear of losing B., but was under the impression that because of that B. had the upper hand and that Eva's life was one of sacrifice and abject devotion, through fear, in order to hold B. from everyone. But you give a more inner and subtle aspect."

He added, "It seems impossible that E's studies of occult and Oriental philosophies could not have taught her more wisdom in this relationship—an example of the utter stubbornness and relentlessness of human instinct and feeling, once directed and fed by emotion. And that emotion, in this case, a dark well of power."

The husband of Bella's niece—a prominent Danish neurologist and political figure named Mogens Fog—visited a number of times, and there was briefly talk of moving Bella to Denmark. In the end, she remained in the nursing home in Croyden. An increasingly frail Toto Norman remained her most loyal friend, visiting whenever she could. On the back of a card bearing a black-and-white reproduction of Christian Krohg's portrait of her at the piano, Bella wrote to Toto, "I thank God every day for your friendship, it will help me to the end."

Another friend also helped her to the end. Late in 1952, after Eva's death, Lyell Barbour wrote to Toto, "I am glad Arthur left something to Bella." Henri Deering was no doubt surprised and relieved to learn of this bequest. When Bella's end came, in March of 1954, Deering wrote, "I trust that now she and Eva are together once more and that they will even be with their old friend Shattuck too."

It was left to Toto Norman to deal with some of Bella's personal effects. A number of items were sent to close friends, such as Barbour and Deering, but most of their possessions went to Isobel

Weber. Janet Weber recalls that once her grandmother and Bella were both gone, "we got a huge amount of stuff that went into the garage—a cello and viola, a clavichord and harpsichord, statues, papers. But there was a lot of pressure to get rid of it all." Janet's mother was not well, and went into the hospital. Soon thereafter, her parents separated. "My father stayed on in the house for a time," Janet said. "He may have gotten rid of everything then." Janet added that financial strain prompted her mother to sell at least one Munch lithograph of Mudocci. "It went for a song—not much more than £25 [about $750 today]."

According to Janet, Bella Edwards died without ever casting doubt on her assertion that the twins' father was Edvard Munch. Eva Mudocci died without ever contradicting Bella or disclosing the father's identity. Everyone was left with questions. It would take another sixty years for the backstory to come to light.

Part II

Do not ring unless an answer is required.

*Plaque on the outside door of
Eva Mudocci's Notting Hill Gate flat*

11

Tremors

"*Edvard Munch døde barnløs*" – "Edvard Munch died childless."

So begins the Norwegian National Archive's commentary on a prized holding—the artist's Last Will & Testament. The will bequeathed most of Munch's vast trove of artworks to the municipality of Oslo. Munch also left his writings to the municipality, stipulating that experts should determine the extent to which they should be made public. He excluded his correspondence—the thousands of letters and drafts of letters, stuffed into suitcases, that he entrusted to his sister Inger. After going through the letters and removing those she thought unfit for public scrutiny, Inger donated them to the municipality of Oslo with the understanding that they would be archived at the planned Munch Museum.

In the years after Munch's death, no one cast doubt on the childless condition of the famously lonely, unmarried man who gave indelible form to human desolation: not the sister or niece who survived him; not the acquaintances who heard him declare repeatedly his unfitness for fatherhood; and certainly not the Oslo

Psychiatrist Otto Lund. LUND FAMILY COLLECTION

officials who found themselves in possession of a priceless collection. As the years passed, no one troubled these officials with the possibility that Munch offspring might surface—no one, that is, except for a tenacious physician named Otto Lund, chief physician of Denmark's Vordingborg Mental Hospital, who in the early spring of 1962 announced himself in the Oslo offices of the soon-to-open Munch Museum.

Dr. Lund had arranged a meeting with Johan Henrik Langaard, the man tapped to direct the new museum. Eighteen years after Munch's death, the building that would house the collection was still under construction. Its doors were set to open the following year, in May 1963, in time to mark the centenary of the artist's birth. Museum officials were vibrating with excitement—in a cultivated, minimalist way.

The meeting was out of the ordinary for Dr. Lund, whose trips to Norway usually took him to meetings of the Scandinavian psychiatrists' union or to ski lodges. It was no less unusual for the museum director. The calendar on Johan Langaard's well-appointed, blond desk was densely populated by city officials, patrons, architects, and art restoration experts. Like Munch himself, who went to great lengths to hold onto his paintings, Langaard jealously guarded the collection and was known to parry questions from visitors. A half year before Lund's visit, the widely published American critic Hilton Kramer, then chief editor of the prestigious monthly *Arts*, had traveled to Oslo to preview the collection and was turned away. Kramer assumed that officials were avoiding exposure of the poor condition of many Munch canvases. He wrote that his request had sent "a tremor of anxiety" through Oslo officialdom.

If Kramer's routine inquiry caused a tremor, Otto Lund's mission was likely to set off a more powerful quake. The psychiatrist understood that the theory he was about to present, if proven, could throw into doubt the ownership of the entire collection, shaking the new museum's foundations. It had the potential to rock not only Norway's art establishment, but also its government. In the postwar era, establishing Edvard Munch as a cultural hero was a key to Norway's effort to enhance its prestige in the international community. The sudden appearance of unexpected heirs would be a most unwelcome development. At the meeting with Lund, the museum's urbane director would have been unlikely to betray concern, but by training and instinct, the psychiatrist was prepared to detect any seismic activity beneath Langaard's polished surface.

At age sixty-two, Director Johan Langaard was a familiar figure in Oslo's cultural scene and the obvious choice to head the new museum. He had a long acquaintance with Munch's work and with the artist himself. As a young man in the 1920s, Langaard had served as assistant director of Norway's National Museum, the institution to which his father, a brewery magnate and one of Oslo's wealthiest men, had willed his private art collection. Langaard rose quickly, and in the 1930s, as a leading figure in Oslo's museum world, exchanged numerous letters with Edvard Munch. In 1946, two years after Munch's death, Langaard became director of a municipal agency called the City of Oslo Art Collections, established largely to look after the Munch legacy.

A third man joined the meeting. Beginning in the early 1950s, Langaard had co-authored several studies of Munch with an ambitious young art historian named Reidar Revold. When Langaard became the Munch Museum's founding director in 1962, he brought his co-author along as senior curator. Revold, a tall man with dark hair and horn-rimmed glasses, had a studious, casual look, at least in comparison with his buttoned-up boss. The senior curator's new responsibilities must have weighed heavily. Revold was entrusted with thousands of Munch's paintings, prints, and drawings, many in deplorable condition. He also became responsible for a vast collection of the artist's journals, letters, and other documents. The position was a stretch for a man who had been a journalist before earning a master's degree in art, and whose most recent post had been art critic for the Oslo daily *Aftenposten*. But he enjoyed the confidence of art experts, who considered Langaard and Revold a dream team. In 1964, Hilton Kramer wrote that the two men "undoubtedly know more about Edvard Munch's life and art than anyone else now writing."

Once formalities had been dispensed with, Dr. Lund explained the reason for his visit. More than a half century earlier, in 1908, the unmarried violinist Eva Mudocci had given birth to twins—a girl and a boy. In time, her daughter became a pianist, married, and by 1962 had a family of her own in England. Mudocci's son, a painter, had been an in-patient at Dr. Lund's psychiatric hospital for three decades. As a long-term resident, the painter had been assigned to a nursing home operated by the hospital in Sakskøbing, not far from his birthplace on Denmark's southern coast. Dr. Lund came right to the point: he suspected that Edvard Munch was the father of his patient and his patient's twin sister. He was hoping to find evidence in the museum's archives; in particular, he wanted to review any correspondence between Munch and Mudocci.

Letters following up on this 1962 meeting have remained in the Munch Museum's administrative files for the last fifty years. Their language and tone make it easy to imagine the tense discussion: Dr. Lund's précis of his theory delivered with a medical researcher's practiced detachment; the officials' demeanor—their mild disdain painted over with exaggerated deference; their eagerness to end the exchange.

Langaard and Revold acknowledged familiarity with the name Eva Mudocci, and the outlines of what Langaard, in subsequent correspondence, called her "undoubted affair" with Edvard Munch. Indeed, as they met with Lund, the two museum officials had a book in press, *Edvard Munch: Paintings and Prints*, that featured *The*

Edvard Munch. MUNCH MUSEUM

Louis Levy. ROYAL DANISH LIBRARY,
PHOTOGRAPH BY SIGURD TRIER

Kai Ellson at about age 20. WEBER
FAMILY COLLECTION

Brooch—Eva Mudocci on its cover. But they assured the doctor that
Munch was not the father and turned the conversation to another
candidate—the Copenhagen writer Louis Levy who had died in
1940. The officials said that they would nevertheless consider the
psychiatrist's request to examine the archived letters—once they
themselves had reviewed the materials.

The museum officials then steered Dr. Lund to a topic they considered more appropriate for his consideration—a diagnosis of Edvard Munch that had appeared in an article published forty years earlier: "degenerative mental illness with alcoholic frenzy and violent paroxysms." What did the psychiatrist think of this diagnosis?

As he said goodbye to Otto Lund and wished him a safe return to Denmark, Director Langaard may well have recalled that the letters Edvard Munch had sent him thirty years earlier harped on one subject in particular—his distrust of Danes.

Dr. Otto Lund was not given immediate access to Mudocci's letters when he visited the Munch Museum in the spring of 1962. As he later told his family, his inquiries had been met with barely disguised hostility. This was not surprising. The museum's doors had not yet opened, and here was a man with considerable credibility raising the possibility of children—non-Norwegian children—who could conceivably turn up and lay claim to Munch's work. Whether or not it was likely to succeed, such a claim had the potential to create legal knots that would take years to untangle. The museum officials were not about to release anything from its archives without first scouring the documents themselves.

Director Langaard and Senior Curator Revold took several weeks for their review and then responded. On April 25, 1962, Langaard sent Lund typed copies of fifty-six letters from Mudocci to Munch, stressing the need for strict confidentiality—an odd role reversal, given that the psychiatrist had been discussing his patient with the museum officials. Some of the letters were undated, but judging by their content, they spanned the years from April 1903 to October 1907 and then resumed in October 1909, with no explanation for the two-year gap covering the time when the twins were conceived and born.

"As you will see," the Director wrote, "there is here no evidence for your theory about the children, but we are sending the documents anyway, both because they surely will interest you, and because we would greatly appreciate getting your technical analysis and assessment of the letters and the undoubted love affair." By "technical analysis and assessment," Langaard presumably meant psychiatric appraisal.

As soon as he received the copies, Dr. Lund wrote back, acknowledging receipt of the documents and offering in return the photograph of "our patient" as a young man. He wrote, "I am not inclined to give too much weight to any similarities," adding that "our patient's appearance does not directly contradict the notion that he could be a cross between Eva Mudocci and Edvard Munch," and at the same time, "does not speak against his being a cross between Eva Mudocci and the other putative father, Louis Levy."

Over the next two years, Dr. Otto Lund devoted his days to rounds, case reviews, and administrative tasks at the psychiatric hospital. In the late afternoons, he would return home to his book-lined study, where the mystery of his patient's parentage awaited him. He read and re-read the Munch-Mudocci correspondence, taking copious notes that he handed off to his secretary, or sometimes his wife, to type. Dr. Lund and the Munch Museum officials stayed in contact over the next two years, exchanging occasional letters. To the usual buffed surface of professional correspondence, both sides added a thick coat of flattery, betraying a certain wariness. Dr. Lund bent over backwards to acknowledge his lack of stature in the art world, repeatedly apologizing for presuming, "as a layman," to interfere "in matters for which, I freely admit, I lack the necessary technical knowledge." Nevertheless, as he researched Edvard Munch and worked his way through Mudocci's letters, Otto Lund thought he was onto something.

The museum officials had assured Lund that the immense collection of Munch's letters to friends and family in their archives included only a few innocuous references to Eva Mudocci, and certainly none that suggested a pregnancy or children. But from a psychiatrist's standpoint, silences can be freighted with meaning. In one letter, Lund asked Langaard a question that showed his way of thinking about the evidence. He noted that Munch did not hesitate to mention other women, notably Tulla Larsen, and asked, "Is it not peculiar that the relationship with Eva Mudocci was so 'sacred' to him that he would not mention it in letters to his family or his friends?"

Lund received no answer to that question, nor to his inquiry about whether the museum had asked Mudocci's daughter, Isobel Weber, for any letters from Munch that might be in her possession. Lund suggested that such a request would need to be made delicately, and considered Director Langaard the best person to approach Mrs. Weber.

Work on the letters proceeded slowly. Not all of them were dated, and Lund wanted to know enough about the protagonists' activities and whereabouts, month by month, to sequence them, and to work out whether Eva and Edvard had crossed paths in the early spring of March 1908, when the babies would have been conceived. He read everything he could find on Munch's life. To establish a chronology of Mudocci's travels and concerts, he borrowed from Isobel Weber a scrapbook of clippings that Eva and Bella had compiled. He considered linguistic evidence, including Eva's increasing comfort over time with writing in Danish (which in her day was even closer to written Norwegian than it is now). It took time, but eventually he came up with a detailed, annotated chronology, disagreeing in several instances with the museum's sequencing of the letters. His cautious notes reflected his sense that the task required delicacy and tact.

Early in 1962, Dr. Otto Lund began a correspondence with his patient's sister, Isobel Weber, hoping to extract facts that would shed light on the twins' parentage. And here Isobel's daughter, Janet Weber, enters the story. Soon after that correspondence began, twenty-two-year-old Janet enrolled in a summer weaving course at a Danish folk arts college and made plans to visit her Uncle Kai.

Kai, now in his mid-fifties, was a long-term resident of a nursing home in Sakskøbing known as Sakskøhoj. A Danish passport listed his occupation as "wood sculptor," but it was painting that absorbed him. More than fifty years earlier, in 1908-09, Dr. Daniel Jacobson had arranged for Edvard Munch to turn his room in a Danish psychiatric clinic into a makeshift studio. Dr. Otto Lund made the same accommodation for Kai Ellson. Then as now, Sakskøhoj operated a farm where patients could grow produce and sell it to local people. Taking a new interest in this longtime patient, Dr. Lund arranged for Kai to mix farm work with painting, and provided studio space in an enclosed gazebo on the clinic's peaceful grounds.

Janet Weber remembers spending time there with her uncle. The studio remains standing today—a squat, half-timbered, mustard-yellow tower with checkerboard windowpanes and a thatched roof. Her Uncle Kai was, Janet says, a gentle person who could seem quite present at one moment, and off in his own world the next. Janet found his hallucinations fascinating, and when she visited, she tried to follow along on his fantasy adventures.

During her visit, Janet stayed with the doctor and his wife in Vordingborg, in their comfortable house on the hospital grounds. Dr. Lund was a thoughtful host. He noticed Janet's interest in mental illness and took her through the wards. At home, he showed her his collection of Kai's paintings, as well as work by other patients. Otto Lund also had in his possession pencil sketches of Eva Mudocci playing the violin that he suspected were the work of Edvard Munch. He wrote to Munch Museum Senior Curator

Revold, "Although I am obviously not in a position to evaluate these sketches, you will probably easily judge whether they could be sketches from Munch's hand."

It was Dr. Lund who first told Janet, during her visit to Denmark, that Edvard Munch was very likely the twins' father—and Janet's grandfather. His source was Copenhagen art dealer Poul Rée, a former diplomat and longtime acquaintance of Eva and Bella. Rée was interested in mounting an exhibit of Kai's paintings. Dr. Lund arranged for Janet to meet Rée so she could hear firsthand his account of her grandmother as well as his proposal to exhibit and sell her uncle's paintings.

Janet was unsure what to make of a story she was hearing for the first time. She knew who Munch was, but knew little about him and had never heard of his possible connection to the family. She had gone to Denmark to study weaving, not to unravel family history, and so she did not ask the questions that would become so compelling later in her life. It was clear to Janet that Lund and Rée wanted her to act as a go-between—to persuade her mother Isobel to agree to an exhibit of Kai's artwork—and that they wanted to promote him as the son of Edvard Munch. The story started to mean more when Janet returned home and told her mother what she had heard from the psychiatrist and the art dealer. "That's when it all opened up between my mother and me," Janet says.

In mid-June 1963, more than a year after he received the copies of Mudocci's letters, Dr. Lund opened a curt note from Director Langaard, requesting return of the copies and asking for an assessment of their contents. The psychiatrist was out of time. Two weeks later, Lund wrote back to Langaard, enclosing a copy of his carefully annotated chronology and reporting his finding: Munch was not the father. The word NOT was written in capital letters.

Kai Ellson, *Untitled*, undated. This portrait is based on the 1891 photograph of his mother as "Miss Rose Lynton" (p.19). A Star of David was drawn at the left edge. LUND FAMILY COLLECTION

Kai Ellson, *Untitled*, undated. LUND FAMILY COLLECTION / AUTHOR'S PHOTOGRAPH

When Dr. Otto Lund's words "NOT the father" were read, and the typographic emphasis was absorbed, sighs of relief must have been audible in the offices of the Munch Museum. If you listen carefully, you can hear their echoes today in the overlapping academic, cultural, governmental, and corporate spheres that constitute Norway's Munch-industrial complex.

Kai Ellson, c. 1963. WEBER FAMILY COLLECTION

Construction is now underway on a huge, impressive glass museum and research center in central Oslo that will house Munch's works and archives, as part of the nation's effort to create a global brand around the artist whose work Norwegians were slow to appreciate during his lifetime. The Munch Museum in Oslo's Toyen district has for some time been considered past its prime—cramped, inconveniently located, and all in all unworthy of its subject. But in 1962, the museum's opening was anticipated with elation and pride. Many works in its collection had never been seen—in Norway or beyond its borders. Never before had the work of a major artist been concentrated to such a degree in one museum. The works of most masters are scattered in the collections of descendants and patrons, as well as in private collections and museums around the world. Munch's was an exceptional case. As Langaard and Revold wrote in a joint biography, from 1914 on, the artist was averse to selling his paintings, storing them in his own home and relying on multiple issues of prints to earn a living. During the last years of Munch's life, a uniquely hostile

Sketches of Mudocci, believed by Otto Lund to be the work of Edvard Munch. They most likely were drawn by Arthur Shattuck, the American pianist and artist. LUND FAMILY COLLECTION / AUTHOR'S PHOTOGRAPH

cultural context redoubled his resolve to hold back his work. He was determined to keep his canvases away from Nazi officials, who deemed his work "degenerate."

When Munch died, more than half of his paintings and many of his works on paper became part of his estate. The fact that Munch was childless proved to be a tremendous boon to the city of Oslo and its Munch Museum. The municipality not only owned most of Munch's work; it also shared rights to his work (and revenue from the licensing of his images) with descendants of Andrea Ellingsen, Munch's niece.

In recent years, Norway has reclaimed its favorite son in a huge way, and the celebration of Munch's 150th birthday in 2013 permeated Norwegians' daily experience. But as preparations were underway, dissatisfaction surfaced. In October 2012, the *Wall Street Journal* reported, nearly one thousand people "packed the streets of Oslo carrying torches to the music of a marching band demanding that Oslo City Council members find a better home for Munch's work" than the inadequate Munch Museum. The article quoted Elisabeth Munch-Ellingsen, a great grandniece of the artist, who "jokes that the 11 family members who share rights with the city of Oslo should 'claim our inheritance back' because of the artist's mistreatment.'" Presumably, Oslo officials were not amused.

And presumably officials had not been amused half a century earlier when the Danish psychiatrist appeared in their offices, threatening the status quo. Dr. Lund's reversal would certainly have occasioned relief. But why did Otto Lund send museum officials such an emphatic conclusion? Nothing in his notes or annotated chronology either proves or disproves Munch's paternity. And why, after disavowing his theory, did Dr. Lund continue to pursue it?

12

Unsettled

"**B**oth Otto Lund and Poul Rée were quite definite that Munch was my grandfather," Janet Weber told me.

It was February 2013. A half century had passed since Janet was first told that Edvard Munch was her grandfather; a half year had passed since she made that story public on Norwegian television. I had driven from New York to meet Janet in her New England home and to learn more about her grandmother. When she met me outside the door of her apartment, she seemed immediately familiar. She reminded me of my own relatives.

I knew from a mutual acquaintance that in the world of contemplative studies, Janet is highly regarded as a spiritual director who leads retreat experiences grounded in solitude, silence, and prayer. I was struck by her openness. She described her early years studying at London's Royal Ballet School, her interest in dance drama, and her time in the theater. She talked about her experiences teaching children of all ages. She said that family members, who were not Catholic, were initially distressed by her decision to take vows. It occurred to me that her grandmother had also been drawn to the Catholic Church. Eva Mudocci wrote to Edvard Munch from

Paris that she would, at times of sorrow or stress, walk to nearby Sainte-Clotilde to light candles and pray.

Janet shares her grandmother's focus on the non-material world, albeit in a different context. She described her ongoing work with individuals who want to explore questions of the spirit, to integrate into day-to-day existence what she called "the moreness of life"—the dimension of human experience that is beyond thought, that may seem at the edge of peripheral vision, just out of reach, and yet can be deeply felt. She had a way of talking about religious sensibility that made it seem both unremarkable and momentous.

Janet had earned a doctorate from Columbia Teachers College. "Maxine Greene took me under her wing," she said, and told me about her work with the distinguished educational philosopher. Janet had mixed work in education with anthropology, linguistics, and phenomenology, and had written about how language conveys "insiderness" and "outsiderness." I found myself wondering how that opposition had played out in the life of a woman who belongs to a religious community but started out in the theater and had put her quest for identity in the public eye. This was my first glimmer of a tension that would animate and constrain our conversations over the next several years.

We had spent nearly an hour together before the conversation turned to Eva Mudocci. Janet broached the subject of her grandmother first, saying she had been surprised to receive my inquiry. I explained that I am an amateur violinist and had become curious about historical figures (Albert Einstein, Thomas Jefferson, Henri Matisse) who devoted countless hours to such an unforgiving instrument. I knew that famous amateurs sometimes persuaded virtuosos to play duets with them. Looking for violinists in biographies of Matisse, I had come across Eva Mudocci, whose "passionate violin playing spoke directly to Parisians in the first winter of [World War I]." I had never heard of her.

Yes, Janet said, Matisse knew her grandmother. She looked through some papers she had gathered and handed me a photocopy of a Matisse portrait. Dating to the First World War, the portrait showed Eva with sunken cheeks. Compared with Munch's spirited lady with a brooch, this Mudocci seemed drained. When Matisse drew her, she was in her mid-forties. "This portrait captures Grandmother as I remember her," Janet told me. That would have been when Mudocci was in her seventies.

Janet said that she did not remember much about her grandmother. Eva died in February 1952, when Janet was not quite twelve. "We rarely met and always in conjunction with my mother," she said. "Eva never came to our house."

She had one vivid memory of a visit to Eva and Bella's London flat. She had just turned seven and was taken to see them before a ballet lesson. A strong smell of burnt food greeted them. Eva, or perhaps it was Bella, had cooked lunch in the kitchen and forgotten it. The two other rooms were indescribably cluttered—"shambolic," Janet said. In the bathroom stood a stack of poetry books that her grandmother had published under a male pseudonym, and Janet was given a copy as a birthday gift. She still has the volume, inscribed "To darling Janet with love from Granny." On a second line Granny had signed "Harry Brander," and on a third, with a flourish, "Eva Mudocci."

I thought such a gift would make a strong impression on a child, and assumed that Janet would have admired Eva. Janet corrected this impression. "I did not admire my grandmother," she said. "I just knew her as my grandmother."

Janet explained that at some point, her mother changed her name from Isabella to Isobel, "perhaps to distance herself from Bella," she suggested. It seemed to her that her mother did not wish to be identified with Eva's lifelong companion. "The relationship between Mother and Grandmother could not be called close," she continued.

I asked what came between them.

"You have to understand the times," Janet said. "These were children born out of wedlock. Grandmother could not acknowledge them. It was an impossible situation. Very difficult for my mother."

Janet described her television interview, and told me how her offer to take a DNA test had come about. In the months since the broadcast, Janet had discovered that DNA testing was not as straightforward as she had imagined. Whose DNA could be compared with her own? Edvard Munch had no known children, and of the artist's four siblings, only one had a child—a daughter named Andrea. Andrea's granddaughter, Elisabeth Munch-Ellingsen, would be the closest living relative, and the American art collector Sally Epstein had put them in touch with each other. I had to jot numerous lines and circles on a notepad to figure out that Elisabeth is Edvard Munch's great-grandniece. If Janet was indeed Edvard Munch's granddaughter, that would make her Elisabeth's second cousin once removed.

Elisabeth readily agreed to a DNA comparison, telling a Norwegian Broadcasting audience, "This is fun for us, if it's true." But Elisabeth and Janet were soon told that establishing paternity, or "grand-paternity," is not always as simple as reality television would suggest, especially when the chain of Y-chromosomes passed from male to male has been broken. With DNA samples from distant cousins, a laboratory would gauge the probability of kinship, but could not promise a definitive answer. This did not seem to faze Elisabeth Munch-Ellingsen. With or without a genetic study, she seemed open to the possibility that she and Janet were related. When she met Janet in person, Elisabeth was struck by a family resemblance, as were other family members.

During our first visit, I asked Janet how confident she was that

Munch was her grandfather. "Ninety percent," she said. "Perhaps less." Janet explained her reasoning: "It was Bella who told my mother that Edvard Munch was her father. She was very certain, and she had no reason to lie." Moreover, Janet's mother had some memory of being taken, with her brother, to meet Edvard Munch when they were very young, perhaps five or six. Isobel had the impression that Munch had drawn a portrait of the twins.

"And then there's the artistic inheritance," she continued. Janet's mother became a pianist, as did one of Janet's brothers. But her Uncle Kai—her mother's twin bother—had been an uncommonly talented artist. And like Edvard Munch, Kai suffered from severe psychiatric problems. She added that a number of her nieces and nephews have turned out to be very gifted artistically.

"You know," Janet said, as the afternoon light dimmed, "some people think my grandmother and Bella were lesbians."

Her "some people" took me aback, given that the two women lived together for half a century.

"That's not your impression?"

"They were artists." Janet continued, "Their lives were entirely wrapped up in music." She did not believe there was a physical dimension.

"I see," I said, taking a few seconds to gather my thoughts. "Of course one can't be certain, if there are no letters between them." She shook her head.

"But, you know," I ventured, "they did choose to live on the Left Bank in Paris for more than twenty years." Janet looked unimpressed by this argument. "And," I went on, aware that we were coming at this from very different viewpoints, "there are memoirs from the time that talk about Eva and Bella playing regularly at certain salons—I mean, salons frequented by Gertrude Stein." I had in mind gatherings at the Montparnasse home of Stein's friend Janet

Scudder, whose memoir recalled that Eva and Bella "came often" and played "very passionate music," but I mentioned neither Scudder nor other, less celebrated lesbian or bisexual women in their Paris circle, such as writer Mildred Aldrich or sculptor Malvina Hoffman.

As Janet went to the kitchen to make us tea, I realized that I had a decision to make. "Perhaps I should mention," I said when she returned with a tray, "that I live with a woman—I've been a lesbian since my twenties." Janet did not appear shaken by this disclosure. "I did not come to this research with an agenda," I added, hoping I didn't sound too defensive. "I started with the violin and Matisse. But based on what I know so far, I think it very likely that they were lovers."

Janet thought for a minute. "Mother would be very unsettled by that idea," she said. "She was very open-minded, but it was a different era."

"How people choose to live is their affair," she added after a few moments. "I have no desire to judge. But my grandmother and Bella did not lay claim to that relationship, so I don't think others should claim it for them, when they're not here to agree or disagree."

"I understand," I said, "But of course your grandmother and Edvard Munch weren't public about their relationship either, and yet—."

Janet saw where I was going with this. She was willing to make public her grandmother's liaison with Munch, although Eva and Edvard were not here to agree or disagree.

"That's different," she said. "That's something I heard directly from my mother. And I have nieces and nephews who would like to know about their heritage—beyond family lore."

We sat quietly. I stirred sugar into my tea, conscious of the clink of my spoon against the china cup.

"And I do think Eva and Bella were totally devoted to their lives as artists," Janet continued. "It was an artistic bond. Music was their God."

Another pause.

"And my mother would be very unsettled."

So much about this story, Janet told me, was difficult for her mother Isobel: the long separations from her own mother; the frayed patches in the fabric of family history; the unanswered questions. The twins were left wondering where they came from, but Eva made it clear that the subject was not to be broached. In 1978, when Isobel was nearing her seventieth birthday, she wrote a letter to John Boulton Smith, who had interviewed her about her mother's life:

> I have always felt very proud of my mother's artistic talent, but sad that I have not always felt I could speak freely about her for fear of it leading to questions which would be awkward or embarrassing. I certainly *do* remember with great clarity the difficulties which used to arise in this respect in my childhood years. They were something of a nightmare to me. However, I have some consolation through the kindness of a few good friends and through my children and *their* children, who have made life worth living. Already several of my grandchildren show signs of being very artistic and musical which is a pleasure for me.

Janet told me that even after Bella divulged the identity of the twins' father, Eva refused to discuss the subject. Later, when Isobel married and became a mother herself, she did not speak to her own children about Munch. The silence was broken only in the early 1960s, when Janet returned from her trip to Denmark with new questions about family history.

I asked how she had felt, while growing up, about the blanks in that history. "My mother would tell me tidbits about her childhood," she said, "but if it got to who was her father, it usually stopped there." Janet added, "I didn't push it because I grew up in the art world, so I didn't see it as anything peculiar, didn't see it as something romantic. But then I did become interested when I met Dr. Lund and began to ponder what he was telling me."

"Louis Levy was *not* the father," Janet Weber said emphatically toward the end of our conversation. "Of that I'm quite certain." She pronounced his name "Louie," in the French manner.

I looked up from my note-taking. At that point, I didn't know the name Louis Levy—there was a great deal I had not yet learned about her grandmother's history—and while I was ready to believe that many men were "not the father," I wondered why this one warranted such strenuous disavowal.

Janet described Louis Levy as a Danish poet, the author of clever nursery rhymes. "As I understood it from my mother, he just offered his name," she added, explaining that Kai had at some point (she wasn't sure when) briefly been known by the surname Levy.

I had noticed a "name variation" described on the Muddock family genealogical website, stating that Eva's son was referred to as Levy, "which was not his correct name." No such note existed for Eva's daughter. I asked myself why a man would lend his name to a child who was not his own, and why he would claim the boy but not the girl. And I wondered when and why Mudocci's son discarded the name—if indeed he had ever used it. I asked Janet how she had first heard of Levy. "My mother told me about Louis Levy way back," Janet replied, adding once more, "She was very clear that he was not the father." She thought Levy could have inspired the name of the fictitious "author" Louis Ellson, whose name appeared on her parents' marriage certificate as the bride's father.

I wondered aloud why Louis Levy would claim paternity of another man's son. He had many children of his own, Janet told me, and was not averse to claiming one or two more to help out his friends. "These were artists," she emphasized. Janet herself had been active in London's theater and dance worlds as a young woman, before taking her vows. "I know from my own experience, the art world has such different ways of dealing with these things," she said. "They do these things for each other."

That prompted another memory. Levy had dedicated one of

his books of verse to several children, including Mudocci's twins. Janet thought the book with the dedication might be in a box of her mother's possessions that was stored in the London flat of a close family friend, and said she would try to retrieve it when she could. It was an offhand comment, and I soon lost track of it. I had no glimmer then that the box would hold answers to some baffling questions—and raise new ones.

Thinking that stories about Mudocci or her twins might have been passed down to Louis Levy's descendants, I decided to try to track them down. Looking online, I found a genealogy webpage that included a Louis Nikolai Levy whose vitals matched those of the writer. It was moderated by a Danish woman named Gy Hentze. I contacted her in Copenhagen, and during my next visit to Denmark I arranged to meet her at the entrance to the Frederiksberg Garden, not far from her home. An energetic woman in her sixties, Gy arrived on bicycle and pointed the way toward a nearby coffee shop. As we walked, she said with a wry smile, "I'm wondering why I'm here."

I quickly explained my interest in Mudocci, including the theory that Louis Levy had fathered her twins.

"I see," she said. "Well, that would not be out of character. He was not the most faithful husband."

And then Gy told me the sad story of her grandmother's sister, Birgitte Marie Andersen, who had been listed on her family's genealogical web page as Levy's wife but was not in fact married to him. Birgitte grew up in Copenhagen with three sisters, all artistically inclined and all active in the city's cultural circles. In 1904, Birgitte conceived a child with Louis Levy, who was then married to his first wife, Clare Angelica Larsen. Birgitte spent a lonely confinement in Dresden, and died just days after giving birth in late December 1904. Birgitte's distraught sister (Gy's grandmother) rushed to Dresden with the intention of adopting the baby.

"But when my grandmother got to Dresden, Louis Levy was there," Gy continued, "and he wanted the child. He took the baby home and presented him to his wife as their son. Well, you can imagine how the wife felt about that! But what choice did she have?"

The boy was named Johannes Louis Levy. The Andersen family tried to stay connected to Johannes, but that proved to be difficult. "His childhood was not a happy one," Gy said. Louis and Clara Levy had three other children. "Johannes was never really treated as one of them."

I asked whether Birgitte had left any letters. "My grandmother had letters from Dresden," Gy said. "Sad letters. She kept them, of course, and I remember reading them. Poor Birgitte was so very far from home." Gy did not know what happened to the letters. "I always wondered why Dresden," she added. "There were closer places to go. My son lived there for a time and I used to take the bus to see him. It is a very long trip from Copenhagen, I can tell you."

Why Dresden? The question had not occurred to me.

"I'm afraid this has taken us very far from your Eva," Gy said. I stood up to refill our coffee cups.

"Maybe," I suggested when I sat down again, "Mudocci is involved in this story after all." I had wondered why Eva and Bella shared their secret with Louis Levy, despite having concealed the twins' existence from everyone else. I had considered the possibility that they needed help finding a Danish doctor who was both sympathetic and competent. A surgeon's son, Levy had studied medicine in Copenhagen before turning to writing.

Now the Dresden connection prompted another thought. Levy was not rich, and making arrangements for Birgitte would have been difficult. I told Gy that Mudocci's family had for years lived in Loschwitz, a suburb of Dresden. And Eva and Bella were touring in Germany, not far from Dresden, just at the time that Birgitte was there. Perhaps Eva and Bella came to the rescue at a desperate moment by helping Birgitte get settled in Dresden and acting as a go-between for the couple. That could explain why, two years later,

Eva and Bella would share their own situation with Levy, despite going to great lengths to hide it from others. And it would explain why Levy, returning an immense favor, would offer his surname to Mudocci's son.

But these were guesses. It was time to look for Louis Levy.

"Looking for Louis Levy in Danish literary histories or reference books, one looks long and almost in vain," literary scholar Kim Ravn wrote in 2003. "He is mentioned and that's it."

That was certainly my experience. Wherever I looked, I found the same photograph and the same brief description: Levy was born in Copenhagen to a military surgeon and his wife on October 9, 1875—as it happened, Eva Mudocci's third birthday. He began writing early and published his debut novel, *Letters from Loneliness*, at the age of twenty-two. Levy is remembered primarily as a writer of witty children's verse that appealed as much to adults as youngsters. As Ravn wrote, "The rest of his writings are described as tired, disconnected and impersonal. Nothing could be further from the truth."

Correspondence archived at the Royal Danish Library shows that Levy was, in his day, a prominent figure in literary Copenhagen. He helped to found a Danish literary journal called *Young Blood*, edited *The Children's Magazine*, and from 1913 to 1923 was a drama critic for *The Spectator*. He reported on cultural affairs in France and elsewhere for Copenhagen and Berlin newspapers. He was close to major writers, theater figures, and publishers of his day.

History is often kinder to artists who are easily classified than to those who may be versatile and strikingly original, but fall outside movements or schools. Levy was impossible to place—not a prolific novelist, not a monumental poet, not a noted philosopher, not a celebrated dramatist or screenwriter, not a massively influential critic. But he worked in all of these genres and excelled in each one.

He was an original—especially in his writing for adults. His experimental novel, *Kzradock the Onion Man and the Spring-Fresh Methuselah*, ventured far beyond the conventions of Danish fiction. The novel has its surrealist moments: a movie theater shows silent films of the protagonist's hallucinations; a character turns out to be the product of his psychiatrist's imagination. This was not run-of-the-mill fare when it appeared in 1910, five years before Franz Kafka published *Metamorphosis*.

Levy's reputation no doubt suffered because his work broke conventions and defied categorization, but there may have been another factor as well—his public stance on Judaism as an international force for peace. In 1918, Levy published a series of free-form poems called *The Jew as Peacemaker*. Two of the poems first appeared in 1914, when there was still faint hope that a cataclysmic world war might be avoided, but uncertainty about who might be strategically positioned to negotiate among nations. Levy's introduction said that he was calling on the people "whose race and history are mine" to help mediate conflict because a thousand years of experience had taught Jews to appreciate the blessings of peace—"often in the same brutal way that Finns have come to appreciate bread—by not having it." Because Jews were scattered among virtually all nations, and among key institutions within those nations (finance, medicine, government, the press), they could, in an emergency, represent an international will and resolve differences. If his call, written in the neutral language of a neutral nation, were to find "the right men of my race, ready to sacrifice all for peace, then it was perhaps not written in the sand."

Levy's words were preserved, but not as he would have wished. In the years that followed, and in subsequent decades, they were quoted out of context by anti-Semites eager to prove the Jewish people's quest for world domination. In this perverted form they remain in use today. In his own time, some literary acquaintances offered Levy support, but others avoided him. Levy wrote to a friend that he felt let down by the Danish Writers' Union, on whose board he had served for ten years.

When Hitler came to power in the 1930s, *The Jew as Peacemaker* and its author were viciously attacked in the Nazi outlet *Der Stürmer*. In 1936, Levy boldly refuted the charges in a published interview. Along with his friends Georg Brandes and Henri Nathansen, he spoke out in favor of sheltering German-Jewish refugees—a position that was far from unanimous in Denmark. None of that was mentioned in Levy's obituary.

The picture I was getting of Louis Levy was intriguing but sketchy. Hoping to fill it in, I turned to his fiction.

That's when Eva Mudocci turned up—along with Bella Edwards, Edvard Munch, and Kai Ellson—on the pages of Louis Levy's book, *Kzradock the Onion Man and the Spring-Fresh Methuselah*. The oddly named novel first appeared in 1910, while the twins were still in diapers. It was soon translated into German, but would not appear in English for another century.

Kzradock is a modernist, sometimes surreal murder mystery told in the first person. To someone immersed in Mudocci's history, it soon becomes apparent that Levy fractured her complicated story and tossed the pieces into a literary puzzle box. Around every corner are people (Eva, Bella, Edvard) and places (Paris's Left Bank, Brighton) from Mudocci's biography. Even Mudocci's absentee father, the detective writer James Edward Muddock, aka Dick Donovan, makes a cameo appearance in the person of a gumshoe named Dick.

A mental hospital is the setting of the opening pages. A psychiatrist recounts the murder of two women, united by music, who are slain in the Paris studio they share near the Pantheon—precisely where Eva and Bella lived in the years before the twins were born. The crime makes the intimacy between the two women hideously literal: "These two who had loved each other so . . . these two sisters and friends, wed at the altar of music! Now their blood runs together into a large pool that seeps into the carpet." The "altar of music" is totally unmotivated by the plot—a sly clue to the victims' identities for all to see.

The slain women make no live appearances, but Levy introduces another character whose resemblance to Mudocci is unmistakable. She is Lady Florence, an alluring, enigmatic Englishwoman who frequents Brighton and harbors a secret. Lady Florence "has encased her secret" within the brain and soul of the protagonist.

This Englishwoman seems to have leaped directly out of Munch's *Brooch*. Lady Florence's thick black hair, the narrator says, falls "over her shoulders in a dark, heavy stream." She is "tall and slender and dark, boyish in her slenderness, restless as if filled with a mysterious nerve-fire. Everything about her, her black hair and infinite pallor, showed spirit, as did the blending of gentleness and cruelty around her mouth." The narrator concludes: "She looked like she belonged more to death than life, looked like a dream, an adventuress, a criminal."

Edvard Munch appears as well. In this novel, written within months of Munch's release from Jacobson's clinic, Levy transformed the artist into the mental patient Kzradock. The patient is not actually insane, the narrator discovers. Rather, "love or hate had driven his soul into abnormality." Like the narrator, Kzradock is privy to Lady Florence's secret. But he "himself was in Lady Florence's power. She had sealed his mouth with seven seals so that he could not divulge her secret, and now he wanted to make use of me to break her hold over him."

From his own inner terrors, the mental patient has "inhabited the darkness with images and visions," and emits a shriek that is a clear echo of Munch's scream of nature: "Kzradock's face showed no emotion—he might as well have been a corpse . . . But how he screamed! Leaves in the primeval forest would have turned over at this screaming; all of night's horror and all of its depth were in it."

Near the novel's end, the plot takes a turn that is predictable only for those acquainted with Mudocci's history. Lady Florence, the narrator explains, always wished to have a child, "a child not of flesh and blood but of soul and spirit, a child whose mission was free expression and whose sphere of action would range from the aether up to the Pleiades." Levy had endowed Lady Florence not only with Mudocci's Theosophist bent, but also with her exalted view of procreation—in Eva's words, "two natures . . . perpetuated in one life stream."

The narrator reveals that Florence has given birth to a son. She is unwilling to name the boy's father, and prevails upon the narrator to claim paternity. The narrator demurs: "I will not be a father to a ghost child who belongs to another." The book is fiction—and rather fantastical fiction at that—but for anyone wondering about the origins of Mudocci's twins, it nevertheless sharpens the impression that Levy, in the same year that he was writing his novel, had been asked to claim paternity for another man's child.

In the end, Lady Florence outwits the narrator, declaring, "You have destroyed my talent. It is time that I lay down my magic wand." And here, Lady Florence seems to merge with the tragic Birgitte Andersen, mother of the novelist's real-life son. She says: "I will die and leave you behind with a ghost child . . . With that, Lady Florence thrust the dagger into her heart and fell to the ground."

13

Some Correspondence

Janet met me by the elevator, as usual, when I visited in 2014, ten days before I was due to leave for Scandinavia. She was curious about my itinerary and recalled her own trips to Denmark. I told her about reading Louis Levy's novel. Until coming upon it, I'd had doubts about Munch's kinship to the twins. *Kzradock* was a game changer. I was struck by its parallels to Mudocci's story—not least by Lady Florence's demand that the narrator take responsibility for another man's offspring. As I described the plot to Janet, dwelling on telltale clues, she looked back at me with unsurprised eyes. Hadn't she said from the start that Levy was not the father?

Janet's attention was directed elsewhere that day. She had found a thirty-year-old tape recording of the funeral service for her mother, Isobel Weber, at London's Danish Church, and she was eager to play it for me. In particular, she wanted me to hear her brother Sven's poignant rendition, on the piano, of Debussy's *Adieu*, beautifully played despite the fact that Sven had not fully recovered from a motorcycle accident that broke both of his arms. We listened and Janet described the setting, including the candles and flowers clustered at the end of each pew.

She played the pastor's eulogy. He began with a quote from *John 14*, in which Jesus speaks to the Disciples: "There are many rooms in my Father's house; if there were not, I would have told you." I knew this passage, had felt somehow consoled by it weeks earlier at a sorrowful funeral service for one of my students, but this time it struck me differently. I tried to repeat it to myself, but kept tripping over the logic. I couldn't get past the literal meaning. Eva and Bella and Edvard and Louis were getting in the way. Where, after all, was Isobel's father's house? And what was true? And if what she believed turned out not to be true, would anyone have told her?

The pastor recounted Isobel's time on earth, a life "surrounded by music from the day she was born," a life scattered, "sometimes here and sometimes there," a life filled with courage and risk-taking. He talked about art and religion, and how they directed Isobel to important questions about the meaning and value of life. He paraphrased Ibsen's character Peer Gynt, who travelled all over the world and finally asked: "Where have I been all those years when I was away?" The answer: "You were never away, you were always in my love." The pastor added, "We are always in God's love." He was talking about Isobel. I thought of Eva. Munch came to mind as well. I recalled reading that Munch had quoted *Peer Gynt* from his bed when his friends first visited him in Jacobson's clinic. So many wanderers.

Janet clicked off the tape recorder and began telling me about her mother's passing. "Just as mother lost consciousness, the pastor of the Danish Church arrived," she said. "Then a sister from my religious order came, and they both kept vigil with me until she died." Soon after they left, Janet began getting competing calls from the university's anatomy department and from a local undertaker, each concerned that the other would get to the body first. Finally, the doorbell rang and some young men stepped in, dressed in scruffy student garb but wearing top hats, and announced that they had come for Isobel. Janet laughed. "Mother would have enjoyed that scene. It was a true Ibsen moment."

That surprised me. We had talked so much about Isobel's sorrow and sense of abandonment that I had missed her wit. It occurred to me then how little I had learned about Isobel, compared with the story's other protagonists. That she became a pianist aroused no surprise or curiosity. She was simply the girl who had dearly loved her foster family and made the best of her Danish girlhood. It was a life with all the dignity and grace that ordinary existence brings. She studied music. She married and raised three children. She took Janet to Denmark to see where she had grown up, and they visited Kai, Dr. Lund, and Isobel's old schoolteacher. There was suffering: a self-absorbed mother; a twin brother ravaged by mental illness; a cancer diagnosis in her early forties; a separation that left her in financial difficulty. But these facts had been narrated to me with no sense of drama.

The photo of Kai that Dr. Lund sent to Director Langaard in 1962 remains among the Mudocci materials archived in the Munch Museum, and when the library director showed it to me, he set it beside photographs of Munch and Levy as young men to allow a comparison. No thought had been given to comparing Isobel's features with those of Munch, despite some similarities. It was Kai who was briefly given Levy's surname, Kai who was taken to Paris after the First World War, Kai whose gift for painting became the subject of intense speculation, Kai who was considered by the twins' mother to be a "genius."

In fact, Isobel had been a very gifted pianist, Janet told me, and loved to improvise. That made her a very sought-after accompanist for dance classes at a variety of ballet schools. Her main source of income was an administrative job at the BBC, but at some point she ran her own small music school. Janet remembers meeting some of her mother's acquaintances from the ballet world, including the formidable Alexandra Danilova, a Russian-born prima ballerina.

"I feel protective of my mother," Janet said, when we touched on the subject of Eva's relationship with Bella. "She just wanted a normal family life." All afternoon, Janet's love for her mother had filled the room. "I've been more blessed," she said. "My mother was a wonderful woman, but she had a hard time. I haven't had that kind of hardship. So yes, I'm here, with nieces and nephews—a new generation with its own giftedness. It's wonderful. It comes down to family somehow."

As I folded my laptop, Janet wished me safe travels and suggested that I visit with her acquaintance Tove Munch, a distant relative by marriage of the artist.

"**M**unch had a fantastic relationship with Mudocci," Tove Munch told me in May 2014, when I visited with her in Oslo. Tove has devoted years to Munch studies and has been a moving force behind the Munch Museum's Friends' Association.

"You could see that he liked Mudocci," she said. "With her, he was in a relaxed state. Also, they could understand each other. He was a very intellectual man, very intellectual." Tove contrasted Munch's cerebral connection to Mudocci with the rancorous Tulla Larsen affair, with its violent denouement.

"What do you think happened at the dramatic Åsgårdstrand meeting between Munch and Tulla Larsen?" I asked Tove. All of the published descriptions of the shooting are ambiguous.

Tove laughed. She said she had once spent hours with a busload of Munch experts who were travelling from a Berlin conference to the ferry that would return them to Oslo. "We all spent the entire trip discussing the shot, nothing but the shot," she recalled. No one could agree. "In Munch's day, all the men had revolvers," she said. "I think Tulla picked up Munch's revolver and said 'I'll shoot myself,' and he put his hand over it to prevent it. Of course, she would never have actually shot herself, she was too dramatic for that." I could picture the scene just as Tove described it.

Some time later, I heard an account of the same bus ride from

Munch scholar Frank Høifødt, who devoted an entire book to the subject of the gunshot. He told me that the story of a violent struggle following a feigned suicide was a romantic tale whose only source was Tulla Larsen. He believes that Munch and Larsen were together at Åsgårdstrand, and that, as usual, Munch was drunk. He fell into an alcohol-induced stupor with the revolver in his hand, awoke with a start, and accidentally shot himself. Once again, I could picture the scene, this time just as Frank described it.

"Edvard and Tulla were certainly a handsome couple," I remarked to Tove Munch. I had been greeted by a larger-than-life photograph of the pair at the entrance to the Munch Museum. She agreed, but she thinks of Mudocci as the real love of Munch's life. "It was surely his most peaceful relationship," she said. "They were soulmates."

Yes, I thought, in some ways they were kindred spirits. They shared some temperamental traits and had overlapping aesthetic and spiritual commitments. On both sides there were moments of infatuation, though not always the same moments. Their bond was intense—sometimes brittle, sometimes ardent. But peaceful? Edvard tormented Eva, kept her off balance. On a dare, before ever setting eyes on her, he had conspired to bend to his purpose whatever vulnerabilities she might have, whatever muddled feelings or inchoate desires. In time, he won her trust and affection, sometimes meeting them with gallant gestures, sometimes with cruel pieties or alcoholic self-pity. Edvard could be tender, then, without warning, prosecutorial. His insinuations— some based on the day's sexology and pop psychology—confused Eva, made her doubt her own feelings and perceptions, at times drove her to desperate acts, including (as she confessed in her post-Elgersburg letter to Munch) sleeping with a man she did not love to refute Edvard's "not normal" charge. Had there been other such refutations involving other men? Whether or not he was the twins' father, I realized, Edvard Munch was implicated in the act that produced the twins.

Months passed before my next meeting with Janet. In the interim, I had been deeply immersed in her grandmother's story. I was excited to tell Janet what I had learned, but as soon as I arrived, I sensed that she had disengaged from our search. Janet was still hoping to know the identity of her grandfather, she said, but the way forward was murky. Elisabeth had written from Norway that she had looked into comparing her own DNA with Janet's. A consultant had suggested using a sample from an earlier generation—perhaps by exhuming the body of Elisabeth's father. Janet was horrified at the turn the search had taken.

It occurred to me that Munch himself would have been intrigued by this gruesome development and by the whole DNA project. He was, after all, deeply concerned about passing on hereditary diseases, and he was fascinated by all kinds of physiological processes, especially those related to conception. A doctor's son, Munch went so far as to study spermatozoa. Picturing him peering through a microscope, it is easy to imagine that if Edvard Munch were alive today, he might want to make a personal study of Janet Weber's DNA.

If genetic testing offered no certainty, then it made sense to return to less modern methods. I recalled Janet's sound bite, aired on Norwegian television in 2012: If Munch knew about the twins, "it would be hard not to have some correspondence." I would dig deeper into the whereabouts and contents of letters exchanged by Eva and Edvard.

At the Munch Museum, I once again pored over a binder of handwritten letters from Eva to Edvard. Eva Mudocci wrote, late in life, that she and Edvard had a sustained correspondence, interrupted only by wartime. The museum's binders reflect a more sporadic exchange, including a two-year gap. In late 1907, Mudocci mentioned a recent visit she and Bella had made to Munch's beach house. This was followed by silence until late 1909, when Eva thanked Edvard for the cherries and wine he had served to her and Bella in his garden at Kragerø.

It would indeed be hard not to have some correspondence—at the very least, to arrange the Kragerø visit. Moreover, in writing to Munch, Eva occasionally referred to something she had said in a previous letter that cannot be found in the existing correspondence. As I worked my way through the binder, I had a keen sense of missing pages.

It is of course possible that letters were misplaced, perhaps borrowed and then misfiled. Edvard Munch's will had gone missing for forty years until it was found in an attorney's files. "These things happen," Library Director Lasse Jacobsen told me when he mentioned that the Munch Museum's only copy of the Knupffer manuscript had disappeared. Or perhaps some of Mudocci's letters had been intentionally removed or destroyed. But who would have done this? The suspects presented themselves for inspection.

Edvard Munch? The artist famously saved every scrap of paper that came his way, including both incoming mail and drafts of posted letters. As unlikely as it seems, Munch could have gotten rid of some letters from Eva, either to protect his own privacy or to abide by her wishes. By the same token, he could have destroyed his own drafts of letters to Eva.

The prime suspect was Inger Munch, Edvard's sister. After his death, Inger went through all of his papers, placing any sensitive correspondence in a suitcase that was locked in a bank vault. She preserved everything—except those documents she considered too scandalous to see the light of day, as in the case of Jappe Nilssen's 1902 letter proposing that Munch seduce Eva Mudocci. It seems likely that letters mentioning Eva's illegitimate children would have fit Inger Munch's definition of scandalous. But as the library director told me, Inger seemed to be conscience-stricken after she destroyed letters, and turned over copies or summaries to the officials overseeing her brother's archives.

That raised one more possibility—albeit less likely. In 1962, before Mudocci's letters to Munch were copied and sent to Dr. Otto Lund, they were reviewed by Director Johan Langaard and

Senior Curator Reidar Revold. It seemed unlikely that scholars of their stature would remove papers from Munch's archives, but it was always possible that they were saving dramatic reveals for their own books. They could have had another, equally powerful motive: avoiding any challenge to their oversight of Munch's legacy.

Even if they were convinced that Munch was not the twins' father, Langaard and Revold had good reason to quash speculation. In the 1960s, DNA testing would not have been available to settle the question. If Mudocci's descendants had been able to document contact between Eva and Edvard during the critical timeframe, a claim to his estate would have been difficult to refute. For all of these reasons, I could not dismiss the museum officials from my line-up without taking a closer look. I began searching Norwegian newspaper archives for insight into these men.

The story of Reidar Revold's arrest stunned me when I came across it. When the story broke in 1968, it received scant mention in the foreign press, but was closely followed by Norwegians. In that year, an art appraiser noticed the Munch Museum stamp on the back of an Edvard Munch woodcut and contacted the museum. When inquiries were made, Revold admitted to stealing three woodcuts from the collection. An investigation followed, and the indictment eventually listed seventy-one works of art filched by the curator. Revold went to jail.

Museum Director Johan Langaard had retired three years before the thefts were discovered and was living in Italy. When he was called home to help determine the scope of the crime, Langaard appeared to be as shaken as the public by Revold's actions. No evidence pointed to his involvement. But for years, Langaard had been criticized for mishandling Munch's legacy in other ways. In the 1960s, complaints aired in the Norwegian press accused him of profiting from the use of research materials that he kept from other Munch scholars. One writer demanded that the Oslo City Council investigate Langaard's "personal and arbitrary control" over public property. Langaard responded that "by virtue of my position, I have a moral obligation to know more than everyone else" about Munch's life and work. He hinted that in time he would reveal all, telling an interviewer that "when everything is unraveled one day, then one will be able to write the most remarkable book about Munch." Controversy about willful control of Munch's archive has continued to erupt from time to time. A quarter-century after Langaard's death, in 2012, Munch biographer Ketil Bjørnstad complained on the pages of *Aftenposten* that "Munch's literary work and the foundation for modern Munch research [have been] withheld and concealed from the public by art historians with strong vested interests."

To be sure, none of this proves that letters were stolen, destroyed, or suppressed. Current Munch Museum officials stress that Langaard was totally committed to promoting Munch's legacy. Revold would not have taken or destroyed letters, they say, because he was only interested in the easy money that stolen artwork would raise. Documents would not have suited his purpose. Moreover, other conscientious museum staffers were on the scene and would have reported irregularities. I had to wonder why officials expressed such confidence in a staff that did not notice the theft of seventy-one artworks.

In the end, I was left with unanswered questions about apparent gaps in Mudocci's archived letters to Munch. I had questions as well about the whereabouts of Munch's letters to Mudocci. The Munch Museum has only the drafts that Munch routinely wrote and saved before dispatching letters, as well as several typed pages of excerpts from posted letters. The original letters are said to be lost, and their whereabouts puzzle Munch scholars. "If you could find Munch's letters [to Mudocci]," one told me, "that would be a real coup!"

Late in her life, Eva Mudocci wrote to Waldemar Stabell that she cherished every one of Munch's letters, but in the end, had saved some and lost others:

During the last war that box was stored with other valuable things against bombing, but when it was returned to me the lock had been forced & only these few letters remained. Enquiry brought nothing & I can only believe that someone believing the box to be a jewel case—(which it somewhat resembled)—in searching it scattered the letters & did not take the trouble to replace them. It has been a bitter loss—of so much that should be treasured.

Eva's convoluted explanation made me wonder whether she might have saved only those letters she was willing to make public. What happened to the letters from Munch that survived?

Toward the end of my search, documents turned up that offered a partial answer. In the mid-1950s, Isobel Weber sold her mother's collection of letters from Munch. The buyer was Waldemar Stabell—the Norwegian painter who corresponded with Mudocci in 1950 and interviewed her for the BBC. Isobel told Otto Lund about the sale. Lund, in turn, informed Johan Langaard.

In September 1964, Director Langaard phoned Stabell in Bergen to try to get hold of the letters. They apparently came to an understanding. Langaard followed up with a letter expressing appreciation for "the loan of Eva Mudocci's letters and a copy of them." Within days, Stabell confirmed to Isobel Weber that (as Lund wrote to Langaard), "The letter collection had been handed over to the museum." Lund also heard from Senior Curator Revold: "Attached are the copies of the materials borrowed from W. Stabell. Please be so kind to return them after your review."

The correspondence indicates that in September 1964, Director Langaard was in possession of Edvard Munch's letters to Eva Mudocci. The puzzling part of the story is that today, the museum's holdings include neither originals nor copies of this letter collection. Rather, it has several typed pages of excerpts from Munch's letters. A number of questions remain. What, exactly, did Stabell send to the museum in September 1964? If Stabell turned over the letters, as Langaard's confirmatory letter to Stabell suggests, what happened to them?

The next time I visited with Janet Weber, I told her that the known correspondence between her grandmother and Edvard Munch could not clear up the question of her lineage. Moreover, I could not rule out the possibility that some letters had been suppressed, perhaps to prevent a claim on Munch's legacy by Mudocci's heirs.

"If that's what happened, it was all for naught," she said. "We wouldn't have made such a claim."

I had hoped to find "some correspondence" that would clear up the mystery. That had not happened, and now Janet seemed to be focusing on other work. Perhaps it was time for me to do the same. But by this time, the search had taken on a life of its own. Some weeks earlier I had spent a few days looking for Louis Levy. On a hunch, I had searched online for Danish writers and journalists with Levy family connections, and had come up with a widely published science writer whose mother was a Levy. He had forwarded my inquiry to his cousin, the unofficial family historian. Just as Janet and I were backing off from our search, a long message arrived from Copenhagen.

"There has never been any doubt in my family that my grandfather Louis was [the twins'] father," Morten Levy had written in English. He added that his grandmother, Louis's second wife Margrete, "told me that for a fact."

I had been contacted by Louis and Margrete's eldest grandson. Born in 1939, Morten Levy is a musicologist and composer, and, coincidentally, an expert on the Norwegian folk violin repertoire. Morten said that his grandmother was fond of the twins and proud of her husband's association with the famous violinist. Margrete had no reason to be jealous, he wrote. She had appeared on the scene

Louis and Margrete Levy, c. 1929. LEVY FAMILY COLLECTION

after Louis's presumed affair with Eva Mudocci.

"My father knew the twins very well," Morten wrote, "and I have as a child seen several photos of the two together with my father and my aunts and uncles (unfortunately, I have not seen these photos since then)."

In our e-mail exchange, I said that I had been in contact with Mudocci's granddaughter Janet, who had been told emphatically by her mother that Louis Levy was "not the father."

Morten responded, using the Danish spelling of Kai's name: "Many years ago (I think it has been in the 1960s) I heard someone in my family (I don't remember who) tell me that a psychiatrist, who worked at a Danish asylum where Kay was a patient, had gotten the idea that Kay perhaps was a son of Munch; this was based on the fact that Kay (according to the psychiatrist) had shown talent as a painter. The person who told me this (possibly one of my aunts) found the idea very funny and ridiculous. This was the first time I heard of such a view."

He continued, "Then, one or two years ago, I read somewhere about Janet Weber's beliefs regarding [her kinship to] E. Munch. I don't think she is right, and I don't see any reason why my grandmother and grandfather should lie about such a thing." He came back to that point at the end of his message: "Naturally, I have no way to be sure if what my family has told me is the truth, but I see no reason why they should lie."

No reason to lie—Janet had used the same reasoning about Bella's disclosure that Munch was the twins' father, and about Isobel's conviction that Louis Levy was not. My thoughts spiraled in the direction of DNA. Morten was apparently thinking along the same lines. "I read someplace, that Janet Weber had planned to make a DNA test," he wrote, "and I should naturally be very interested in the result of that, if she goes this way."

The following month, I visited Morten in his third-floor flat in the Søerne district of Copenhagen. He showed me into a study that was clearly the reflection of a lively mind. On the table, he had set out first editions of Louis's books, as well as his grandmother's sketches and whimsically illustrated book and journals. Across from the table, under papers and journals, were hints of an upright piano. He plays on a keyboard kept in another room, he explained.

High on the wall adjacent to the piano was a large, luminous black-and-white photograph of handsome Louis Levy in his sixties, with cherubic Morten on his knee. "It was taken a few months before his death, when I was less than one year," the grandson explained, adding that he was born in late January 1939. I looked carefully at the photograph—the season, the size of the baby. It must have been taken in the autumn of 1939, as Hitler's armies were on the march. Morten spoke with admiration about his grandfather, "a charming, beautiful, very gifted man." Louis was shy, he later wrote to me, but at the same time very conscious of appearances. When Morten looks at photos of his grandparents in their later years, Margrete strikes him as the cool one—playful and bohemian, while Louis seems a bit boyish in his self-conscious effort to keep up his man-of-the-world façade. I asked about Louis Levy's roots. Morten replied that Louis's forebears, going back at least four generations, were without exception Ashkenazi Jews. Morten had produced a detailed, handwritten genealogical chart as part of an eighty-page family history written years earlier as a birthday gift to his father. He had called it *Vores Jøder—Our Jews*, and explained that the title was meant to have an ironic tinge. Morten himself had only one Jewish grandparent.

Studying Morten's account of the family, I counted thirteen Levy children: three born to Louis's first wife, Clara; six born to his second wife, Margrete; and four born to women who were not his wives. Morten had included on his family tree the son born to Birgitte Andersen in 1904, the twins born to Eva Mudocci in 1908, and a son born to Danish writer Olga Ott in 1911 ("the same year my father was born," Morten remarked). "There were many women in those years," he told me, with a shy smile. "My grandfather spread his seed across Europe."

I showed Morten pictures of Isobel and Kai as children and he took a close look. Yes, he said, he could see a strong family resemblance. I laughed and told him that some of Edvard Munch's relations had been struck by the resemblance to *their* family. We looked together at grainy photos of Louis Levy's many children— dark hair, deep-set eyes, animated features. "I can see some resemblance to Janet's family," I told him, "but on the other hand, they also could be *my* relatives."

What was undeniable was the Levy family's embrace of the twins, especially Isobel, into their family. He showed me his grandmother's whimsical, brilliantly illustrated book, *Freckle's Diary*, and explained that Freckle was the family's nickname for Morten's father, Robinson. One entry announced that Robinson had received a postcard from "his two aunts in Paris," showing a statue of Robinson Crusoe at one of the suburban treetop bars where fashionably dressed Parisians would spend Sundays clambering up ladders to drink hot chocolate in the trees. This was the first hint I had that long after the twins were born, Eva and Bella remained on friendly terms with Louis Levy and his children.

In 1926, a subsequent volume of *Freckle's Diary* reported the arrival of a letter from London, addressed to Louis at the offices of a Copenhagen newspaper where he sometimes published. "Perhaps something about a translation? No, it was a daughter, Isobel Elson (*sic*), near the age of adulthood, who wanted to visit her father for her eighteenth birthday." How did Louis and Margrete react? "Immense delight. Strong feeling. Which spread to the entire family."

Over the next year, Margrete reported the arrival of "letters, many letters from England, where Isobel lies ill." In 1927, as Isobel recuperated from rheumatic fever, she made two more visits to the Levy family. Kai, who had been struck by the same illness, stayed in London. It was precisely at this time that his mental health was deteriorating.

Morten's store of family history included information about the twins, mostly accurate: the identity of their mother, their birthplace, the name of the doctor who attended their birth and later took them in. As we talked, he mentioned details that Janet had not yet mentioned but later confirmed. He recalled hearing, for example, that Isobel ran a music school. He told me that his Aunt Germaine—then an aspiring dancer—had gone to visit Isobel and her husband in London. Germaine later found her own place and remained in London for several years, Morten said. There, she sometimes visited with Eva and Bella. Something about the name Germaine was ringing a bell. I looked back at my notes and saw that Janet recalled as a child meeting someone named Germaine who lived on a houseboat. She had the impression that this Danish woman was Bella's relative; she had not connected her with Louis Levy. I later found Germaine mentioned in a letter from Lyell Barbour, who recalled meeting the "little Danish dancer" at a gathering at Bella and Eva's house.

Morten had a first edition of his grandfather's novel *Kzradock*, and I pointed out passages in which Lady Florence prevails on the narrator to lay claim to another man's child. Morten knew the book but had never noticed that twist. I wondered whether, in his mind, that called into question his grandfather's kinship to Mudocci's twins. "Of course, anything is possible," he said. I mentioned to Morten my theory that Levy may have claimed paternity of Mudocci's children out of gratitude for her assistance in Dresden to Birgitte Andersen, the mother of Levy's son Johannes.

Morten was well aware of Birgitte's story. He remembered her son—his uncle Johannes, whom he knew as Hans. "A nice man," he said. He was a grocer who later worked as a projectionist in a Copenhagen cinema. Most vivid in Morten's memory was a day in the 1950s when Hans helped twelve-year-old Morten get into a sold-out American movie that he was eager to see.

I learned more about Olga Ott, the mother of Louis's son Niels Ott. Soon after giving birth to Niels, she wrote two well-received plays about mothers, their illegitimate children, and the crushing weight of public scorn. Both plays were sardonic about the fathers of such children, whose lives are minimally affected. In one play, a young mother sees her newborn for the first time and exclaims: "Thank God, a boy! So he can have no illegitimate children." In Ott's world, only women have illegitimate children; men just have children.

One of Ott's plays, in particular, caught my attention. *Little Eva*, which premiered in 1913, featured a woman who helps the daughter of an unwed mother investigate her roots. The play mentions an annual sum of money sent anonymously by the father, using as an intermediary an accommodating family doctor. My thoughts flew in the direction of Dr. Lemvigh-Müller.

When I returned from Denmark, I got in touch with Janet to tell her about the visit. She was interested to hear that I had found a Levy grandson who was certain that they were cousins.

"Louis Levy did claim the children as his own—Mother told me that," Janet said after giving some thought to this development. "So it's not entirely surprising that the family would welcome Mother and Kai." Her tone suggested that Morten's impressions would not override the conviction, born of her mother's emphatic assertion, that Levy was not the father. I had found Morten Levy's account compelling, but sitting with Janet, I could feel my internal pendulum begin to swing back toward Munch.

I had one more piece of news to report. I told her that Morten would like to compare DNA.

Eva Mudocci's granddaughter and Louis Levy's grandson began an email correspondence and later met in person. As I had imagined, they seemed to get on well. They were Europeans of one generation, born a year apart into artistic families that had staked out the uneven terrain between nonconformity and respectability. Both Janet and Morten had lively, curious minds; they disliked pretension and shared a keen sense of irony. Both had a philosophical bent. While

Morten Levy beneath a 1939 photograph of himself with his grandfather, Louis Levy. AUTHOR'S PHOTOGRAPH

Janet Weber beneath Munch's portrait of her grandmother, Eva Mudocci.
NORWEGIAN BROADCASTING COMPANY

not inclined to boast, they conveyed love for their families and pride in the rising generations.

I had enjoyed conversations with both, but now I had to get out of the way. It would be up to Janet and Morten whether to proceed with DNA testing, and if they did, whether to share the results with me. There was nothing to do but wait.

I knew Morten was eager to proceed, but I wondered about Janet. A number of years had passed since she first raised the possibility of DNA testing at the end of her Norwegian television interview. Now that the possibility was real, I could imagine she might feel some ambivalence. She seemed eager to put aside family history, to feel anchored in the present, in her community and her work. But then again, she had gone to some lengths to learn about her origins. I had no idea what she would decide.

And in any case, I was not at all sure that the test would solve the mystery. Considerable evidence pointed to Munch: Bella's assertion that Munch was the twins' father; the same claim by Eva and Bella's acquaintance, Poul Rée; Kai's artistic gift and psychiatric history; the recognition by Munch descendants of a family resemblance.

I had given weight to the fact that Mudocci's son was named Edvard—while also noting the second name, Ludvig (the German form of Louis). I had factored in Munch's presence in Paris in the early spring of 1908, when the twins would have been conceived, and his choice of a hotel very close to Eva and Bella's studio. I was struck by the fact that Munch passed through Nykøbing in the summer of 1908, by the timing of his breakdown in Copenhagen that fall, two months before the twins' birth, and by his parting gift to his doctor—his portrait of Eva and Bella. I found the Adam-and-Eve narrative that Munch wrote during his stay at Jacobson's clinic to be highly suggestive: *Alpha and Omega* depicted two illegitimate offspring pursuing their father; one key illustration seemed to feature Mudocci's distinctive face. Finally, the contents of Levy's 1910 novel seemed consistent with Janet's sense that Louis Levy had lent his name to another man's progeny.

Morten Levy had offered a persuasive counternarrative, revealing considerable contact between Eva's children and the Levy family. I also considered the "father's name" listed on Isobel's marriage certificate—Louis Ellson, author. But weighing the evidence, I thought it likely that a DNA comparison would rule out Louis Levy as Janet's grandfather. That would raise the odds of descent from Munch, but there would be no certainty. I was puzzling over what would come next.

And then one afternoon, without warning, unceremoniously, news arrived. Both Janet and Morten had been tested. Once the two sets of results were entered into a computer program designed for this purpose, the answer had been spit out in less than a second. Janet and Morten's most recent common ancestor was two generations back. A grandparent. Louis Levy.

14

Double Helix

"**M**aybe Bella never knew the truth and thus surmised," Janet Weber wrote to me, once she'd had time to absorb the news that Edvard Munch was not her grandfather. "Maybe Eva just never said."

It was Bella who named Munch as the twins' father, Janet had said from the start. But DNA said otherwise. How could Bella have gotten it so wrong? Could Isobel have misheard or misconstrued Bella's disclosure? Perhaps the secret Bella shared was Eva's love affair with Munch—leading Isobel to assume that he was her father. With this thought, we crossed from the firm ground of research to the jagged terrain of speculation, and there we wandered for a time.

Alternatively, was Eva herself somehow muddled about the question of paternity? There is always the possibility that Eva was seeing both men and did not know which was the father, but based on all I had learned about her, that seemed unlikely. Was Eva so deeply committed to combining natures with a "great artist," as she once wrote to Munch, that she embraced that fantasy and began to believe it herself? Again, unlikely. Eva was eccentric and, like many of her contemporaries, wrapped up in Eastern mysticism, but she was not delusional.

Perhaps Eva misled Bella, thinking Bella would tolerate an affair with one man, but not two. Perhaps, given Bella's history with Grieg, Eva thought her own attraction to a charismatic, famous artist would be more easily understood and forgiven than a tie to a less celebrated lover. Or perhaps Eva dreaded confessing that the father was a member of Bella's Copenhagen circle—a man she had met through Bella. That Bella was misled has, at least, an emotional logic. As their friend Gertrude Norman once wrote, what motivated Eva most fiercely was her fear of losing Bella. Protecting their relationship was, for Eva, a reason to lie—a reason sufficiently powerful to produce decades of silence.

But if Eva misled Bella, how did she persuade Louis Levy not to divulge the truth? How did she get him to pretend to be what he actually was—the twins' biological father? What a convoluted scheme! And what inspired Levy to invent, in his 1910 novel, a plot in which the narrator is asked to claim paternity for another man's child?

As I considered what I knew about Levy, I thought that posing as the gallant paternal stand-in for his own children may have suited him. Tortuous plots obviously intrigued him. He already had many children. And, like Eva Mudocci, he viewed the next generation with some detachment. A photograph sent by Morten showed Louis on a country outing with his family, looking aloof and out of place. Levy once wrote to a fellow children's writer: "You love the children. I think I admire them more than I love them. . . . I want to make them understand all I have experienced, while you give to them out of your feelings and your heart."

So perhaps Eva would have reached an understanding with Levy without much difficulty. But what about Edvard Munch? Would Eva have confided in him? How would she have guarded against the possibility that Bella would confront Munch? Once again, I thought back to the trio's meeting in the garden at Kragerø in the summer of 1909, just seven months after the twins' birth. What in the world had transpired there?

Several months later, I visited Janet. The DNA result had answered the question that sparked her search, so this was a moment for closure. But toward the end of our visit, Janet reminded me that some of her mother's possessions had been stored for years in the London flat of a close family friend. The friend had recently passed away, and during a visit to England, Janet had retrieved a pile of photographs and papers. Among the papers were eight letters written to Isobel in 1962 and 1963—five from Dr. Otto Lund and three from art dealer Poul Rée. Because they were in Danish, Janet had no idea of their contents. At the same time, through a separate line of inquiry, I came across a file of letters from Poul Rée to a prospective American client—an avid Munch collector. Over the next several weeks, I began making sense of all of these papers.

I turned first to Otto Lund's typed letters to Isobel. I had come to think of the Danish psychiatrist as a studious fellow traveler, given his abiding interest in Mudocci's biography and his painstaking annotations of the Munch-Mudocci correspondence. Based on all I had learned, I thought him a mild, compassionate man—generous to Kai and hospitable to Kai's relatives. As I read Dr. Lund's letters to Isobel Weber, a more complex picture emerged.

"I am writing to you regarding your brother, Kai Ellson, who resides at our nursing home in Sakskøbing," Dr. Lund began in early 1962, at about the same time that he visited the Munch Museum. This was his first contact with Isobel, although as he told her, Kai "had been a patient in this hospital for many years before I became the chief physician of the hospital in 1954." His aim in writing, he explained, was to learn more about his patient, since he had "only the information contained in the [medical] record," which was "not very detailed."

The psychiatrist, I quickly realized, had taken no special interest in Kai until he learned of the possible Munch connection. News of that connection had come from Poul Rée, who had traced Mudocci's son to Sakskøbing and paid him a number of visits.

Louis Levy on a family outing, c. 1929. LEVY FAMILY COLLECTION

When Janet first mentioned her 1962 meeting with Poul Rée, I assumed the art dealer would have a walk-on part in the story that was unfolding. But as I dug deeper into Mudocci's biography, Rée kept turning up. Only now, reading this stack of letters, did I begin to understand his role. He grew up in Copenhagen, where his parents moved in social circles that included Eva Mudocci and Bella Edwards, and probably Louis Levy as well. Rée had known Eva and Bella since his childhood, and had visited them in Paris in December 1919 and in London in 1946 and 1947. The two London visits took place during a period of decline, when Eva and Bella were fragile and had few contacts with people who had known them in their heyday. That may explain how Rée became privy to a surprising amount of confidential information about the musicians, including details about Eva's twins. In a 1961 letter to an American collector (written in English), he included these details:

[When I visited in the 1940s], Bella made some comments as to the relations between Eva and Munch. If I repeated them, Eva's daughter might sue me. Eva got twins 19/12 1908, the boy Edward is in a lunanetic (*sic*) asylum. He paints and cuts in wood. The daughter is married to an Englishman in London and has 3 children. The father to the twins is indicated to be a married man, Mr. L.

I was surprised that in 1961 Rée was aware of Louis Levy as the twins' putative father. Indeed, it now seems likely that he was the source of the Munch Museum officials' knowledge of Levy. But the dealer clearly preferred the Munch theory and eagerly promoted it. He followed his revelation about Mr. L. with these points: "According to Munch's letters, he was in Paris in March 1908. Munch had his breakdown in 1908."

In another letter to the American collector, Rée wrote that his wife, upon meeting Eva Mudocci's son, had been startled by his resemblance to Edvard Munch. He acknowledged that Kai lacked Munch's height and that his features suggested Jewish origins, but explained this by describing Eva as a "little Jewish-looking girl."

At about the same time, Rée stunned psychiatrist Otto Lund with the news that Lund's middle-aged, psychotic patient was in all likelihood the son of the great Norwegian artist. Rée's revelation had a commercial motive. The dealer wanted to mount an exhibit of Kai's paintings, promoting him as the son and artistic heir of Edvard Munch. To do so, he would need the hospital's cooperation.

Intrigued by Poul Rée's disclosure, Dr. Lund began making inquiries of his own. It was at this juncture that he contacted the Munch Museum and arranged to meet with the director. As for the proposed exhibit, Dr. Lund agreed to write to his patient's sister to seek her approval. He proceeded cautiously. Lund's first letter to Isobel Weber made no mention of the art dealer, or of Edvard Munch, but did broach the possibility of selling Kai's artwork, with proceeds to be used "solely for your brother." Lund added, "While he is not incapacitated and has no guardian, it will probably make sense in this case for the hospital to help him manage the revenue."

Lund asked Isobel for documents and data about her family, urging her to provide "as much detail as possible about [Kai's] birth, upbringing, and life," ostensibly to inform his patient's treatment. Lund quoted a letter, found among Kai's records, that Isobel had once written to one of her brother's doctors, declaring that Kai "has our mother to thank for much of the state he is in." Now, eight years after assuming his post, Dr. Lund asked Isobel to explain what she meant.

Isobel answered promptly, demurring on the proposed exhibit. According to Janet, Isobel did not want to expose her twin brother to public scrutiny, especially since she lived too far from him to offer the emotional support he would need. Dr. Lund replied six months later, telling Isobel that the idea of an exhibit had been scuttled. "Like you, I feared all along that it could get out that the pictures were painted by a psychotic patient," he wrote.

Dr. Lund added that since writing to her, he had chanced upon Kai's link to Eva Mudocci, "who played a significant role in the great Norwegian painter Edvard Munch's life at the beginning of this century." This was disingenuous at best. When he began writing to Isobel, Otto Lund was well aware of the possible Munch connection and was already in touch with Munch Museum officials.

Over the next year, Dr. Lund won Isobel's trust, offering to foot the bill with hospital funds if she wanted to visit her brother, and reassuring her that her brother's disease, although hereditary, would not inevitably afflict her or her children. By October 1962, when he was deep into his analysis of the Munch-Mudocci correspondence, Dr. Lund succeeded in eliciting the information he was after. Toward the end of a long letter to Isobel, Dr. Lund wrote: "Finally, of course, your insistence that Edvard Munch cannot be your and Kai's father aroused my interest. Now that you yourself directly mention this, I can confess that this possibility had crossed my mind."

Isobel's side of this correspondence has not survived, but Lund's response makes it clear that in 1962, she denied kinship to Munch. Moreover, she confided to Dr. Lund her connection to Louis Levy. Dr. Lund wrote, "I understand from your letter that you have known and associated with Louis Levy, and that he regarded you as his daughter. This Louis Levy would not do, of course, unless he was certain that he was your and Kai's father, and thus this, as well as some other questions that you touch on in your letter, must be considered fully resolved."

Now I understood how Dr. Lund could so emphatically assure Munch Museum officials, in 1963, that Munch was "NOT the father." His source was Eva Mudocci's daughter.

Suddenly nothing was making sense. As I worked out the chronology, I realized that Isobel had denied kinship to Munch during the same season that Janet returned home from Denmark and heard from her mother about Bella's disclosure. In other words, in the fall of 1962, Isobel told the psychiatrist that her father was not Munch, but Levy, and conveyed to her daughter that her father was not Levy, but Munch.

To further complicate matters, Dr. Lund clung to the Munch theory even after writing to Isobel that the matter must be considered "fully resolved." He continued his research into the intersecting lives of Munch and Mudocci, and in subsequent letters to Munch Museum officials, proposed returning for additional discussions. Perhaps it was his patient's accomplished artwork, as well as Poul Rée's compelling arguments, that made it hard for the psychiatrist to part with his theory. According to Dr. Lund's heirs, he gave up his research only because Oslo officials proved to be so uncooperative. For the rest of his long life, Otto Lund remained resentful that they had treated him dismissively.

I had spent years unraveling a mystery at the heart of Janet Weber's family history. Then, unexpectedly, a stack of letters called into question the very premise of the search. It now seemed that in 1962, when Janet was first told that her grandfather was Edvard Munch, her mother Isobel actually believed otherwise. Had there been a misunderstanding? Multiple misunderstandings?

I had thought long and hard about why Eva Mudocci would withhold information from her children. Now I had to ask myself why, decades later, Isobel Weber would do the same. What would keep her from confiding to her adult daughter and sons the distinct possibility that Louis Levy was her father—and their grandfather? Was it eagerness to claim a link to Munch? Or perhaps reluctance to claim kinship to Levy?

To be sure, many parents are reticent about chapters of family history that they fear may burden the generations that follow. I wondered whether, in the context of post-Holocaust Europe, Isobel was reluctant to claim Jewish heritage for herself and her children. Morten Levy, more oriented to the facts of family life, offered a different perspective: "Perhaps [Isobel] has had thoughts about Louis as a womanizer," he suggested. After all, Levy had fathered thirteen children by five women, three of whom were not his wives. "Perhaps she didn't like to be part of such a menagerie."

That menagerie, Morten told me, was readily acknowledged by the Levy family. Isobel and Kai were welcomed into the family and written into the family tree. Louis's children and grandchildren all seemed to know the twins, or to know about them. Their kinship was settled family history. Psychologically and temperamentally, Eva Mudocci and Louis Levy were very different people, and their family dramas played out against different cultural backdrops. Levy's greater openness no doubt reflected, as well, the social reality stated so tersely by Olga Ott, the mother of another Levy child: only women have illegitimate children; men just have children.

Finally, I asked Janet Weber for her thoughts about the letters that had come to light at the end of our search. Isobel was never completely sure who her biological father was, she told me, and did "move between possible choices depending on societal impact and who she was talking to." But she was not confused about whom she loved and who loved her: "HmHm [Dr. Lemvigh-Müller] and his extended family—*they* were her family. She spent holidays with them, only visiting the Levys, I think, very intermittently. The others were a swirl around her. They were there only when they wanted to be."

This swirl was a nightmare for Isobel as a child, and perhaps always, Janet said. "She grappled with how to make sense of it. She didn't know what or who to believe. She certainly wouldn't have minded having Jewish heritage. I don't know how she talked it out with HmHm, but the love he and his family gave her was—I think—the foundation of her very loving, generous and forgiving nature."

"Mother never talked ill of people," Janet continued, "but, every now and again, without her voicing it in words, I was aware of how deeply painful the whole situation had been for her. She suffered for Kai too. I think she had a very uneasy relationship with Bella, but mostly she kept it all within, which was the societal norm, even expectation, of the time."

The secrets guarded by Eva and kept by Isobel lay dormant for decades, but eventually unsettled the next generation. Family secrets, it turns out, do not always fall away with time; more often, they multiply, creating dense tangles of unanswered questions. Over time, memories become suspect. As inconsistencies and contradictions are exposed, vividly recollected events and conversations may begin to blur. Family resemblances, once distinct, begin to seem imperfect, tentative. New questions arise, but the people most likely to have answers are out of reach. The effects may be long-lasting. The century-old knot of secrets surrounding Eva Mudocci has now been unraveled, but a fresh set of questions that arose in the process may never be answered.

On an intensely contested stretch of family history lies a question that has yet to be squarely addressed: What was the nature of Eva's relationships with Edvard and Bella?

Some art historians believe that Eva and Edvard had a close, fraught, but ultimately chaste relationship—that they were more akin to siblings than lovers. That is a minority opinion, however. Most take for granted an affair (or an attempted affair). Some simply refer to Mudocci as Edvard Munch's "muse." Scholars tend to agree that Munch's liaison with Eva provided some respite from his exhausting fixation on Tulla Larsen.

Viewing Eva through the lens of Munch's life and work, scholars have written telegraphically about her relationship with Bella Edwards. Some assume that the two women were lovers; others play it safe by calling them an "artist-couple." From the start, I was reluctant to try to sort this out. From 1900 through the early 1950s, Eva and Bella lived with and for each other. No one would question whether a man and woman who lived together for more than half a century, making sacrifices and taking immense risks to be together, were actually a couple. But Janet Weber and I had embarked on this search together, and I felt obliged to consider carefully her sense of her grandmother and Bella's relationship as a deep artistic bond, without a physical dimension.

Their social inclinations were unambiguous. Throughout their decades together, Eva and Bella socialized with gay artists who, while discreet, were intentional and unapologetic about their sexual identities. Indeed, Knupffer's unpublished account of Eva and Bella's life together at times reads like a crazily evasive who's who of upper-crust gay and lesbian culture. Eva and Bella took part in lesbian salons in Paris and continued to socialize primarily with lesbians and gay men when, in mid-life, they relocated to more conservative England.

Contemporaries considered Eva and Bella a couple. In 1902, Jappe Nilssen confidently informed Munch that the two women

Mudocci's daughter Isabella (Isobel) with her Danish foster father,
Dr. Carl Johan Lemvigh-Müller, c. 1926. WEBER FAMILY COLLECTION

were lovers. For Munch, spending time with them and visiting their home did nothing to dispel the impression. Months after their initial meeting, he was questioning Eva about her relationship with Bella and bruising her with the words "not normal." Bella, feisty and resilient, was the more confident partner; while deeply attached to Bella, Eva was less secure in her identity, more susceptible to the attention of men who saw her as a challenge.

Eva's relationship with Munch certainly had an erotic dimension. She made it clear that her feelings for Munch were not platonic, but her declarations of passion were cast, characteristically, in spiritual terms. When Edvard wrote, "I don't know what kind of kindred feelings these are—whether they are physical or spiritual," Mudocci responded: "My dear, do you believe that body and soul are separated by such a gulf? How do you know they are not one and the same—two yet one, as they say about God and Christ? Just when you experience the ultimate spiritual delight, it probably has a physical basis. . . . So, my dear, what I mean is that—what drew us both to each other began in our blood."

Eva was certainly infatuated with Edvard, and at times was overwhelmed by conflicting feelings and impulses. In early 1906, she appeared willing to risk everything, telling her "lieber Edvard" that she would try to free herself to be with him. The risks were immense. Edvard's letters offered tenderness, spiritual connection, sporadic intensity, but nothing that could be relied upon. Although intent on loosening Eva's ties to her anchor, Munch promised no safe harbor.

In the end, Eva would not leave Bella, but her confusion and self-doubt persisted. As she told Munch in a 1906 letter, she had tried to ward off his "not normal" charge by sleeping with another man. This was not the only occasion. As DNA testing has shown, two years later Eva conceived twins with Louis Levy. Whether her pregnancy was accidental or a deliberate effort to conceive is not known.

In 1906, Eva wrote to Edvard that until he came into her life, she had lived "as a nun." This certainly fits with Janet's view of her grandmother. By "as a nun," did Eva mean "without men," or did she mean "without intimacy"? In the same letter, Mudocci wrote that when she met Munch, she was "so inexperienced, so silly and innocent, that I was at a loss what to do when the time finally came." Was she totally unfamiliar with sexual expression, or just inexperienced with men?

These passages resonate with Janet's view of her grandmother. Had Eva lived as a nun, with music as her God? History offers examples of "Boston marriages"—committed, romantic friendships between women who shared their lives, apparently without sexual intimacy, so called because in the United States, such partnerships were thought to be particularly common in New England. In the nineteenth century, Boston marriages were seen as reasonable alternatives for "new women"—often artists and writers—who were financially independent and valued both self-reliance and loving companionship. Only after sexologists began writing about "inverts" at the outset of the twentieth century were such bonds subject to public speculation and censure.

By now, Janet's televised comment, "it would be hard not to have some correspondence," had become a kind of mantra for me. In years of research, no letters between Eva and Bella had surfaced. Eva's love for Edvard can therefore be established in a way that her bond with Bella cannot. The lack of correspondence struck me as significant. In the early twentieth century, lesbians and gay men had good reason to purge incriminating letters from their personal archives. Writer Willa Cather preserved thousands of letters, but not her correspondence with Edith Lewis, the woman with whom she lived for forty years. The Gertrude Norman-Marcia Van Dresser archive contains hundreds of letters, but none exchanged by the two principals. Most of Eva and Bella's letters to their friends were also purged from that collection.

The times required discretion. A quarter century after Radclyffe Hall's obscenity trial in England, those of her acquaintances who remained on the scene were shaken by the news that Sir John Gielgud had been arrested by Scotland Yard's "pretty police"—attractive young men stationed at public lavatories to entrap gay men. The scandal nearly ended the actor's career. In 1953, a particularly repressive time, even Gielgud's recent knighthood could not protect him from public excoriation. As Lyell Barbour wrote to Toto Norman, Gielgud had broken the Edwardian commandment: "Thou shalt not be found out."

When the recipients of incriminating letters did not destroy them, heirs often took it upon themselves to do so. And that, apparently, is what happened in the case of Eva and Bella, as I learned from one of the letters that had turned up in the box from London at the end of our search. "I quite agree with your comments about your mother's letters," Dr. Lund wrote to Mudocci's daughter in 1963. "They should not, of course, be read by others. Also, I completely agree with your comments about your mother's and Bella's relationship." We cannot know what was in those letters, or what Isobel had written about Eva and Bella's relationship. But there can be little doubt about the kind of revelations that "should not, of course, be read by others."

In the end, this is what mattered most: Eva and Bella loved each other, shared a primary bond, were considered an indivisible unit by all who knew them. Eva's love for Munch did not eclipse her deep attachment to Bella, nor did her love for Bella preclude her attraction to Munch. The two strands of Eva's emotional life—her two most powerful relationships—were tightly wound together. It was this double helix, I decided, that was the key to Mudocci's life. To disentangle it was to lose its complexity and its beauty.

Dr. Lund counseled Isobel to destroy her mother's letters, but offered contrasting advice about another set of papers that had come into Isobel's possession—the letters from Edvard Grieg to Bella that revealed her role in a brief romance. When he learned that

Isobel had these letters, Otto Lund asked to see them. He agreed with Isobel that they were "of an intimate nature," but nevertheless passed them along to Poul Rée, who, in turn, arranged for antiquities dealer Dan Fog to negotiate their sale. In 1963, Poul Rée reported to Isobel that the letters had been sold for one thousand kroner (about $1,000 today). That is how they found their way to Norway's Bergen Library.

Once again, Poul Rée had turned up. His letters show how persistently he insinuated himself into the family's history, teaming up with Kai's psychiatrist to shed light on Mudocci's life and relationships, making multiple visits to Mudocci's hospitalized son, and proposing to exhibit Kai's paintings. While brokering the sale of letters and memorabilia in Isobel's possession, Rée hoped to locate works by Munch left behind at Eva's death. In a 1963 letter to Isobel, Rée described a painting he dimly recalled seeing in Eva and Bella's flat, depicting Eva dressed in white. He wrote to Isobel, "[S]omewhere in your deceased mother's property there might be a small fortune for you, if you are able to find it." He was no doubt anticipating the commission he would make in the process.

With Poul Rée in mind, I once again considered the origin of Janet's impression that Edvard Munch was her grandfather. According to Janet, Bella was the source of her mother's information about Munch's role in their family history. Poul Rée also pointed to Bella as *his* source for knowledge of Mudocci's relationship with Munch. Could it be that Isobel heard the news from Bella—but only indirectly, with Rée as the unmentioned middle man? I began to wonder whether it was actually the meddling art dealer who not only promoted and perpetuated, but also originated the idea that Edvard Munch was the twins' father in hopes of profiting from the sale of paintings by "the son of the great Norwegian artist." He could have suggested this connection to Isobel when he visited London in 1947, or perhaps in a follow-up letter that was not saved.

Poul Rée was destined to turn up one more time before my search was over.

15

The Mona Lisa of Expressionism

"It was his ambition to make the perfect portrait of me," Eva Mudocci recalled toward the end of her life, nearly fifty years after she first met Edvard Munch. But each time Edvard began a painting of her, Eva wrote, "he destroyed it because he was dissatisfied with it." Accounts of Munch's life and work agree that he created three lithographic portraits of Eva Mudocci, but no oil paintings. "I've never seen a reference to his actually painting Mudocci," one Munch expert told me.

I had no reason to doubt this—until in 2017 I found myself in the dining room of a handsome prairie-style house in southern Minnesota, face to face with a large, full-length Eva Mudocci on canvas. This portrait has been called the "Mona Lisa of Expressionism"—perhaps because Mudocci's expression is inscrutable, or perhaps because her pose, especially the distinctive position of her hand, mirrors the iconic pose of the woman in Leonardo da Vinci's masterpiece.

The portrait of Mudocci is unfinished and unsigned. A brass nameplate on its frame identifies the artist as Edvard Munch, but

Unsigned, unfinished, oil on canvas 45-1/2 x 34-1/4 in. (115.5 x 87 cm) FLATEN
MUSEUM, NORTHFIELD, MINNESOTA /AUTHOR'S PHOTOGRAPH

Mudocci's pose seems inexplicably awkward until the portrait is viewed side-by-side with Leonardo da Vinci's *Mona Lisa*. LOUVRE MUSEUM, PARIS

St. Olaf College, which owns the painting and has hung it in its president's house, has for more than a decade taken the stance that the artist is unknown. Standing before this haunting portrait, I realized that one more mystery about Eva Mudocci and Edvard Munch had yet to be solved.

Munch intended to paint Mudocci—of that there is no doubt. In a letter drafted to her in mid-1903, Edvard complained that the photograph she had sent him was attractive, but did not do her justice. "Your expression and character are missing—I will paint you sometime," he wrote. He reiterated this intention in other letters. But did he follow through? For decades, the answer has been hidden in plain sight. Letters archived at the Flaten and at the Munch Museum suggest that Munch attempted at least two oil portraits of Eva Mudocci—one painted in Paris and the other in Berlin.

The Paris portrait was referenced in a 1903 letter from Eva to her mother. Eva's letter (quoted in Chapter 3) described a Norwegian's "beautiful" painting of her wearing a silver cross and playing the violin. Like Munch's *Madonna* images of the 1890s, it placed her head against a crimson halo. Eva wrote that the painting showed her in a blue silk blouse against "a black ground intensely black." The Flaten's painting does place Mudocci against a black ground, but otherwise does not accord with her description of the Paris painting. That painting has never surfaced and was apparently destroyed.

The Berlin portrait was referenced in a letter from Max Linde to Munch dated February 1, 1904—two weeks after Munch reported to his friend Jappe Nilssen, "I am painting and drawing— and am together with Eva M." Linde's letter asked Munch, "How is it going with the painting of the woman violinist [*violinistin*]?"

Could this Berlin portrait be the one that now hangs in the Minnesota dining room?

I first came across mention of the Flaten's unfinished Mudocci portrait in a 1973 journal article by Waldemar Stabell, published in Norway, that reproduced the painting in black and white and gave its date as 1903-04. When I asked Janet Weber about Stabell's claim, she said that she had heard about an unfinished portrait from her mother Isobel—not once, but on several occasions. Her mother had the definite impression that the painting was by Munch.

The 1973 article left many questions unanswered. Where had the black-and-white photo come from? On what basis had the author concluded that Munch had painted the portrait? And if it was an authentic Munch, why wasn't it catalogued with his other paintings? I found some answers in the Munch Museum's administrative files. In late 1959, Senior Curator Reidar Revold learned from a conservator at the National Gallery of Denmark that a painting of Eva Mudocci had surfaced at a Copenhagen auction. The painting had been sold as part of the estate of Mudocci's friend, the artist Kay Nielsen—the same Kay Nielsen whom Eva and Bella had looked after when, as a young man, he attended art school in Paris. The painting was listed as "Lady in a Black Dress." It was not identified in the auction catalogue as a Munch, but instead was grouped with several works by Nielsen. It was purchased at the auction by the Danish art dealer Poul Rée, who had known Mudocci personally and recognized that she was the portrait's subject. Rée had gone to school with Kay Nielsen, was familiar with his art nouveau style, and knew that the portrait was not his work. He believed that the portrait was, rather, a previously unknown Munch.

When he learned of Rée's purchase, Revold looked into the matter. He corresponded with Rée and then reported his findings to his boss, Johan Langaard:

> A few months ago we received from dealer Poul Rée, Holbergsgade 11, Copenhagen, a photographic copy of a painted portrait of Eva Mudocci, allegedly carried out by Edv. Munch. The photo does not prove this, but the dealer Rée says that the painting belonged to illustrator Kay Nielsen who was an art foster son [*en art plejeson*] of Bella Edwards and Eva Mudocci during his stay in Paris 1904-1910, and was sold at an auction of his belongings in Copenhagen in 1959. The dealer Rée sold the picture to an American who wants to remain anonymous, and it should now be deposited in an American museum.

When I read this memo, two facts jumped out at me. First, crucial links in the painting's provenance (Eva Mudocci to Kay Nielsen to Poul Rée) were considered questionable. To trace the painting's origins, I would have to investigate those links. And second, the unsigned portrait was said to be in the U.S. But where?

Over several weeks, I checked the digital collections of American museums that own works by Munch, but found no reference to a Mudocci portrait. Then one afternoon, as I went through a stack of materials hunting for an elusive citation, I came across a passing reference to the portrait in a 1983 book on Frederick Delius and Edvard Munch. A painting of Mudocci, it said, had been purchased by Richard N. Tetlie of Washington, D.C. With this bit of information, I located the painting at Tetlie's alma mater—St. Olaf College. The portrait had not turned up in an internet search because it hangs in its president's house rather than in its Flaten Museum, and had therefore not been photographed for the museum's digital collection.

I wrote to Flaten Museum Director Jane Becker Nelson, planned a visit, and soon had a chance to see the imposing painting, which measures forty-five by thirty-four inches. Mudocci stands on an oriental rug in a room with walls the color of cognac. She wears a black gown; a decorative green ribbon is looped around her right hand. There is a large black square behind Eva's lithe figure and to her left, a Buddha is sketched in pencil. Eva lists slightly to her right, recalling the full-length figure of Mudocci in Munch's lithograph, *The Violin Concert.*

In time, I was able to establish that the painting had indeed been sold on September 2, 1959 by the Brun Rasmussen auction house in Copenhagen as part of Kay Nielsen's estate. Rée paid 50 Danish kroner—about $60 today. What happened next is documented in the Flaten Museum's files. Thrilled to have gotten his hands on what he believed to be a previously unknown Munch, Poul Rée showed his painting to several experts, and they applauded his discovery. National Gallery of Denmark conservator Poul Lunøe (the man who contacted Reidar Revold about the painting) wrote to Rée that he believed the painting was by Munch. Rée also heard from Harald Holst Halvorsen, who had known Munch personally and was, over three decades, one of his most important dealers and collectors. Halvorsen's letter congratulated Rée on his find and predicted that it would cause a sensation. The Norwegian dealer knew that Rée was a small-time operator, without access to the well-placed Munch collectors who comprised his own Oslo clientele, and he offered to handle the sale of the Mudocci portrait. In particular, he wrote that Rolf Stenersen—Munch's friend and biographer and an avid collector of his work—was eager to buy the painting. Of course, Halvorsen would have taken a cut, and Poul Rée was not eager to share the profits, so he made no commitment to him. Then, in 1960, Halvorsen died.

And so, when a wealthy collector appeared in Copenhagen, eager to have a look at the painting, Rée jumped at the opportunity. The collector was Richard Tetlie, an American of Norwegian descent and a 1943 graduate of St. Olaf College. He had learned of the portrait from two independent sources: Anne Birgitte Bjerke, who had taken over her father Holst Halvorsen's business and told Tetlie that her father believed the painting to be a "real" Munch; and the Danish artist Knud Pedersen, who arranged for Tetlie to see the painting at Rée's home. Tetlie was eager to buy the painting, but he was an experienced collector who owned other works by Munch, and he asked for documentation of its authenticity. He returned home without the painting.

Over the next several months, Rée sent Tetlie several long letters, written in English, describing his relationship with Mudocci, his familiarity with private details of her biography, his conversations with Bella Edwards, and his correspondence with Mudocci's daughter, Isobel. Rée sent written accounts of his conversations with museum officials, such as the National Gallery of Norway's eminent director, Sigurd Willoch. According to Rée, Willoch needed no convincing that the painting was a Munch and dismissed out of hand the notion that it could be a fake. At the time that Mudocci would have posed for the portrait, Willoch told Rée, Munch's style was not yet in vogue; no one would have thought it profitable to imitate his work.

Rée's letters to his prospective buyer also offered stylistic analysis, pointing out that the painting was fully consistent with Munch's composition and style: its off-center placement of the subject; its use of color; its characteristic use of lines and planes to create the sense of depth that draws the viewer into its world. He noted the rather crude representation of the hand—something Munch had been criticized for—and observed that the portrait reflects Munch's peculiar habit of leaving some of the canvas exposed where other artists would have applied white paint.

After considerable back and forth, Tetlie was satisfied by the accumulation of evidence and in 1960, he paid $10,000 for the portrait. Rée shipped it to him. Years later, Tetlie recalled that he had brought the portrait to the United States "to help lessen the inadequacy of Munch's representation in this country." He called his painting "the only Munch outside of Norway which Norway needs." American institutions were satisfied by documentation of the painting's provenance. In 1967, Tetlie lent the painting to the Los Angeles County Museum of Art, where it was exhibited for nearly a decade. In 1971, the museum proposed buying the portrait for $250,000 (about $1.5 million today). The offer was tempting, as Tetlie had become overextended. But unwilling to part with the portrait, he turned down the offer and instead borrowed $300,000 from a Washington, DC bank, using the painting as collateral. Tetlie lived for four decades after buying the painting, never doubting its authenticity.

As for Poul Rée, for several years after selling the portrait, he continued to pursue and forward evidence linking it to Munch. In 1962, through his acquaintance with psychiatrist Otto Lund, Rée got hold of Eva and Edvard's correspondence (despite Langaard's request to Lund that the letters be kept confidential). He sent Richard Tetlie a copy of one of the letters, begging Tetlie not to divulge to Munch Museum officials the "indiscretion" that had put the letter in his hands. The letter revealed that Munch and Mudocci had quarreled early in 1904 and that they abruptly broke off contact.

Rée concluded, not unreasonably, that Mudocci was left with an unfinished painting. This explained how an unsigned, unfinished Munch appeared at auction half a century later, despite the fact that the artist seldom parted with unfinished canvases and was known to sign paintings before showing or selling them.

That leaves the question of how the portrait ended up in the estate of Danish painter Kay Nielsen. A major clue turns up in a letter archived at the Munch Museum. Writing from Berlin's Hotel Sans Souci, Eva Mudocci told Munch, "There is a young painter here who would terribly like to meet you—Since he is the son of the greatest Danish actress—Oda Nielsen who is also with us—it might also be amusing for you—especially since he himself is a very gifted boy, as a painter." Eva proposed that Munch join them at the hotel the following day.

This letter places Kay Nielsen in Berlin, with Munch and Mudocci, at the time the painting would have been worked on and abandoned. It also establishes Nielsen's strong interest in the older painter. These facts support the notion that the unfinished painting ended up in Kay Nielsen's hands after Mudocci's break with Munch.

Nearly sixty years have passed since Tetlie purchased the portrait, believing it to be a Munch. Given its credible provenance, as well as Max Linde's 1904 letter to Munch asking about progress on his painting of the woman violinist, I wondered why the portrait had not been authenticated in the interim.

The Flaten Museum's records tell that story. In 2004, Gerd Woll, a Munch authority who then held the post of senior curator at the Munch Museum, declined to include the portrait in the *Catalogue Raisonné* of Munch's paintings. In a letter to the executor of Tetlie's estate regarding other Munch canvases in the Tetlie collection, Woll wrote: "As for the portrait of Eva Mudocci, I am sorry to tell you that there are serious doubts about its authenticity, and we do not find the information from Poul Rée too convincing. We shall, however, look carefully into the matter before making a final decision."

The Flaten never received that final decision, and Woll offered no specifics when she declined to include the Mudocci portrait in the authoritative catalogue of Munch's paintings. To be sure, Woll had good reason to be cautious. The unctious tone of the dealer's letters to Tetlie would have raised a red flag. And while the letters included accurate details about Mudocci's life known to few (i.e., the existence of her twins, the date of their birth, and the involvement of a married man with the initials L.L.), they also included glaring errors (notably, the dates and circumstances of Mudocci's relationship with Munch). Rée believed that the painting dated from 1896—a time when Eva lived in Germany and had not yet met Munch—and to this day, that date is inscribed on the painting's nameplate.

But Rée was not wrong about issues at the heart of the provenance, including Eva and Bella's close relationship with Kay Nielsen and the quarrel that broke off contact between Eva and Edvard early in 1904, when Munch was known to be at work on a portrait of a woman violinist.

Since receiving Woll's letter in 2004, the Flaten has listed the portrait's painter as unknown, and the painting has been effectively erased from Munch's biography and oeuvre. No one revisited the question. Such is the power of a single institution that, in effect, controls the legacy of an internationally celebrated artist.

In 2017, I raised the question of the portrait with a number of experts in Denmark and Norway who agreed on one point: today, most museums are unwilling to risk authenticating a painting. The benefits to the museum are minimal, compared with the problems that ensue if an opinion is challenged or reversed. Unofficially, museum officials offered opinions on the Mudocci portrait (based solely on photographs) ranging from *probably a Munch* (compelling provenance; Munch-like composition; similarity to other portraits of the same period) to *probably not* (background too messy; hand too lifeless). Those who thought it was probably authentic measured their words carefully: "It is not unlike a Munch," one said. "It looks like a Munch, it smells like a Munch, perhaps it is a Munch," another offered. They agreed that the provenance—as I had described it—sounded persuasive.

The expert who doubted the portrait's authenticity was more specific, calling the brush strokes of the background and the carpet "too random." Munch was always intentional and systematic. Yes, the portrait was unfinished, but Munch did not build paintings that way—by starting out messy and then layering in structure.

I asked who else could have painted the Mudocci portrait. I had in mind a letter from Eva to Edvard: "Don't you want to paint me? I have just promised a French painter [Matisse?] to sit for him sometime since he is somewhat more interesting than the rest. Otherwise I have always, always said no because I think to myself that there is only <u>one</u> who can paint me."

"People have faked his style," I was told. "You wouldn't believe some of the cases I've seen." In the end, this expert too held open the possibility that the portrait was authentic, saying that it had never been inspected first-hand by Munch Museum curators, and that the museum has filed it in a "we-have-our-doubts" folder, not in its folder of outright fakes.

I had thought that sorting out whether Munch was responsible for Mudocci's pregnancy would be difficult; determining whether he was responsible for her portrait was proving to be even more problematic. It seemed that I had reached a dead end, and then I remembered the observation Janet Weber had made at the end of her Norwegian television interview: these days, scientific testing can help determine a person's origins. Could the same be true for a portrait? I raised the question with the leadership of St. Olaf's

Jennifer L. Mass of Scientific Analysis of Fine Art, LLC, takes a minute sample of paint from the oil painting of Eva Mudocci, 2018. AUTHOR'S PHOTOGRAPH

Flaten Museum.

In October 2018, the Flaten Museum engaged two scientists to study the Mudocci portrait. Jennifer L. Mass and Adam Finnefrock, of Scientific Analysis of Fine Art, LLC, spent two days in Minnesota examining the unfinished canvas. With a surgeon's steady hand, Mass collected minute samples from the painting. Over the next several weeks, they used a variety of sophisticated tools to conduct an "elemental and molecular analysis" of its materials.

A leading scholar in the field of art authentication and conservation, Mass had previously published an analysis of the materials that Munch used in the 1910 version of his iconic painting, *The Scream*. She and Finnefrock also had access to inventories of Munch's materials compiled by the Munch Museum and a team of collaborating scientists. With all of this information in hand, they could compare the collected samples with materials used in a range of Munch paintings created before 1916.

At the Flaten Museum, their report was eagerly awaited. In late November 2018, it arrived. "All of the pigments, preparation layers, and binders inferred or identified here are found in the works by Edvard Munch," they wrote. They pointed to the use of strontium yellow, a pigment in use in the last years of the nineteenth century and the first years of the twentieth that "dates this work to within the expected timeframe for the Mudocci portrait." They also noted the absence of specific blue and green pigments used later by expressionist painters, but not available in 1904. Finally, they said that the combination of pigments in one of their samples (vermilion, Prussian blue, cobalt blue, strontium yellow, zinc yellow, and likely viridian green) was consistent with Munch's "complex mixtures."

In short, the scientists concluded that the unfinished portrait is fully consistent with Munch's materials and working methods. By establishing the timeframe, they punctured the theory that the painting was a fake created mid-century to exploit the posthumous rise in Munch's reputation. That leaves the possibility that the portrait was painted by another acquaintance of Eva Mudocci who was familiar with her home and used a palette and style similar to Munch's—but who could that be? Neither Matisse nor Nielsen, the other painters who were known to spend time with Mudocci, ever produced a canvas that remotely resembled St. Olaf's portrait. No one has offered a plausible alternative.

Who painted the evocative portrait of Eva Mudocci? All of the evidence now points to Edvard Munch. The stylistic link to Munch paintings of the same period has long been observed. Given new information about its provenance and materials, the time has come to re-evaluate this important work and to include it in the *Catalogue Raisonné* of Munch's paintings. When that happens, the art world will finally come to know the Mona Lisa of Expressionism a century after it was created, and the unfinished story of Eva Mudocci will have a new ending.

Epilogue

Eva Mudocci and Bella Edwards lived together for fifty-two years. When Eva died in 1952, her ashes were scattered. On her death certificate, under "occupation," were the words: "Widow of Louis Muddock, a journalist." In one of the last known photos of Mudocci, she is wearing the brooch that Munch depicted a half century earlier in his celebrated portrait.

The death of Bella Edwards two years later went unnoticed in the press, but there was a flurry of headlines forty years later, in 1985, when Edvard Grieg's love letters to her were made public. The Reuters wire service picked up the story, and American newspapers ran it under such headlines as "Letters Reveal Passion of Famous Composer."

Mudocci in her seventies, wearing the brooch depicted in Munch's 1903 portrait. WEBER FAMILY COLLECTION

Edvard Munch spent his last decades mostly in seclusion at his compound on the outskirts of Oslo, known as Ekely. Today it is a national monument. In the 1930s, the Nazis declared Munch a degenerate artist and removed scores of his works from German museums. Nevertheless, when Munch died in January 1944, Nazi propaganda minister Joseph Goebbels commandeered the funeral, festooning his casket in swastikas. To the dismay of Munch's friends and relatives, this left the mistaken impression that the artist was a Nazi sympathizer. He died without issue.

"Tulla Larsen married twice, grew old, became a lovely, nice old lady," Tove Munch has said. She added that on Edvard Munch's eightieth birthday, Tulla sent him a big box of leftovers from her father's days as a prominent wine merchant. "She knew he liked good wine."

Louis Levy died at age sixty-four on March 9, 1940, one month before Nazi forces landed in Denmark. Morten Levy, who was one year old when his grandfather died, was later told that Louis, an avid swimmer, had taken a dip in the wintry sea and caught a chill that developed into pneumonia. Levy's obituary noted that the writer "was already forgotten even when he was alive." In 2017, his novel *Kzradock the Onion Man and the Spring-Fresh Methuselah* was reissued in Denmark, renewing interest in Levy's work.

After the death of Maud Warrender in 1945, Gertrude "Toto" Norman moved from Leasam to Lady Maud's London house at Holland Park. She continued to be an active supporter of the Musicians' Benevolent Association. Lady Maud's mansion, Leasam, provided housing and agricultural training for boys who attended Rye's local school, and later became a boarding house. Today, it is privately owned.

Pianist Arthur Shattuck remembered Bella in his will, easing her final days. After his death, *The New York Times* wrote: "His career was cut short by illness, but it lasted long enough for critics to classify him as one of the world's leading pianists." Today, historians of music mention Shattuck only in passing.

Founding director of the Munch Museum, Johan Langaard,

spent his retirement in Italy. Senior Curator Reidar Revold began serving a five-year prison term in 1969, after the Norwegian Supreme Court turned down his appeal for clemency. He wrote poetry in prison, became ill, and died in 1974 at the age of fifty-four.

Neurologist Daniel Jacobson ran into Edvard Munch on the street, some twenty years after Munch's confinement at his clinic. Munch did not initially recognize his physician.

After entering a Danish mental hospital in 1930, Mudocci's son, Kai Ellson, spent the rest of his life in its long-term care facility in southern Denmark, near his birthplace. He died in his seventies. To date, neither the circumstances of his death nor the disposition of his remains have been divulged to his next of kin. His psychiatrist, Dr. Otto Lund, retired and moved to a country home, where he was visited by Isobel Weber and her daughter Janet. Several of Kai's paintings now belong to Otto Lund's heirs, who have hung them on the walls of their homes in Denmark and the United States. The psychiatrist never gave up his theory that Edvard Munch was his patient's father. According to his stepdaughter, when Norway's art establishment proved to be "like a closed world," and his thesis was dismissed, Otto Lund "got very disappointed and just let it die out."

The early-state print of Eva and Bella that was left rolled up in the attic of Linden Villa is still owned by the family that bought the house from Lucy Muddock in 1935.

The unfinished, unsigned painting of Eva Mudocci owned by the Flaten Museum is finally being recognized as the work of Edvard Munch.

Mudocci's Emiliani Stradivarius violin remains in the hands of virtuoso Anne-Sophie Mutter.

Eva Mudocci's dream of "two natures perpetuated" did, over time, produce a "life stream" consisting of three grandchildren, nine great-grandchildren, and ten great-great-grandchildren who live in England, the Netherlands, Poland, and the United States. Mudocci's descendants have included several musicians and artists.

Janet Weber continues her work as a spiritual director and

seems to be at peace with the results of the DNA test. She has met her newly discovered cousin, Morten Levy. One additional DNA comparison, in 2017, yielded a totally unexpected finding: Morten Levy and I turned out to be fourth cousins, related through his only Jewish grandparent, Louis Levy. Our likely common ancestor appears on Morten's family tree as Bendit Scheyer, apparently a forebear of my grandfather, Ben Shore. Of course, if Morten Levy is my distant cousin through Louis Levy, then so is Janet Weber. In the end, my search for Janet's ancestors somehow led to my own.

The Brooch, Edvard Munch's exquisite portrait of Eva Mudocci, became one of his best known and most admired images. Some eighty years after it was created, the image inspired Andy Warhol to produce a series of psychedelic prints known as *Eva Mudocci (after Munch)*, reinterpreting for a new generation the mystery and allure of the lady with a brooch.

Coda

Another kind of legacy informs the story of Eva Mudocci.

When he died, Munch left behind thousands of paintings, prints, and sketches. Bella Edwards left several published compositions, including the score of a ballet now archived at the Royal Danish Library. Louis Levy left books, articles, and much-loved nursery rhymes. Mudocci left prose and poetry, but in the absence of recordings, all traces of her musical artistry are gone. We can only speculate about her sound, her technique, the colors she achieved with subtle variations in bowing and vibrato, or the musical ideas she brought to particular compositions. What survived was not the music, but the instrument.

To suggest that Mudocci's musical DNA inheres in the instrument she played might seem far-fetched—but not to musicians. Violinist Joshua Bell once explained that a virtuoso who plays a violin for decades, "playing in tune and milking the instrument for all it's worth," leaves an imprint. He believes that the way a violin has been played, the way its potential has been intuited and stretched, alters the instrument's physical characteristics as well as its soul. Bell was talking about his experience playing an instrument that had been owned, a century earlier, by the eminent violinist and composer Henri Vieuxtemps. Listening to the interview, you may think at first that Bell is reaching for a metaphor that can express the kinship he feels with a cherished musical ancestor. But he wants to be taken literally. He says, "maybe someday scientists will figure out how this works."

Eva Mudocci played the Emiliani for at least four decades. She played for hours every day over four decades—perhaps forty thousand hours or more. If Joshua Bell is right, the Emiliani she played in mid-life was not exactly the same Emiliani she first tucked under her chin as a young woman. And perhaps some trace of Eva Mudocci's musical imprint has been felt by the celebrated German virtuoso Anne-Sophie Mutter, who today owns Mudocci's Emiliani Stradivarius.

What kind of imprint would Mudocci have left? In Europe's salon culture of the early twentieth century, Mudocci played primarily in recital halls and drawing rooms. She was esteemed for the elegance and intimacy of her performances and for her passionate interpretations. Mutter, in contrast, is celebrated for bravura performances of an immense array of music—from the cerebral unaccompanied Bach partitas and sonatas to the muscular Brahms violin concerto to the profound *In Tempus Praesens*, composed for Mutter by the Russian composer Sofia Gubaidulina.

When Mutter first played the Emiliani, she has told interviewers, its sound was a revelation. "It opened my ears," she said. That sound can be heard in the recordings she made with Herbert von Karajan. Then in 1984, after performing exclusively on the Emiliani for five years, Mutter acquired a second Strad. The Emiliani sounds "superb," Mutter explained, but it is "dark in timbre." It lacks "a dimension—it has no edginess. I miss the unbridled power. I need this roughness for the eruptive moments of the Beethoven sonatas. You need it for Brahms, Sibelius and contemporary works." To meet these challenges, she plays the 1710 Lord Dunn-Raven Stradivarius, which provides the depth of color and the dynamic potential she was seeking. "You need the masculine side as well," Mutter says.

Young Anne-Sophie Mutter plays the Emiliani Stradivarius for conductor Herbert von Karajan. PHOTOGRAPH: DEUTSCHE GRAMMOPHON GMBH, © SUSESCH BAYAT / DG

Mutter's description of the Emiliani—offered without any thought of its previous owners—captures both the beauty and constriction of Mudocci's playing. By all accounts, Mudocci's playing was indeed superb, and, judging by reviews, opened the ears of many listeners. Her instrument's timbre gave voice to what she called, in her poetry, "the dark Gods." But she failed to earn a place in violin history that approaches Mutter's. Something was missing. Mutter named it: edginess, roughness, unbridled power. Thinking about Mudocci's life, it is easy to imagine the pressures and burdens that may have drained her energies. And, to be sure, she lived in a time and place that rewarded women for displays of delicacy, not power. But her playing may also have been constricted by a habit of inwardness, a lifelong commitment to refinement, and a fear of "waking the dark Gods stirring round."

Leading Mudocci's life took courage. She mastered the language of "insiderness," but was often overwhelmed by the demands of "outsiderness." "I wish you could just be a little polite," Mudocci once wrote to Edvard Munch. I find myself wondering whether Mudocci might have earned a more prominent place in the pantheon of virtuosos had she been a little less polite. We lack the recordings that would allow a fuller understanding of her musical achievements and limitations. What is clear is that her sound was exquisite, and that for two tumultuous decades, Eva Mudocci and Bella Edwards offered to a loyal following across Europe passionate expression of a generation's hopes and heartbreak.

Acknowledgments

In 2012, I began looking into the life of Eva Mudocci without any sense of where the research would lead. In the interim, I have relied on many guides. My greatest debt is to Mudocci's granddaughter, Janet Weber, who made time over several years for long conversations and extended e-mail exchanges, and generously gave me access to family documents, letters, and photographs. In the few cases where our conclusions differ, I offer mine with deep respect for the commitments that underlie hers. I am also indebted to Bent Weber and Morten Levy, who graciously offered crucial materials and unique perspectives on their remarkable grandparents. Morten also translated portions of his grandfather's letters and poems.

As the project grew, Karen Weiss was an astute reader and a constant source of advice and encouragement. As always, the extended Shore and Weiss/Ghent families offered nonstop support. Dan Greenwald and Marisa Gold cheered me on, read multiple drafts, and made important suggestions along the way. My mother Florence Shore, who reached her hundredth birthday as I worked on this project, closely followed its progress, as did my sister Barbara Shore and my brothers Bradd Shore and Ken Shore.

Special thanks to violinists Nadia Ghent and Eva León and to translator and researcher Lisbeth Dore, who added immeasurably to my understanding of Mudocci's life and work. For invaluable comments on various drafts, I gratefully acknowledge (in addition to many of those named above): Gergana Alyakova, Vera Chalidze, Janet Cutler, Trent Duffy, Marlene Ellin, Rosemary Goldford, Jack Herskovits, Sydelle Kramer, Lucy Liben, Ludmila Nigelska, Kevin O'Connor, and Louise Schneider. Anne-Sophie Mutter graciously reviewed the Coda. Book designer Niki Harris and editor Barbara Shore spared no effort as they helped ready the manuscript for publication, and in the process challenged and extended my thinking.

This project took me to several countries. In Germany, the current and former owners of Linden Villa were generous informants. In Norway, I profited from exchanges with Tove Munch and Ketil Bjørnstad. The curatorial and research staffs of the Munch Museum in Oslo have been extraordinarily helpful.

In Denmark, Jens-Otto Lund, Birgitte Folmer, and Vibeke Kjær acquainted me with the life of Dr. Otto Lund, and Gy Hentze shared a tragic episode from her family history. Peter Larsen of the National Gallery of Denmark and Katherine Eriksen of Bruun Rasmussen offered helpful information. In Nykøbing, the Pedersen family kindly invited me into the house where Mudocci's twins were born.

In the U.S., Sarah Epstein generously shared her knowledge of Munch and guided me through her amazing collection. Jane Becker Nelson and Mona Weselmann of the Flaten Museum at St. Olaf College offered access to important materials and shared my excitement about investigating the origin of St. Olaf's Mudocci portrait. Jennifer Mass and Adam Finnefrock offered fascinating explanations of their methods and findings.

My research benefitted from the assistance of librarians and archivists at the Getty Research Institute (Malvina Hoffman papers), Huntington Library (Kay Nielsen papers), Morgan Library & Museum (Pierre Matisse Gallery archives), New York Public Library (Gertrude Norman-Marcia Van Dresser collection), Tate

Gallery Library (Kenneth Clark papers), British Library (Ernst Henschel collection), Bibliotèque Nationale de France Département de la Musique, Bergen Offentlige Bibliotek (Edvard Grieg papers), Det Kongelige Bibliotek (Bella Edwards letters and scores; Louis Levy papers), Munchmuseet Biblioteket, Staatliches Institut für Musikforschung, Universität der Künste, Stadtarchiv Dresden, and Sächsische Landesbibliothek-Staats-und Universitätsbibliothek. I also want to acknowledge the work of researchers whose interest in Mudocci predated my own, including Patricia Berman, Alison Chang, Bruce Durie, Atle Næss, Carol Ravenal, and Jane Van Nimmen.

I am grateful for all of this help, but claim as entirely my own any errors of fact or judgment.

Finally, this book would not exist had not Adria Schwartz coaxed me to open my neglected violin case some twenty years ago. It held so much more than I ever imagined.

Permissions & photo credits: Every effort has been made to obtain permission to use or quote from copyrighted materials. Works by Henri Matisse are used with permission of Succession H. Matisse/Artists Rights Society (ARS), New York, NY. I gratefully acknowledge the institutions that make available digital images of their collections, including: Art Institute of Chicago, Flaten Museum at St. Olaf College, Metropolitan Museum of Art, Munch Museum, National Gallery of Norway, and Royal Danish Library.

Notes

These notes refer to page numbers, and make use of the following abbreviations:

BPL   Bergen Public Library, Bergen, Norway

FM   Flaten Museum, St. Olaf College, Northfield, Minnesota.

LFP   Levy Family Papers held by Morten Levy.

MM   Munch Museum, Oslo, Norway.

NYPL   Gertrude Norman-Marcia Van Dresser Papers, New York Public Library, New York, New York.

RDL   Royal Danish Library, Copenhagen, Denmark.

WFP   Weber Family Papers held by Bent Weber and Janet Weber.

Brackets indicate that a date has been established based on a letter's contents or by a postmark.

9   **own chamber orchestra**   Eva Mudocci's maternal grandfather, Robert Hann, was a distinguished violinist, and Robert's three children (Emily, Lucy, and Charles) were all musicians and/or music teachers. Robert's brother (and Eva's great uncle) William Henry Hann was a noted viola player. A history of London's promenade concerts at Covent Garden noted that fifty years after W.H. Hann's death, his name was among those "still remembered by veteran concert-goers in London." See Adam Carse, *The Life of Julien: Adventurer, Showman-Conductor and Establisher of the Promenade Concerts in England, together with a history*

of those concerts up to 1895 (Cambridge: W. Heffer & Sons Ltd., 1951), 15. William Henry Hann's daughter (Marianne) was a mezzo-soprano. His sons included violinists (Edwin and Lewis), cellists (William and Clement), and a violist (Sidney). Several of the musical Hanns also composed, played other instruments, and sang, and quite a few were professors of music. Violinist and composer Lewis Hann was devoted to the education of female violinists, wrote a book on the subject, and taught at Cheltenham Ladies' College and Malvern Girls' College. A genealogical study of the family reports that the "Sherborne Hanns are a bit of an enigma in that they arrive from nowhere in 1689." See Eddie Hann, "Hann Family History," http://www.hannfamily.org.uk/sherborne_dist.htm.

10 **civilization in America** For background on J.E.P. Muddock, see Bruce Durie, "Dick Donovan, the Glasgow Detective, and His Creator, James Edward (Joyce Emerson Preston) Muddock," *Clues* 26, no. 2 (Winter 2008): 23-38. Some sources say that the use of "dick" to mean detective in popular literature originated with Muddock's character; others say that the term came from Britain's criminal slang of the 1860s.

10 **old family name** A handwritten note on a Rose Lynton program by Mudocci's daughter, Isobel Weber, says: "My mother was called Rose Lynton (an old family name) as a child prodigy." *WFP.*

10 **prospects uncertain** See Bruce Durie, "Did Edvard Munch Have Children with Eva Mudocci: Genealogy and DNA," in Ellin Galtung Lihaug, ed., *Genealogica & Heraldica. Proceedings of the XXXIst International Congress of Genealogical and Heraldic Sciences Oslo 2014* (Oslo: Slektshistorisk forlag, 2015), 125-36. According to Durie, after a nervous breakdown in 1874, Muddock applied to the Royal Literary Fund for emergency funds, citing poverty and claiming that he suffered from "utter nervous prostration" as well as lung congestion. He requested support to travel abroad to recuperate, as well as "at least one pound a week" (equivalent in purchasing power to about $80 today) to maintain his "wife and children" during his absence. He received a total of £40 (about $3,200 today) and left for the Azores.

10 **make a go of it** *The South London Courier* was established and edited by W. Harnett Blanch in 1869, in the Conservative interest, and remained under his management until November 1870. An account of Blanch in the February 15, 1894 edition of *The Surveyer* (p. 150) suggests that Muddock had been forewarned about the difficulty of keeping the newspaper in the black: "[Blanch] has ever since been eloquent on the

unwisdom of relying on political enthusiasm taking the form of financial support."

10 **out of business** J.E.P. Muddock was destined to declare bankruptcy at least three more times during his lifetime.

11 **grave and enduring** Ginger Frost, *Living in Sin: Cohabiting as Husband and Wife in Nineteenth-Century England* (Manchester, England: Manchester University Press, 2008).

11 **half brothers and sisters** Gai Eaton, *A Bad Beginning: The Path to Islam* (Cambridge: Archetype, 2010). This memoir by James and Eleanor Muddock's grandson, Gai Eaton, notes that the families had no contact.

12 **Niccolò Paganini** Lucy de Knupffer, *Music and Friendship or: Two Artists of Life or: On Wings of Music* (unpublished, c.1945), WFP (hereafter referred to as the Knupffer account), Ch.I,3. The typescript, provided by Janet Weber, has been a source for information about Mudocci's early years. Knupffer's account was based on written recollections sent to her in the early 1940s by Eva Mudocci and Bella Edwards. Knupffer's account contains notable errors and omissions; other than family lore, identified as such, I have not used information from Knupffer unless it could be confirmed by another source.

12 **Louisa Chapman** British census information cited in this book can be found in the U.K. National Archives, available online at www.nationalarchives.gov.uk/help-with-your-research/research-guides/census-records/. Danish census information comes from the Dansk Demografisk Database, available at http://www.ddd.dda.dk/ddd_en.htm.

13 **documents claim** Schneider was born in August 1853. The census added two years to his age. The Hann family may indeed have had roots in Germany. A memoir by Eva Mudocci's second cousin Frank Hann (son of Lewis) recalled that the family descended from German court musicians. See Frank Hann, *Autobiography* (undated manuscript), Frank Hann Collection, The Library of the University of British Columbia.

13 **sole teacher** Eva had occasional instruction from distinguished violinists, such as the eminent Belgian Lambert Massart (1811-92), whom she was taken to see in her late teen years (and who is credited with popularizing the sustained vibrato), but there is no evidence of prolonged early study with anyone but Schneider.

14 **'most enthusiastic'** "[Miss Rose Lynton] has been heard as far back as 1882 when she played at the Atheneum at the first concert, given by Mr. H. Francis Gregg; her solos that time were de Beriot's Fantaisie 'Scene

de Ballet' and Vieuxtemps's 'Air Varie.'" *The Strad* 2, no. 13 (May 1891): 4-5.

14 **'Bach's Chaconne'** *Truth* 19 (June 24, 1886): 974.

16 **'front ranks of violinists'** *The Strad* 1, no. 12 (April 1891): 230.

16 **'a finished piece'** *Musical Times* 1, no. 13 (May 29, 1891): 255.

16 **'lady violinists of the day'** *The Strad* 2, no. 15 (July 1891): 46.

16 **'London critics'** *The Strad* 2, no. 19 (November 1891): 127-28.

16 **competed for readers** London-based publications launched during the late Victorian and Edwardian eras included *The Fiddler* (launched 1884), *The Strad* (1890), *Violin Times* (1893), *Strings* (1894), *The Cremona* (1906), and *The Violin and String World* (1908). See Mark Katz, *The Violin: A Research and Information Guide* (New York and London: Routledge, 2006).

16 **'Grand' Caprice Fantastique** *The Strad* 2, no. 14 (June 1891): 37.

17 **costs of musical education** Simon McVeigh, "Women Violinists in London's Concert Life around 1900," in *Essays on the History of English Music in Honour of John Caldwell: Sources, Style, Performance*, ed. Emma Hornby and David Nicholas Maw (Woodbridge, Suffolk: Boydell & Brewer, 2010), 238. According to McVeigh, at the turn of the century tuition at the Royal Academy of Music could be £40 per year (equivalent to nearly a quarter of a senior clerk's salary), although especially talented students could sometimes secure scholarships.

17 **'takes their place'** "Violinists At Home," *The Strad* 3, no. 34 (February 1893): 185.

18 **'excellent technique'** Review excerpts quoted on a Rose Lynton concert program, *WFP*.

18 **recital halls** Rose Lynton's contemporaries included prodigies Anna Hegner, Maud McCarthy and Vivien Chartres. Vivien Chartres's mother later wrote a novel called *The Devourers* (1910) about the fate of parents who raise child prodigies.

20 **teacher of Carl Schneider** It appears that Straus did not actually own the Emiliani. Rather, it was loaned to him on a long-term basis by an Englishman from Brighton named Edward Shrubsole Cunliffe, a member of the Shrubsole family that to this day is prominent in the sale of antiquities. This was a common arrangement. Collectors know that putting an instrument at the disposal of a well-known musician magnifies its value. After Cunliffe's death (November 28, 1905), the violin passed into the estate left to his daughter and her family, and was sold at auction. The sale, orchestrated by the London dealers Glendining

& Co., took place on March 7, 1906. Mudocci could then purchase the Golden Emiliani for £300—equivalent to nearly $52,000 in purchasing power today. The money left to the family by Carl Schneider would have made this purchase possible.

20 **viola player**   Ludwig Straus was known both as a violinist and violist. He had trained in Vienna, appeared as a soloist on the Continent, then at age thirty, emigrated to England. Within a year, he had been named concertmaster of the London Philharmonic Society. In addition, he often appeared with the prestigious string quartet led by Joseph Joachim, which primarily toured on the Continent but gave frequent concerts across the Channel. When the Joachim Quartet performed in London, Straus was usually its violist.

20 **'joints so unmannerly'**   Sir Charles Hallé, *Life and Letters of Sir Charles Hallé: Being An Autogiography (1819-1860) with Correspondence and Diaries* (London: Smith, Elder & Co., 1896), 341.

20 **his last years**   Freed from his orchestral duties, Straus continued playing, but was willing to part with the Emiliani violin because he had acquired another amazing instrument. In an 1894 letter to Joseph Joachim, archived at Staatliches Institut für Musikforschung in Berlin, Straus wrote, "I am enjoying my Guadagnini and can't wait to hear you play it." When Straus died in 1899, the Guadagnini was bequeathed to London's Royal Academy of Music, but the Emiliani remained with Eva Mudocci. See David Rattray, *Masterpieces of Italian Violin Making: Important Stringed Instruments from the Collection at the Royal Academy of Music* (Lanham, MD: Scarecrow Press, 2000), 132.

21 **rather than power**   Mudocci's training differed, in these ways, from that of rising stars of her day who were trained in the Russian tradition, such as Jascha Heifetz.

22 **quarter of the cost**   Probate records indicate that in 1891, Harriet Hann left an estate valued at about £400, equivalent in purchasing power to approximately $43,000 today.

23 **name Linden Villa**   In 1901, a hillside railway was built connecting the village to a landing and lookout at the top of the cobbled path where Linden Villa is located.

24 **visit England**   Eva Mudocci to Edvard Munch, June 22, [1903], *MM* K 1806.

24 **Madame Eva Mudocci**   As an adolescent, Eva had spent time in Paris with Carl Schneider, attending concerts and visiting his favorite haunts.

25 **new stage name** The note was written by Mudocci's daughter, Isobel Weber.

25 **based in Berlin** *The Strad* announced in 1892 that Miss Rose Lynton would be traveling to Berlin to play for an eminent European agent, accompanied by her teacher, Carl Schneider.

26 **taking it all in** The Ernst Henschel Collection at the British Library has a comprehensive collection of turn-of-the century programs from Berlin concert halls.

27 **'favourite pupil'** Concert program, April 25, 1918, *WFP*. The claim that Eva Mudocci was Joachim's favorite student also appeared in Georg Brandes's 1913 article about Mudocci and Edwards, which was offered by a wire service and picked up by several U.S. newspapers. See Brandes, "Some Women": 2.

28 **'carrying a violin case'** Knupffer, IV, 10.

29 **'unprepared for a lesson'** Harvey Sachs and Donald Manildi, *Rubinstein: A Life* (New York: Grove Press, 1995), 26.

29 **down the stairs** Knupffer, IV, 11.

30 **'united the two ladies musically'** Brandes, "Some Women": 2.

30 **'sick with nerves?'** Mudocci to Munch, 1903, *MM* K 1795.

31 **'how it is for all of us'** Bella Edwards to Ferdinand Prior, November 28, 1919, *RDL*.

34 **future star** The best known of Bella's classmates at the Gade Academy was violinist Carl Nielsen (1865-1931), who became a prominent conductor and composer.

34 **'Teddie'** Eva refers to Bella as Teddie in an undated (1903) letter to her mother, *FM*.

34 **over many years** Collection of letters to Bella Edwards, *RDL*.

36 **renew the acquaintance** According to the Knupffer manuscript (VIII,2-4), Bella had previously been introduced to Grieg at a large reception given by his publishers in Kristiania, and was seated beside him at the dinner that followed. I have found no independent source to confirm this.

36 **leaving for Germany** Edvard Grieg to Bella Edwards, *BPL*. All subsequent quotes from Grieg's letters to Bella Edwards come from this collection.

36 **'home in January-February?'** Bella was no doubt aware that Grieg often accompanied his wife Nina's performances of his songs.

37 **'composer and his wife'** Katharine Metcalf Roof, "Edvard Grieg: Norway's Tone Poet," *The Craftsman* 13 (1908): 278.

38 **'relationship with Grieg'** Lionel Carley, *Edvard Grieg in England* (Woodbridge, Suffolk: Boydell Press, 2006), 237.

38 **understated English style** This was the same small residential hotel where James Joyce found lodgings in Paris twenty years later.

39 **'easy friendship'** Edith Wharton, *French Ways and Their Meaning* (Lee, MA: Berkshire House Books, 1997), first published in 1919, 116-17.

39 **'most famous pieces'** A notable exception to such *heures de musiques* was the serious musical salon established in Paris by Winnaretta Singer.

39 **'perfect acoustics'** Cited in Mark Mitchell and Allan Evans, eds., *Moriz Rosenthal in Word and Music: A Legacy of the Nineteenth Century* (Bloomington: Indiana University Press, 2005), xix.

39 **'newcomers warmly'** "Spectacles et Concerts," *Le Figaro* (May 12, 1901): 4.

40 **'delicious changes'** Leonora Raines, "Falling off of Musical Events in Paris," *Musical America* 26 (August 4, 1917): 25. Bella's compositions were published in Paris under the name Bella Edvards.

40 **'more fabulous'** Gustav Hetsch, "Danske Kunsterinder i Paris: Bella Edwards, Magnus Malkine," *Paris,* May 2001.

42 **break into a polka** Gustav Hetsch, "En kvindelig Komponist Frk Bella Edwards," *Hversdag,* July 19, 1923: 1.

42 **'succeed without me'** Ibid.

43 **'poetry of snobbery'** The phrase "poetry of snobbery" is attributed to—and personified by—Robert de Montesquiou, who was said to have instructed Marcel Proust on its fine points. See Cornelia Otis Skinner, *Elegant Wits and Grand Horizontals* (Boston: Houghton Mifflin, 1962), 54.

43 **'to be noticed'** Arthur Shattuck, *The Memoirs of Arthur Shattuck* (Neenah, WI: privately published, 1961), 39.

43 **'anti-Semite'** Skinner, *Elegant Wits and Grand Horizontals,* 18-19. Gyp was the nom de plume of Sibylle Riquetti de Mirabeau, Comtesse de Martel de Janville.

44 **'in their veins'** "Eva Mudocci og Bella Edwards," *Svensk Musiktidning* 3 (February 1, 1902): 17-18.

44 **Jewish lineage** In at least one public document, the family name is given as Hahn. A genealogical website devoted to the Hann family suggested that there were Jews among the Sherborne Hanns, the branch of the family from which Eva descended. However, no specific link has been found. See http//www.hannfamily.org.uk/sherborne_dist.htm.

44 **parliamentary debates** Susan Sarah Cohen, *Antisemitism: An Annotated Bibliography*, vol. 4 (Jerusalem: Vidal Sassoon International Center for the Study of Antisemitism, 1997).

45 **charming violinist** Their interest in Mudocci is evident in the correspondence between Brandes and Nathansen, and in the 1910 novel by Louis Levy discussed in Chapter 13. See Georg Brandes to Henri Nathansen, December 22, 1912, and; Nathansen to Brandes, December 25, 1912. Both letters are quoted in http://www.henrikpontoppidan.dk/ text/seclit/secbreve/nathansen/1912_12_25.html#fod3. See also Georg Brandes, "Some Women," *Pittsburgh Gazette Times* April 20, 1913, sec. II: 2.

45 **'bring along a piano'** Count Hubert de Pourtalès to Bella Edwards, *RDL*.

45 **'musical expression'** Review by Dr. Wilh. Altmann, *Die Musik* 2, no. 10: 310.

45 **'Grieg's C moll'** The piece referenced in Mudocci's letter was Grieg's *Violin Sonata No. 3 in C minor, op. 45*, the most popular of his three violin sonatas and a personal favorite of the composer. It became a key element in the duo's programs.

46 **'day and night'** Hetsch, "Danske Kunsterinder I Paris."

46 **'we are one'** Adolf Langsted, "Kendle Danske i vor Pariser-koloni": 1.

47 **spring of 1903** Late in life, Mudocci recalled that her first encounter with Munch took place at a Paris café (Waldemar Stabell, BBC Norwegian Service interview of Eva Mudocci, recorded May 18, 1950, *WFP*). Some scholars believe there was a 1902 encounter in Berlin, but I have found no evidence of such a meeting. Lucy Knupffer's unpublished book is the likely source, since it mentions an early Berlin meeting, but that account contains many inaccuracies (especially in chronology). A possible source of confusion is a letter that Mudocci wrote in Berlin, telling Munch she was eager to attend the Secession with him (*MM* K 1813). It may appear that Mudocci was referencing the 1902 Secession, where Munch's paintings caused a sensation, but her letter could not have been written in 1902 since it declares that "we are back" from a tour with tenor Raimund von zur-Mühlen that began in November 1903. The letter's timing and content point to a different event—the winter 1903/04 Berlin Secession exhibit of works on paper.

48 **'hallucinations'** Cited in "Contributions," *Minneapolis Institute of Art Bulletin* 44-47 (1956): 50.

48 **likenesses as well** In the years leading up to the First World War, Theodore Spicer-Simpson made a bas-relief of Mudocci and Edwards; Agnes de Frumerie exhibited a porcelain bust of Mudocci; and Clement John Heaton used Mudocci and Edwards as models for a stained glass window.

48 **musical receptions** Among the patrons mentioned in the Knupffer manuscript are la Comtesse Lafond, la Marquise de l'Aigle, le Duc de Guise, and Count Potacki.

49 **gallery owners** For a full discussion of Delius's ties to Munch and Norway, see Andrew J. Boyle, *Delius and Norway* (Woodbridge, Suffolk: Boydell & Brewer, 1916).

49 **'Bella's clutches'** Biographers sometimes reflect Jappe Nilssen's view of Eva and Bella's relationship. See for example Atle Næss, *Munch: en Biografi* (Oslo: Gyldendal Norsk Forlag, 2004), "[It] was whispered that Bella was a lesbian and that Eva was, more or less voluntarily, her lover."

50 **'become natural'** Arne Eggum, *Munch and Photography*, trans. Bergit Holm (New Haven, CT: Yale University Press, 1989), 199. According to Eggum, after Munch's death, his sister "Inger systematically went through the letters and sent them to director Johan H. Langaard in portions. Before she destroyed some of the letters she made some 'witnessed copies', which were also sent to Langaard and the Munch Museum. The quoted letters exist only in these copies." See also Lasse Jacobsen, "Edvard Munch's Writings after 1944: Fragments of a Research and Publication Chronicle," trans. Francesca M. Nichols, https://www.emunch.no/ENGART_emunch_jacobsen_1_eng.xhtm.

50 **'fear for her life'** Sue Prideaux, *Edvard Munch: Behind the Scream* (New Haven, CT: Yale University Press, 2005), 130.

51 **'half dead'** Edvard Munch, draft letter to Jappe Nilssen, *MM* N 1903.

51 **'after-effects'** Næss, *Munch*: 192-93.

51 **'short and stiff'** Edvard Munch to Karen Bjølstad, February 27, 1903, p. 2, *MM* N 859.

52 **'understandable reasons'** Ibid.

52 **on the upswing** Gerd Woll, *Edvard Munch: The Complete Graphic Works* (London: Philip Wilson Publishers, Ltd., 2012). Appendix IX of Woll's book lists "Important Exhibitions: 1892-1944," and shows none for 1900 and one for 1901, then four in 1902 and eight in 1903.

52 **boulevard Arago** The studio at 65 boulevard Arago was in a complex of artists' ateliers called La Cité Fleurie that had large windows and

skylights constructed with plate glass taken from the dismantled 1878 Exposition Universelle.

53 **foursome** Mudocci to Stabell [postmarked May 16, 1950], *MM*. Parisians generally refer to the venue as simply "Le Dôme." Mudocci mentioned "Café Dôme" in this letter, which dealt primarily with Munch's relationships with other Norwegians in Paris. It is not certain from the context whether it was the site of their initial encounter.

53 **could all navigate** Munch spoke "broken German," according to a letter from Max Linde to Hanni Esche cited in Reinhold Heller, *Edvard Munch: His Life and Work* (Chicago: University of Chicago Press, 1984), 187.

54 **'with many'** Mudocci to Stabell, May 7, 1950, p. 3, *MM*.

54 **'ex-fiancée'** Today, screwed to a wooden tabletop near the bar at La Closerie des Lilas is a small brass nameplate inscribed "Edvard Munch."

55 **'sudden light'** Mudocci to Munch, January 19, [1906], *MM* K 1837.

56 **'help it?'** Munch to Mudocci, *MM* N 2370.

56 **'great disaster'** Gustav Lindke, ed., *Edvard Munch Max Linde Briefweschel 1902-08* (Lübeck: Ackermann, 1974), 25.

56 **'the same city'** The Knupffer manuscript (VIII, 3-4) suggests that Edvard Grieg sufficiently recovered from his infatuation with Bella Edwards to socialize with her and Eva Mudocci. The duo is said to have visited the Griegs in Trondheim, for example, but this has not been confirmed by other sources.

57 **special guests** Edvard Grieg to Bella Edwards, April 26, 1903, *RDL*.

57 **life of their own** The painting was exhibited in Charlottenborg, Germany at an autumn 1906 exhibit of recent work by Norwegian artists that also included eight works by Edvard Munch. See Erik Werenskiold, *Fortegnelse over Kunstværkerne paa den Norske Udstilling* (Charlottenborg: Efteraaret, 1906), http://www.kunstbib.dk/objekter/udstillingskataloger/Udst_0505.pdf.

57 **played a role** Mudocci to Munch, June 22, [1903], *MM* K 1806.

58 **'same as mine'** Draft, Edvard Munch to Eva Mudocci, [1903], *MM* N 2370. Munch's original letters to Mudocci, sold to Waldemar Stabell after Mudocci's death, have not surfaced. However, the Munch Museum's archives include Munch's drafts of some letters. It was Munch's habit to keep such drafts.

61 **black-and-white lithographs** Munch often reworked his lithographs, so this count does not reflect multiple versions or states of his prints.

61 **'sounds beautiful?'** Eva Mudocci to Lucy Muddock, [1903], *FM*. The dating of this letter is based on Mudocci's description of a large gathering of Freemasons at Trocadero, in all likelihood the *Grande Fête Civique de la Raison* held on May 17, 1903 and reported the next day in the journal *Paris*: http://gallica.bnf.fr/ark:/12148/bpt6k7627621t/f3.item. The letter is the only known reference to this painting. Saint Cecilia, who lived in the third century A.D., is the patron saint of music. When the crypt containing her remains was opened in the middle ages, her body was said to be miraculously intact under beautifully draped cloth.

62 *Madonna* Edvard Munch, draft letter to unidentified recipient, December 25, 1913, *MM* N 2739. In this letter, Munch mentioned "Eva Mudocci as Madonna," presumably a reference to *The Brooch—Eva Mudocci*. The Norwegian National Gallery's online commentary says, "There are certain similarities between the figure in *The Brooch* and Munch's famous Madonna. Earlier, this lithograph itself bore that title. Here the erotic dimension is considerably toned down and the figure shows more individual and thoughtful traits." See: http://samling. nasjonalmuseet.no/en/object/NG.K_H.B.00816.

62 **'Thus,** *Lady with a Brooch'* Transcript, Stabell interview of Mudocci, May 18, 1950, *WFP*.

62 **'this occasion'** Woll, *Edvard Munch: The Complete Graphic Works*, 221. Gerd Woll cites this passage from a 1933 recollection by Jens Thiis. Thiis must have presented the brooch to Mudocci in 1901, given that a publicity photo in which Mudocci wears the brooch appeared in a Swedish journal dated February 1, 1902.

64 **'before her death'** Lawrence H. Warick and Elaine R. Warick, "Edvard Munch: The Creative Search for Self," in *Psychoanalytic Perspectives on Art*, vol. 2, ed. Mary M. Gedo (New York: Routledge, 2013), 291.

64 **Eva's breast** Otto Benesch, *Edvard Munch*, trans. Joan Spencer (London: The Phaidon Press, 1960), 30.

64 **word for the sun** Jill Condra, *Encyclopedia of National Dress: Traditional Clothing Around the World* (Santa Barbara, CA: ABC-CLIO, 2013), 564. In Norwegian folk culture (as in other folk traditions), silver was thought to have magical healing properties.

64 **through generations** Kathleen Stokker, *Remedies and Rituals: Folk Medicine in Norway and the New Land* (St. Paul, MN: Minnesota Historical Society, 2007).

65 **events and relationships** The perception of human features on the brooch's surface may reflect the Norwegian tradition of the *glibbsølje*

(face brooch), which uses one or more primitive faces to scare off evil spirits.

66 **her true love** "The Interrupted Wedding" was collected in eastern Norway c. 1836 by Peter Christen Asbjørnsen. See Reidar Christiansen, ed., *Folktales of Norway* (Chicago, IL: University of Chicago Press, 2016), 116-17.

66 **had given her** "Living with the Huldre-folk in a Knoll" was collected by P. Lunde before 1920 in southern Norway. See Christiansen, *Folktales of Norway*, 103-04.

66 **'do me good'** Draft, Munch to Mudocci, [1903], *MM* N 2382.

66 **wrote to Eva** Draft, Munch to Mudocci [1903], *MM* N 2371.

67 **'both my hands'** Mudocci to Munch, June 22, [1903], *MM* K 1806.

67 **'from afar'** Mudocci to Munch, [1903], *MM* K 1804.

67 **'again sometime'** Mudocci to Munch, [1903], *MM* K 1793.

67 **'never bridge'** Mudocci to Munch, [1903], *MM* K 1795.

67 **'pure music'** Draft, Munch to Mudocci, 1903, *MM* N 2381. Another draft (*MM* N 2368) says: "Your picture is hanging over my bed."

67 **'on your letter'** Mudocci to Munch [1903], *MM* K 1798.

67 **'don't love angels'** Mudocci to Munch [1903], *MM* K 1802.

68 **sister to him** Draft, Munch to Mudocci, [1903], *MM* N 2371.

68 **'work forces me'** Draft, Munch to Mudocci, [1903], *MM* N 2382.

68 **'and never could'** Mudocci to Munch, [1903], *MM* K 1807.

68 **'from each other'** Mudocci to Munch, [late August or early September, 1903], *MM* K 1808.

68 **'happy to see you'** Mudocci to Munch, [1903], *MM* K 1811.

69 **'consumption and insanity'** Eggum, *Munch and Photography*, 137.

69 **syntax was awkward** In a letter drafted to Elisabeth Förster-Nietzsche, Munch wrote, "I always have so much to recount—and am always chagrined by my hopeless German" ("Immer mochte ich so viel erzahlen–und immer ärgret mich mein unmoglich Deutsch"), *MM* N 2653. See Sibylle Söring, "My German is in such a poor state: Edvard Munch's letters written in German," tr. F. M. Nichols, https://emunch. no/ENGART_german_English.xhtml.

70 **'what I'm saying'** Mudocci to Munch, [1904], *MM* K 1818.

70 **'non-heroic life'** Mudocci to Munch, January 19, [1904], *MM* K 1812.

70 **from nature** The German title Munch gave to *The Scream* was *Der Schrei der Natur*—The Scream of Nature.

70 **unseen realm** "Music: An Interview with E.A. Neresheimer," *Theosophy* 12, no. 5 (August 1897): 226-31.

70 **spiritual potential**   Hillarion Smerdis, "The Ensouled Violin," *The Theosophist* 9, no. 4, sec. 2 (January 1880). This story ascribes the power of Paganini's "unearthly sounds" to mystical sources. Mudocci was not the only violinist of her day to be intrigued by Theosophy. Another Theosophist was Maud MacCarthy, a British prodigy who left the concert stage in 1906, in her mid-twenties, and devoted herself entirely to her spiritual pursuits.

70 **cosmic ray**   Mudocci, "Infantilia—The Lion's Whelp," in Leon M. Lion, *The Surprise of My Life: The Lesser Half of an Autobiography* (London: Hutchinson, 1948), 259-60.

71 **merging**   Clément Chéroux, *The Perfect Medium: Photography and the Occult* (New Haven, CT: Yale University Press, 2005).

71 **Kodak camera**   See John L. Greenway, "The Photograph as Esthetic Norm in Fin-de-Siècle Scandinavia," in *Fin(s) de Siècle in Scandinavian Perspective: Studies in Honor of Harald S. Næss,* eds. Faith Ingwersen and Mary Kay Norseng (Columbia, SC: Camden House, 1993), 141-49.

71 *Frieze of Life* **series**   Edvard Munch, Note, 1927-1933, *MM* N 122.

71 **'Spirits'**   Edvard Munch, Note, 1908, *MM* T 2785, 94-95.

72 **attempting wit**   Mudocci to Munch, [1903], *MM* K 1799.

72 **get right**   Drafts, Munch to Mudocci [1903], *MM* N 2372-2377.

72 **'to tease you'**   Mudocci to Munch, [1903], *MM* K 1800.

72 **'fit in with you'**   Draft, Munch to Mudocci, [1903], *MM* N 2370.

72 **'madly apprehensive'**   Draft, Edvard Munch to Frederick Delius, [1904], *MM* N 2186.

73 **Sans Souci**   Rolf E. Stenersen, *Edvard Munch: Close-Up of a Genius,* trans. Reidar Dittmann (Oslo: Glyndendal, 1969), 42.

74 **'from my heart'**   See Eggum, *Munch and Photography,* 76, for an account of Munch's unsuccessful attempt at a double portrait of Mudocci and Edwards.

77 **Renoir**   Edvard Munch to Jens Thiis, undated, *MM* N 2083. In this letter, Munch referred to the "strange assertion that I am influenced by Renoir, which I have never been."

77 **birth and death**   See, for example, Shelley Wood Cordulack, *Edvard Munch and the Physiology of Symbolism* (Madison, NJ: Fairleigh Dickinson University Press, 2002).

77 **decapitated head**   Munch and Delius were both interested in the Salome theme in 1903. At that time, Delius wrote to Charles Russell & Co. in London to inquire about the musical rights to Oscar Wilde's play.

Delius lost interest once he'd heard from an acquaintance, Hans Haym: "What a pity that [Richard] Strauss took the material away from you!"

77 **in this era**   Nadia Valman, *The Jewess in Nineteenth-Century British Literary Culture* (Cambridge: Cambridge University Press, 2006).

78 **Neues Theater in Berlin**   The play premiered on November 15, 1902. Various German productions followed, including a 1903 production at Berlin's Neues Theater. See William Tydeman, *Wilde: Salome* (Cambridge: Cambridge University Press, 1996).

78 **sensuous depravity**   Horst Uhr, *Lovis Corinth* (Oakland, CA: University of California Press, 1990), 166. Munch later created set designs for Reinhardt.

78 **later stagings**   See, for example, the case of Maud Allen, described by Philip Hoare, *Oscar Wilde's Last Stand: Decadence, Conspiracy, and the Most Outrageous Trial of the Century* (New York: Arcade Publishing, 1998).

80 **'a little polite'**   Mudocci to Munch, [late 1903 or early 1904], *MM* K 1816.

80 **'together with Eva M.'**   Edvard Munch to Jappe Nilssen, January 12, 1904, Nasjonalbiblioteket, letter 604 PN 706.

80 **without Bella**   This attempt, discussed in Chapter 15, was referenced in a letter, Max Linde to Edvard Munch, February 1, 1904, *MM* 2792.

81 **'run into her?'**   Munch to Delius, [early February 1905], Letter #176, in Lionel Carley, *Delius: A Life in Letters* (London: Scholar Press & The Delius Trust), 252. The original in the Delius Trust Archive.

81 **'charming'**   Frederick Delius to Edvard Munch, February 11, 1905, *MM* K 1771.

81 **her address**   Munch to Delius, [early March, 1905], in Carley: *Delius: A Life in Letters*, 255. Original in the Delius Trust Archive.

82 **'our concerts'**   Waldemar Stabell, BBC Norwegian Service interview of Eva Mudocci, recorded May 18, 1950, *WFP*.

82 **unthreatening**   This argument was advanced in Elizabeth Ingles, *Munch* (New York: Parkstone International, 2012).

82 **Tulla Larsen**   This is Tove Munch's theory.

82 **distinguishing between them**   For a discussion of Munch's journal writing, see J. Gill Holland's introduction to *The Private Journals of Edvard Munch: We are Flames Which Pour Out of the Earth* (Madison, WI: The University of Wisconsin Press, 2005).

83 **between two women** Edvard Munch, sketchbook, *MM* T 2800, 49-59. The notion of coming between two women recurs in Munch's sketchbooks. Here is another example from 1890-91 (*MM* T 2771, fol. 34v):

> Over there they walked arm in arm – in arm – one of the cocottes dashed over to the other and whispered in her ear – then the gentlemen dashed at them and split them up – Now one of the gentlemen had two ladies [one] under each arm – Then two by two they climbed the sun striped rise under the trees that was coloured in a delicate green – There was youth in their gait there was laughter in their shoulders

83 **evident** Biographers may have overlooked Munch's interest in love between women because they have felt compelled to address a different question: Was he a misogynist? Rolf Stenersen, a friend of the artist and a major collector of his work, helped to set this line of inquiry into motion with a 1944 biography that reported many of Munch's disparaging comments about women. See Stenersen, *Edvard Munch: Close-Up of a Genius*.

83 **in 1917-19** See Alison W. Chang, *Negotiating Modernity: Edvard Munch's Late Figural Work 1900-1925* (Ph.D. dissertation, University of Pennsylvania, 2010), and Alison W. Chang, "Sexology and Sapphism: Edvard Munch's Double Nudes," *Kunst og kultur* 2 (2009): 92-111. Chang's work discusses in detail Munch's double nudes. She believes that Munch's fascination with intimacy between women predated his acquaintance with Mudocci and Edwards, but intensified thereafter. Her treatment stands in contrast to that of most Munch biographers, who tend to dismiss this aspect of Munch's oeuvre.

83 **'hardly relevant to Munch'** Prideaux, *Edvard Munch: Behind the Scream*, 295: "It is puzzling. Lesbian erotica was very common in Germany at the time, but that was hardly relevant to Munch."

83 **models to draw upon** As Chang observes, depictions of lesbians were common in turn-of-the-century Europe, both in risqué popular publications and respectable galleries. She noted that these images ranged from depictions of sexually aggressive prostitutes to devoted but asexual companions, and that Munch explored both extremes.

84 **on a lady's lap** Nancy Erber, "In the Flesh: Scandalous Women's Performances in Fin-de-Siècle Paris," *Proceedings of the Western Society for French History* 36 (2008): 182. Erber cites a French medical doctor, Julien Chevalier, who reported a sudden "explosion of lesbian vice" in a book on abnormal sexuality published in 1905.

85 **Strindberg** In her study of Munch's double nudes, Chang draws attention to Munch's familiarity with Weininger's book. The book is among the volumes in Munch's personal library at the Munch Museum.

85 **'conscious maleness'** Otto Weininger, *Sex and Character* (authorized translation from the sixth German edition, New York: G.P. Putnam's Sons, 1906), 189.

85 **maleness in her** Ibid, 350.

85 **'as if we liked it'** Mudocci to Munch, December 12, [1905], *MM* K 1825.

86 **more directly** Smith, *Frederick Delius and Edvard Munch*, 159 n.24: "Her daughter, Mrs. Isobel Weber, has told me that Eva Mudocci showed little interest in Delius's music and attributes this to her mother's great love for the modern French school, especially Debussy, who had shown himself decidedly critical of some compositions by Delius."

86 **reconnect him with Eva** Prideaux suggests that Jelka Rosen played cupid when Munch first made Mudocci's acquaintance in 1903, but it is more likely, in my view, that she had a hand in reuniting them in 1905.

87 **word from you** Mudocci to Munch, October 31 [1905], *MM* K 1823, pp. 1-3.

87 **'heart disease'** Letters written about Eva Mudocci (*NYPL*) over several decades make no mention of heart ailments.

88 **'hung over?'** Mudocci to Munch, [1904], *MM* K 1815.

91 **'non-procreative'** Havelock Elis, *Sexual Inversion* (Philadelphia, PA: F.A. Davis Company, 1901), 238.

92 **about Munch** "Munch, The Norse Artist," *M'lle New York* 1, no. 10 (January 1896): "Edvard Munch, who studied both in Munich and Paris, is known fairly well on the Continent, but so far as I know there is only one of his works—a sketch in coloured chalks—in this country." The magazine included a rendering of *The Scream*, as redrawn by art editor Thomas Fleming from a woodcut in *La Revue Blanche*.

92 **in America** The article in *M'lle New York* is thought to be the first mention of Munch in the American press. See Martin Hopkinson, "Review: *The Symbolist Prints of Edvard Munch* by Elizabeth Prelinger and Michael Parke-Taylor; *Munch and Women: Image and Myth* by Patricia G. Berman and Jane van Nimmen," *Print Quarterly* 17, no. 1, 2000.

93 **house in Åsgårdstrand** Advertisements indicate that in 1907, after delaying their spring tour of Scandinavia, Mudocci and Edwards played concerts in Norway on September 15 and 23. The postmark on a card from Edvard Munch to his aunt indicates that Munch was in Norway

in mid-September of that year.

94 **footprints** Mudocci to Stabell, May 7, 1950: 5-6, *MM*: "It was a correspondence lasting over many years—only interrupted by ill health occasionally, & finally by many vicissitudes preceding & following the first war." It is, of course, possible that Mudocci and Munch simply drifted apart in 1907, and then casually arranged a visit in Kragerø two years later, but at the very least, there would have been correspondence to arrange this visit.

95 **annual crescendo** Taking into account the typical gestation for twins (36 weeks), the most likely date of conception was in mid-April.

95 **'chestnuts in Paris'** Draft, Munch to Mudocci, December 20, 1905, *MM* N 2386.

97 **childbirth** See Fabrice Cahen, "Medicine, Statistics, and the Encounter of Abortion and 'Depopulation' in France (1870-1920), *The History of the Family* (January 3, 2012): 19-35; also Elinor Accampo, *Blessed Motherhood, Bitter Fruit: Nelly Roussel and the Politics of Female Pain in Third Republic France* (Baltimore, MD: Johns Hopkins University Press, 2006).

97 **chose this route** Lucy Delap, *The Feminist Avant-Garde: Translatlantic Encounters of the Early Twentieth Century* (Cambridge and New York: Cambridge University Press, 2007), 130.

98 **'don't talk about it'** Isadora Duncan, *My Life* (New York: Norton, Rev. 2013), 163.

98 **'the pregnant mother'** Duncan, *My Life*, 168.

99 **drowned** *The New York Times*, April 20, 1913: 1.

101 **euphemistic name** Donald S. Connery, *The Scandinavians* (New York: Simon & Schuster, 1996).

101 **into the train car** Prideaux, *Edvard Munch: Beyond the Scream*, 248-49.

102 **'nobleman'** Ibid, 72.

104 **odd ingredients** Such treatments remained the standard of care in Denmark for some time. Anticipating the opening of a new hospital in 1915, psychiatrist Frode Krarup wrote that to protect the sick organ (i.e., the brain), patients needed several months of calm and rest, and ideally confinement to bed. Very disturbed patients would benefit from soothing, warm baths that could last all day, even into the night; they would take meals in the bathtub. Such treatments had to be closely supervised, requiring large staffs. http://www.kulturarv. dk/1001fortaellinger/en_GB/nykoebing-sjaelland-psychiatric-hospital.

104 **'it would be noisy'** Edvard Munch to Ludvig Ravensberg, December 18, 1908, *MM* N 2857.

105 **Munch's breakdown?** I have found only one source that mentions Eva Mudocci's pregnancy in connection with Munch's 1908 confinement: Milton Viederman, M.D., "Edvard Munch: A Life in Art," *Journal of the American Academy of Psychoanalysis* 22, no. 1 (Spring 1994): 73. Viederman wrote that his breakdown "followed the death of two close friends and possibly the news that Eva Mudocci was pregnant."

105 **birth process** Stephen Schloesser, S. J., "From Spiritual Naturalism to Psychical Naturalism: Catholic Decadence, Lutheran Munch, Madone Mysterique" in *Edvard Munch: Psyche, Symbol and Expression*, ed. Jeffrey W. Howe (Boston, MA: McMullen Museum of Art and Chicago: University of Chicago Press, 2001), 75-110.

106 **'depressed'** Edvard Munch to Ernest Thiel, May 12, 1908. *MM* (Thielska Gallery), PN 1180, quoted in Otto Lund, "Notes on the letters from Eva Mudocci to Edvard Munch, with special reference to their dating and consecutive order" (unpublished), *WFP*.

106 **music scene in mid-1908** The dates of Eva and Bella's tours and concerts can be constructed from announcements and reviews in a variety of European newspapers of the day.

106 **gave birth to twins** Given Eva Mudocci's later history of abdominal adhesions (noted on her death certificate), it may be that the children were born by caesarean section.

107 **'as delicious to look at as to hear'** "Notes Musicales," *Gil Blas*, May 8, 1909: 3.

109 **the previous year** In the few archived letters that Mudocci sent to Munch in 1909 and 1910, the tone shifted from fervent to friendly. And unaccountably, at this time, Mudocci began writing to Munch in flawless Danish. Perhaps Eva had spent the months in Nykøbing studying the language. Or it may be that during this period, Bella edited Mudocci's letters to Munch, or drafted them herself.

109 **'looking at it'** Daniel Jacobson to Edvard Munch, October 11, 1909, *MM* K 1554. Dr. Jacobson was no doubt referring to the lithograph entitled *The Violin Concert* (1903), Munch's only known portrait of Mudocci and Edwards.

110 **'little or nothing'** Cited in McVeigh, "Women Violinists in London's Concert Life around 1900," 247.

110 **each had students** Mudocci's students included Americans Max Helmer and Paul Mowrer. Among Bella Edwards's students were Danish diplomat Ferdinand Prior and (according to Knupffer) the young Eva Le Gallienne.

110 **Schneider's bequest** According to his death certificate and will, Schneider was the son of Ludwig and Clotilde (née Schaufelberger) Schneider. He was born in Paris, but spent his school years in Karlsruhe, in Baden, and was there during the Franco-Prussian war. According to Knupffer (I,5), he recalled ducking bullets in his home. It was the violence and outcome of that war that caused the Schneider family to move to London in 1871. When his parents returned to Paris, Carl stayed in London and moved in with the Hann family. According to Knupffer (I,1), Eva was taken to meet Schneider's mother—a "stately Alsation woman" who lived in a lavishly furnished Paris mansion. Knupffer wrote that Schneider came from the "colourful French side" of the Hann family, but there are no clear genealogical ties. Eva's Hann grandparents descended on Robert's side from several generations of English Hanns (or Hands), many named Robert, and on Harriet's side, from several generations of men named Rich. The maternal lines are harder to trace. Eva claimed that Harriet Hann's mother descended from Swedes.

110 **considerable sum** Jonathan Justice, "Bricks Are Worth Their Weight in Gold: A Century of House Prices," *The Guardian*, December 18, 1999.

112 **'wan Danish woman'** Paul Scott Mowrer, *The House of Europe* (Boston: Houghton Mifflin Co., 1945), 275.

112 **'Great Danes'** Scudder, *Modeling My Life*, 234; Hoffman, *Yesterday is Tomorrow*, 133.

113 **'An Evening of Spirits'** Malvina Hoffman, *1910 Travel Journal* (manuscript), Getty Research Institute, Los Angeles.

115 **'two human beings into one'** Herman Bang, "Om Eva Mudocci og Bella Edwards," *Nordenfjeldsk Tidene*, May 26, 1904.

115 **exceedingly boring** Mudocci to Munch, April 17, 1906: "There was someone here recently who wanted to use me as a model for a window in the Strasbourg Cathedral. Just imagine, sitting eternally in a cathedral window. I was afraid I would be too bored!"

118 **not of Edvard Ludvig Kay** If, as seems possible, Louis Levy had consented to be the boy's godfather, as a Jew he would not have been listed in the parish register.

122 **or beyond** For background on enemy aliens in Germany during the First World War, see Peter Liddle, *Britain Goes to War* (Barnsley: Pen & Sword, 2015) and Matthew Stibbe, *British Civilian Internees in Germany: The Ruhleben Camp, 1914-1918* (Manchester, England: Manchester University Press, 2008).

122 **as long as they pleased** John Torpey, "The Great War and the Birth of the Modern Passport System," in Jane Caplan and John Torpey, eds., *Documenting Individual Liberty: The Development of State Practices in the Modern World* (Princeton, NJ: Princeton University Press, 2001), 256-70.

123 **his family** Knupffer (XI,1) recounted this story without mentioning the children; she may have been unaware of their existence.

123 **'enlarged Christmas cards'** According to Alfred H. Barr, Jr., Matisse's fame was spread across Scandinavia by students who worked under the Frenchman at his atelier in the Couvent du Sacre Coeur beginning in 1908. In 1909, the "Matissites" held a landmark show in Stockholm. Barr commented, "For a dozen years thereafter Matisse was the chief influence affecting the course of painting in Norway and Sweden. Scandinavian collectors took their cue from the painters and, later, museums followed suit, Jens Thiis, Director of the Christiania Museum, taking the lead." Alfred H. Barr, *Matisse: His Art and His Public.* (New York, Museum of Modern Art, 1951), 109.

124 **'to trace this'** Smith, *Frederick Delius and Edvard Munch,* 157 n36.

125 **wounded troops** *Trondhjems Adresseavis,* February 16, 1915: 5.

125 **this way:** Cited in Næss, *Munch: en Biografi.*

125 **'didn't mean that'** Perhaps she did "mean that." Eva Mudocci was invested in her family's connection to Gustav Prince of Vasa (1799-1877), the exiled crown prince of Sweden, judging by her adoption of his English moniker (Harry Brander) as her pen name. If there was indeed a historical connection between Carl Schneider and the Hann family, as the Knupffer manuscript suggests, then Gustav was the most likely link. Like Gustav, Schneider spent his youth in Karlsruhe, in a home that was the site of crossfire during the Franco-Prussian war. (Gustav's mother, Queen Frederica of Sweden, had been the Princess of Baden, and when the family was exiled from Sweden, they settled in Karlsruhe.) Schneider moved Eva's family to Loschwitz, five miles from the palace at Pillnitz where Gustav had spent his last years (with his daughter, Carola of Vasa, Queen Consort of Saxony). Perhaps coincidentally, Lucy Muddock's photo album from her years in Loschwitz contains a photograph of the palace at Pillnitz where Gustav died. The connection is very speculative, but intriguing.

125 **Spanish violinist** *Musical America* 25 (August 4, 1917): 25; *Musical America* 31 (February 21, 1920): 15.

126 **a British holding** Daniela L. Caglioti, "Property Rights and Economic Nationalism," *International Encyclopedia of the First World War*. http://encyclopedia.1914-1918-online.net/article/property_rights_and_economic_nationalism. Caglioti writes, "When it became clear that the war would be long-lasting, the government established the compulsory registration of enemy property and then inaugurated the liquidation of British enemy property with the Ordinance of 31 July 1916."

126 **'the very sky'** Shattuck, *Memoirs*, 200.

126 **'arts were concerned'** Frederick James Gregg, "The World's New Art Center," *Vanity Fair* (January 1915): 31.

127 **'look older'** Malvina Hoffman, *1915 Travel Journal* (manuscript), Getty Research Institute, Los Angeles.

127 **wife and three children** John Russell, *Matisse: Father & Son* (New York: Henry N. Abrams, 1999), 9.

127 **'played his violin'** Gertrude Stein, *The Autobiography of Alice B. Toklas* (London: John Lane, 1933), 38.

128 **'popular clamor'** Gregg, "The World's New Art Center": 32.

128 **'madly anxious'** Barr, *Matisse: His Art and His Public*, 53.

129 **brisk** According to the Suzuki Co. website, there was a huge increase in violin sales beginning in 1914. By 1918, the company was exporting up to 500 violins and 1,000 bows in one day.

129 **when she performed** Victor I. Carlson, *Matisse as a Draughtsman* (Baltimore: Baltimore Museum of Art/New York Graphic Society, 1971), 74.

129 ***Concerto in D minor for Two Violins*** Barr, *Matisse: His Art and His Public*, 54.

130 **'outsider women'** Carol Salus, "R.B. Kitaj: Painting as Personal Voyage," in *Out of Context: American Artists Abroad*, eds. Laura Fellman Fattal and Carol Salus (Westport, CT: Praeger, 2004), 149. Salus refers to "Matisse's grand experimental portraits of outsider women (G. Prozor, Y. Landberg, E. Mudocci, S. Stein, the Cones, etc.)."

130 **wavy hair** Stephanie D'Alessandro and John Elderfield, *Matisse: Radical Invention 1913-1917* (Chicago: The Art Institute of Chicago, 2010), 327.

130 **never left her** Bent Weber, personal communication, September 1, 2013.

135 **affected by the conflict** "Arthur Shattuck Aids War Relief Fund," *New York Times*, August 22, 1917. A similar report appeared in *Musical Courier*, August 30, 1917.

135 **'from my soul, unfortunately'** Bella Edwards to Ferdinand Prior, November 28, 1918, *RDL*.

135 **African-American soldiers** Two combat divisions of African American soldiers, the 92nd and 93rd, included some 40,000 troops. See Chad Williams, "African Americans and World War I," in *Africana Age, an online exhibition* (New York: Schomberg Center for Research in Black Culture 2015), http://exhibitions.nypl.org/africanaage/essay-world-war-i.html.

136 **drug stores** Elliot Paul, *The Last Time I Saw Paris*. (New York: Random House, 1942).

136 **make ends meet** Willa Cather, *The Selected Letters of Willa Cather* (New York: Knopf Doubleday, 2013), 291. Returning to Paris in mid-1920, Cather wrote to her mother that since the war, "everything has doubled or trebled in price."

137 **'the immediate present'** Scudder, *Modeling My Life*, 280.

138 **'Spanish violinist Eva Murducci (*sic*)'** "Shattuck Visits Norwegian Artists," *Musical America* 31 (February 21, 1920): 15. The beaming young man leaning over Eva and Bella is identified as Sinding's son, and the woman seated next to Anna Sinding is called a daughter-in-law. But the Sindings were by all accounts childless.

139 **return with his mother to Paris** Interview with Janet Weber, February 16, 2013. Janet told me that young Kay Nielsen was living with Eva and Bella at the time. She conjectured that having both "young men" in residence made the younger boy's sudden appearance easier to explain. The two stories seem to have gotten conflated, as often happens with family history. Nielsen frequented Eva and Bella's home during the period when he was studying in Paris (1904-11); he then went to England. While it is quite possible that Nielsen's artwork influenced Eva's son, their stays in Paris did not coincide.

141 **in a trio** The cellist was American Robert Haven Schauffler (1879-1964), better remembered as a poet. He had been wounded at the Battle of Montfaucon in October 1918, and met Mudocci and Edwards while convalescing in Nice.

141 **'at that time'** Composer Edgard Varèse cited in Caroline Potter, *Erik Satie: A Parisian Composer and His World* (Woodbridge, Suffolk: Boydell & Brewer, 2016), 64.

142 **from the score** *Pauvre Pierrot* (known in English as *Evening with Pierrot*) was a collaboration between composer Bella Edwards and lyricist Hans Hartvig Seedorff (1892-1986).

142 **artistic experimentation** See, for example, Gérard Durozoi, *Paris 1919-1939: Art, Life & Culture* (New York: Vendome Press, 2010).

142 **upending convention** David John Taylor, *Bright Young People: The Lost Generation of London's Jazz Age* (London: Chatto & Windus, 2007).

142 **Danish accent** Bent Weber, personal communication, September 1, 2013. Mudocci's grandson (who was twenty-one when Bella Edwards died) recalled that she spoke English with a thick Danish accent.

143 **Soviet Union** J. P. Wearing, *The London Stage, 1930-1939: A Calendar of Productions, Performers, and Personnel* (London: Rowan & Littlefield, 2014).

144 **with Dr. Lemvigh-Müller** The 1930 Danish census lists Kay Ellson as a resident of Dr. Lemvigh-Müller's home.

144 **through mutual friends** The marriage certificate identifies the groom as Theophile Herman Weber, son of Gottlieb Weber; in England he was known as Geoffrey.

145 **title role** Mrs. Fiske, as she was known to theatergoers, became a good friend of Norman and Van Dresser. The pair were also friends with writer Gertrude Atherton, and were reportedly the inspiration for characters in her 1910 novel, *The Tower of Ivory*. See *San Francisco Daily Times*, October 22, 1910: 12.

145 **to family and friends** A 1905 letter from Gertrude Norman to E. G. Craig is signed "Tommy." It was not uncommon for lesbians of this era to assume male names. Several of the women who later became Gertrude and Marcia's close friends had done so. Clare Atwood was known as "Tony," Christabel Marshall as "Christopher," and Radclyffe Hall as "John." Bella Edwards was called "Teddie."

146 **'artistic acting'** "Topics of the Theatre," *Ainslee's Magazine* 7 (1901): 28.

147 **less predictable** See Maud Warrender, *My First Sixty Years* (London: Cassell & Co., Ltd., 1933). See also Kate Kennedy, "Lady Maud Warrender," *Classical Music's Unsung Heroines*, BBC radio broadcast, March 3, 2015, http://www.bbc.co.uk/programmes/b05402cs.

147 **1902 publication** Unsigned article, *Car: A Journal of Travel by Land, Sea, and Air* 1, no. 1 (May 28, 1902): 17.

147 **'blue-fox'** Unsigned article, *The London Magazine* 10 (1903): 527.

147 **often headlined** Lady Warrender was among the concert-hall and drawing-room singers described in Sophie Fuller, "'The Finest Voice of the Century': Clara Butt and Other Concert-Hall and Drawing-Room Singers of Fin-de-Siècle Britain," in *The Arts of the Prima Donna in the*

Long Nineteenth Century, eds. Rachel Cowgill and Hilary Poriss (Oxford University Press, 2012), 308-27.

147 **Christabel Marshall** Nicky Hallett, *Lesbian Lives: Identity and Auto/Biography in the Twentieth Century* (Sterling, VA: Pluto Press, 1999), 16.

148 **live at Leasam** Daniel M. Grimley, "'The Spirit-Stirring Drum': Elgar and Populism" in *Elgar and His World* (Princeton, NJ: Princeton University Press, 2007), n. 83. This essay quotes the diary of Siegfried Sassoon, who, using a code word of the day, called Lady Maud "a fashionably-attired Amazon with a talent for singing and archery; quite a noble creature and extremely amusing."

148 **Marcie and Toto** Correspondence (*NYPL*) makes it clear that Toto was viewed by all who knew her, including Van Dresser's brother, as Marcie's beloved. Toto was also Marcie's sole heir. As an American who died abroad, Van Dresser was the subject of an official American Foreign Service report, which noted that her brother William had been notified by cable, and that Van Dresser's effects passed "by survivorship to joint owner, Miss Gertrude Maud Norman." Norman also inherited "all stocks etc. held in joint names and bank accounts etc. in joint names." Norman was identified, parenthetically, as "Friend."

148 **'two angels'** Such loving threesomes were not unknown in the lesbian society in which they socialized. For example, during the thirty years that reached from one world war to the next, Lady Maud's friend, the painter Clare Atwood, lived with Christabel Marshall, the dramatist, and also with Edith Craig, the theatrical producer, director, actor, and costume designer.

149 **display it publicly** Unsigned article, *Musical Courier* 81 (September 9, 1920): 26. This article notes that Van Dresser is to be congratulated on her renditions of German songs in English, which benefitted from her having found a "worthy translator" in Gertrude Norman. Other mentions of Gertrude Norman in the press refer to her as Van Dresser's companion or secretary.

149 **corrupt the young** See Diana Souhami, *The Trials of Radclyffe Hall* (London: Quercus Publishing, 2013). Souhami shows that the mails in England were not entirely secure. When *The Well of Loneliness* was published in Paris, the British Home Secretary issued warrants to the Post Office to intercept any letters to its French publisher.

149 **'Indecency by Females'** Ibid, 112.

150 **after her death** Gertrude Norman donated additional artifacts and papers to the New England Conservatory in Boston.

150 **decades of their lives**   Eva and Bella's British friend Gertrude M. Norman should not to be confused with the American silent-film star known as Gertrude Norman.

151 **financial struggles**   Janet Weber, in a note to the author, April 2016, recalled that when she was ten years old and a student at the Royal Ballet School, she was taken to meet two of her grandmother's friends and was presented with a bursary. She thinks one of them may have been Gertrude Norman.

153 **Eva's ailing mother**   Mudocci to Norman, 1937, *NYPL*. Eva wrote that her mother was "unable to move" for the last seven years of her life.

153 **William E. Hill & Sons**   The firm exists to this day, but could not locate a record of the sale of Mudocci's violin. A listing on tarisio.com shows that the violin was owned by Mudocci in 1920 and in 1931 was sold by W.E. Hill & Sons to a collector. See details on the Emiliani's provenance at: https://tarisio.com/cozio-archive/property/?ID=41221.

154 **bills mounted**   According to a listing of historical auction prices for violins made by Antonio Stradivari (tarisio.com), auction prices in the late nineteen twenties and early thirties were typically in the £1,000-£2,000 range (approximately $65,000-$130,000 today). To put this in perspective, a September 1931 *Good Housekeeping* article suggested an annual budget of £410 for a British family. Assuming Mudocci and Edwards, living in London, could manage on half that amount, proceeds from the violin sale could have lasted from five to ten years; high medical and hospital expenses would certainly have drained some of those resources.

154 **trips to France and Italy**   Eva Mudocci, British passport, *WFP*. Stamps in the passport show six trips abroad between 1929 and 1933—three to France, three to Denmark.

156 **condolence messages**   Eva Mudocci to Gertrude M. Norman, 1937, *NYPL*.

157 **impersonal feel**   Mudocci's language appears to derive from William Oxley, *The Philosophy of Spirit, Illustrated New Version of the Bhagavat Gita: An Episode of the Mahabharat, One of the Epic Poems of Ancient India* (London: E.W. Allen, 1888), 230. At the time the book was published, Oxley was a member of the Theosophical Society. In his commentary on the *Bhagavat Gita*, he wrote: "[W]hen the spirit is emancipated from its physical covering, the fetters of these outer conditions are removed, and then it ascends to that state, in conformity with its own specific love or life, and attracted by the magnet of affinity, to that which accords with

its own quality, it joins the company of those who have preceded and there finds its happiness and home."

157 **reunited in the next**   Tim Jeal, *Swimming with My Father* (London: Faber & Faber, 2011), 106.

159 **Fritz**   The surname has been omitted at the family's request.

160 **not unreasonable**   Katharina Knoll, Moritz Schularick and Michael Thomas. "No Price Like Home: Global House Prices, 1870-2012," CEPR Discussion Paper No. DP10166: 15-16: "German house prices rose before World War I, contracted during World War I and remained low during the interwar period. They did not recover their pre-1913 levels until the 1960s."

160 **in June 1938**   Susan Meinl, "The Expropriation of Jewish Emigrants from Hessen during the 1930s," in *Confiscation of Jewish Property in Europe, 1933–1945: New Sources and Perspectives* (Washington, DC: Center for Advanced Holocaust Studies, U.S. Holocaust Memorial Museum, 2003), 100.

166 **designed and then occupied it**   The house at 1 Hanover Terrace Ladbroke Square, where Mudocci and Edwards lived in the 1930s, was designed by the architect Sir Aston Webb (1849-1930) for his family. Webb served as president of the Institute of British Architects from 1902 to 1904. His best known works in London include the Queen Victoria Memorial, the mall approach to and principal façade of Buckingham Palace, and the main building of the Victoria and Albert Museum.

166 **views of the sea**   Unsigned article, *The Builder* 88 (April 29, 1905). An architectural journalist is cited as the source of the date. He describes a drawing of the house this way: "The view of the house, in pen line, shows a square brick block with quoins at the angles, a pediment on the surface of the central portion, and a semi-circular window under it. This kind of architecture certainly does not sin against good taste, as there seems practically to be no architecture in it; but that we suppose is its merit."

167 **'singing to Gawd'**   Warrender, *My First Sixty Years*, 199.

168 **'awaiting her prey'**   Philip Horne, ed. *Henry James: A Life in Letters* (London: Penguin, 2001), 442.

168 **'agreeably dotty'**   Richard Garnett, *Constance Garnett: A Heroic Life* (London: Sinclair-Stevenson, 1991), 32. Alice Dew-Smith was a friend of translator Constance Garnett.

169 **Blitz lay ahead**   Telephone books and electoral registries do not supply their addresses for the war years. By 1945, Eva and Bella had moved down the road to the parlor flat at 10 Ladbroke Square that

they occupied until entering a retirement home in 1950. It is not clear whether in August 1940 they returned to their One Hanover Terrace flat, moved directly to 10 Ladbroke Square, or stayed elsewhere.

170 **exiles in London**   Lucy Knupffer was born Lucy Schmidt in Estonia in 1884, and married Moritz (later Maurice) Knupffer in Saint Petersburg in 1906. Two children, George and Daisy, were born there in 1907 and 1908, making them age-mates of Mudocci's children. Moritz Knupffer, a captain in the Russian Naval Guard, fought with the Whites in the civil war that followed the Bolshevik Revolution. After the Whites' defeat in 1920, the family fled to London, joining a community of monarchist exiles in Belsize Park, near Hampstead Heath. The Knupffers' daughter Daisy studied at the Slade School of Art and became an accomplished painter. Their son George took up the family's monarchist sympathies with zeal, leading the right-wing Mladorus (Young Russia) emigré party in London. Princess Alexandra Mestchersky was his political ally. In 1941, George Knupffer sued the *London Express* for calling members of his party fascists and quislings in what became a landmark libel case. In 1958, he published a book called *The Struggle for World Power: Revolution and Counter-Revolution* (re-published in 1986 by Noontide Press), assailing "usury capitalism" and asserting that Jewish financiers in New York City had bankrolled both Adolph Hitler and Joseph Stalin. For a discussion of George Knupffer's activities as a "long-standing anti-Jewish campaigner," see Nick Toczek, *Haters, Baiters and Would-Be Dictators: Anti-Semitism and the UK Far Right* (New York: Routledge, 2015), 255.

170 **all things Russian**   Alexei Knupffer, personal communication, November 11, 2013 and November 13, 2013. Alexei Knupffer is a pianist and composer. He was eleven when his grandmother died, and—using a word Janet had summoned to describe her grandmother—said that Lucy had always seemed "aloof." He knew of no family ties to musicians. He recalled that his grandparents were very involved with London's Russian Orthodox Church in Exile and that on holidays, congregants and clergy from the Church would fill his grandparents' home. The grandchildren, all born in England, were sent to Russian schools. It was a highly concentrated Russian world in the midst of London. He said that grandmother was sometimes known as "Lucy de Knupffer" or "Lucy von Knupffer"—common usages among Russian nobility in exile. Alexei said that English was Lucy's fourth and last language (she also spoke Russian,

German, and French), but thought she could have written a manuscript in that language if she had someone to proofread and improve the copy.

170 **notorious anti-Semite** Knupffer IX,15. Princess Mestchersky, aka Tola Dorian, was the publisher of *La Revue d'Aujourd'hui*, which published blasphemous articles, including one about the Jewish "worship and conquest of gold." Although signed by "A Lookout," scholars say that this article was likely written by the Princess Mestchersky herself.

170 **White Russian colony** George Knupffer shared the monarchist commitments of Princess Alexandra Mestchersky and undertook joint political work with her after World War II, opposing the repatriation of Soviet prisoners of war.

171 **'devoted friend'** Lucy Knupffer to Eva Mudocci and Bella Edwards, March 2, 1944, *WFP*.

171 **leveled** Tom Vague, *Getting It Straight in Notting Hill Gate: A West London Psychogeography Report* (London: Bread and Circuses Publishing, 2012).

172 **'music for us'** Poul Rée to Isobel Weber, August 19, 1963, *WFP*.

172 **from the other side** See Grace Rosher, *Beyond the Horizon* (London: James Clarke Lutterworth, 1961).

173 **June 26, 1950** Unsigned article announcing the BBC program, *Arbeiderbladet* June 24, 1950: 2: "Along with her friend, Bella Edwards, pianist, she met Edvard Munch for the first time [in Paris] in the early 1900s, and for many years a warm friendship developed among the three artists."

174 **French painting** Herbert Read, *Edvard Munch,* exhibition catalogue (London: London Gallery, Ltd., 1936).

174 **Modern Movement in Painting** Thomas Wade Earp, *The Modern Movement in Painting* (London: The Studio, Ltd., 1935).

174 **'as a leader'** Thomas Wade Earp, "Edvard Munch Works. First Exhibition in London," *Daily Telegraph*, November 2, 1936. Earp was less critical of Munch's drawings and lithographs.

175 **'pedicultural nightmare'** "M. Munch's Goloshes," *Daily Telegraph*, October 21, 1936.

175 **English painters** Sir Kenneth Clark, Typescript appreciation of Munch, Sir Kenneth Clark Papers, Tate Gallery, London, 1944 (8812/1/1/54/164). Clark referred to Mudocci as a singer. See Sir Kenneth Clark, *Feminine Beauty*. London: Weidenfeld & Nicolson, 1980, 184.

176 **'caught up'** Mudocci to Stabell, [postmarked May 16, 1950], *MM*.

176 **'knowing its cause'** Mudocci to Stabell, [May 6, 1950, postmarked May 7, 1950], *MM*.

176 **'from the first'** Mudocci to Stabell, May 7, 1950, p. 5, *MM*.

176 **'after so long'** Smith, *Frederick Delius and Edvard Munch*, mentions an additional meeting of Munch and Mudocci in Paris, in or around 1927, but I have found no documentary evidence for this encounter.

176 **influenza** In those years, Spanish flu swept across Norway in three waves: the summer epidemic of 1918, the autumn epidemic of 1918 and the winter epidemic of 1918-19. See T. Borza, "Spanish Flu in Norway 1918-19," *Tidsskr Nor Laegeforen* 121, no. 30 (December 10, 2001): 3551-4.

177 **'convenience for writing'** Mudocci to Stabell, May 7, 1950, *WFP*.

179 **narcotics** Walter Luedtke, "An Account of [Arthur Shattuck's] Career," in Shattuck, *Memoirs*, 245.

180 **moving Bella to Denmark** Mogens Fog (1904-1990) was married to Bella's niece Elin Hariet Edwards. A prominent neurologist, he co-founded Free Denmark, an organization that resisted Nazi occupation in 1942. He was arrested by the Gestapo in 1944, but escaped the following year. Fog played a role in Danish politics in the decades after the war, helping to found the Socialist People's Party, and served as rector of the University of Copenhagen from 1966-72, introducing democratic reforms in an era of student activism.

185 **Testament** Edvard Munch, *Last Will and Testament*, 1944, Statsarkivet, Oslo, https://www.arkivverket.no/arkivverket/Arkivverket/Statsarkivet-i-Oslo/Norges-dokumentarv-Statsarkivet-i-Oslo/Edvards-Munchs-testamente-og-doedsbo.

185 **his sister, Inger** Nicolay Stang, *Edvard Munch* (Oslo, J.G. Tanum Forlag, 1972), 32: "And his sister, Inger, can tell us that Edvard always had a suitcase full of old letters with him on his travels."

186 **Oslo officialdom** Hilton Kramer, *The Age of the Avant-Garde: 1956-1972* (New Brunswick, NJ: Transaction Publishers, 2011), 102.

188 **'now writing'** Ibid, 100.

189 **on its cover** Johan Langaard and Reidar Revold, *Edvard Munch: Malerier og Grafikk* (Oslo: Forlaget Norsk Kunstreproduksjon, 1962).

190 **'paroxysms'** Einar Brünniche, "Om kunst og sindslidelse," *Spectator* 36, no. 2 (July 1919): 73-80.

190 **museum officials** One additional letter from Eva Mudocci to Munch's friend, attorney Thorvald Stang, dated February 10, 1910, responded to a request for contact information for a Paris-based art-world official.

190 **conceived and born** Lund, "Notes on Mudocci's letters to Munch," *WFP*. Lund suggests that the gap extended from mid-1906 to late 1909. My review suggests that the correspondence continued into 1907.

193 **visit her Uncle Kai** Interview with Janet Weber, April 29, 2014. Janet was unsure whether her visit to Denmark took place in 1962 or 1963. She recalled hearing from Dr. Lund, during that visit, about the proposed exhibit of Kai's paintings. By the summer of 1963, Dr. Lund had written to Janet's mother that he had given up on the idea of such an exhibit. Therefore, Janet's visit must have taken place in 1962.

194 **acquaintance of Eva and Bella** Poul Rée at one time served as Danish consul in the city of Perm, in Russia, and became a source for historians looking into the circumstances of the execution of Tsar Nicholas II and his family. See Greg King & Penny Wilson, *The Fate of the Romanovs* (Morrisville, NC: Lulu Press, Inc., 2014).

197 **earn a living** Kramer, *The Age of the Avant-Garde*, 101-02. Kramer offers this excerpt from the writings of Langaard and Revold: "From 1914 onward, Edvard Munch became increasingly reluctant to part with his works. He sold almost nothing except those pictures that were bought by museums or had been executed on commission. In earlier years he had also been averse to letting his works go but then he had been forced to sell in order to live. Even then, however, there were two groups of pictures which he kept in his possession as long as he could: those works which were linked most closely with his emotional life, and everything that formed part of the cycle of pictures which he called The Frieze of Life."

202 **'first winter of [World War I]'** Hilary Spurling, *Matisse the Master: A Life of Henri Matisse—The Conquest of Colour, 1909-1954* (London: Knopf), 167.

203 **'if it's true'** Nina Berglund, "Views and news from Norway," August 12, 2012, http://www.newsinenglish.no/2012/08/20/tests-to-prove-munch-heirs/.

203 **broken** The most definitive genetic evidence of the twins' possible connection to Edvard Munch had been buried with Janet's uncle, Kai Ellson. It seemed unlikely that Janet would want to pursue that route, and in any case, she had no idea where Kai was buried. Citing privacy concerns, the Danish psychiatric institution where he died in the 1980s has declined to give Janet any information about the circumstances of his death or what became of his remains. If Kai had fathered a son, he too would have carried the Y chromosome, but according to Janet, her

uncle never married and never had children.

204 **portrait of the twins** Smith, *Frederick Delius and Edvard Munch*, 157 n36: "Eva Mudocci's daughter, Mrs. Isobel Weber, says that she, her twin brother and their mother met Munch together somewhere around 1914-16, either in Copenhagen or Germany. Mrs. Weber claims that Munch later made a portrait from memory of her and her brother, but I have been unable to trace this."

206 **'a pleasure for me'** Isobel Weber to John Boulton Smith, August 18, 1978, *WFP*.

207 **'not his correct name'** The source cited on the website is Bruce Durie, a Scottish genealogist who has studied the Muddock family history.

210 **'and that's it'** Kim Ravn, "Louis Levy — dansk pulp fiction," in *Kristeligt Dagblad*, September 17, 2003, https://www.kristeligt-dagblad.dk/kirke-tro/louis-levy-dansk-pulp-fiction.

211 ***Metamorphosis*** Levy's novel was reissued in Danish in 2017 by Escho Press in Copenhagen.

212 **ten years** Louis Levy discussed anti-Semitism in the literary world in letters to Karl Larsen (1918) and Anders W. Holm (mid-1930s), *RDL*.

212 ***Der Stürmer*** Morten Thing, *Antisemitismens Bibel: Historien om Smædeskriftet Zions Vises Protokoller* (Copenhagen: Informations Forlag, 2014). The author documents *Der Stürmer*'s attack on Levy, showing how the Nazis twisted Levy's words.

212 **interview** "Louis Levy om Forfalskningen af hans Digt." *Ekstrabladet*, July 10, 1936.

213 **'seeps into the carpet'** All quotes from the novel have been translated from Louis Levy, *Menneskeløget Kzradock, den vårfriske Methusalem af Dr. Renard de Montpensiers Optegnelser* (Copenhagen: Escho/Sidste Århundrede, 2017). Levy's book was first published in the Danish illustrated monthly *Månedsmagasinet* in 1909 and appeared in book form a year later (Copenhagen: Gyldendal, 1910). A German translation by Hermann Kiy came out in 1912. An English translation was based on the German edition: Louis Levy, *Kzradock the Onion Man and the Spring-Fresh Methuselah: From the Notes of Dr. Renard de Montpensier*, trans. W.C. Bamberger (Rockville, MD: Wildside Press, 2010).

217 **financial difficulty** Henri Deering to Gertrude Norman, May 26, 1952, *NYPL*. The letter mentions Eva's daughter's efforts to extricate herself from financial difficulty. According to Janet Weber, between January 1953 and the early 1960s, Isobel and Geoffrey Weber twice separated and reunited. For the next ten years, they lived separately during the

week and together on the weekends. This worked well for them until 1973-74, when Isobel felt she couldn't leave London for Barton on Sea, where Geoffrey was living in a retirement home they had purchased. Only then did the couple divorce.

219 **the gunshot** Frank Høifødt, *Kunsten, kvinnen og en ladd revolver, Edvard Munch anno 1900* (Oslo: Utgivelsesår: 2010).

221 **attorney's files** Lasse Jacobsen, personal communication, August 16, 2016. Jacobsen explained: "In 1969, Munch's will was taken from Oslo Skifterett [probate office] by Andrea Munch-Ellingsen's lawyer, Jens Christian Hauge concerning a court [case] on the copyright on Munch's works of art. Hauge then forgot about the will and it ended up in his private files in the State Archives, where it was discovered by Mai Britt Guleng and myself in 2009."

221 **seduce Eva Mudocci** Åshild Haugsland, "'…this chaos of letters I have collected…': Edvard Munch, the Letter Writer," n5, http://www. emunch.no/ENGART_emunch_haugsland_eng.xhtml#note5. "During this process Inger went through the papers, and the question has been raised whether she discarded some of the material."

221 **her brother's archives** See Ketil Bjørnstad, "Munch is the State's Responsibility," *Aftenposten*, September 2, 2012. Some Norwegians believe that Munch's decision to leave his work and archives to the city of Oslo was a mistake. According to Bjørnstad, the municipality mismanaged the collection, making policy decisions that resulted in "a catastrophic neglect of the Munch legacy." In addition, he wrote, "Munch's literary work and the foundation for modern Munch research was withheld and concealed from the public by art historians with strong vested interests." In a personal communication (April 8, 2015), Bjørnstad wrote to me that Langaard withheld letters, diaries and literary works.

222 **Munch's legacy** Even if they were convinced that Munch was not the twins' father, Langaard and Revold had good reason to quash speculation. In the 1960s, DNA testing would not have been available to settle the question. If Mudocci's descendants had been able to document contact between Munch and Mudocci during the critical timeframe, a claim to his estate may have been difficult to refute.

222 **followed by Norwegians** There was one notable exception. *The Guardian* (London) carried a page-one story on April 20, 1968, credited to its Oslo correspondent, entitled "Norway's Biggest Art Scandal." The Munch Museum's books of clippings contain dozens of articles on the theft.

222 **woodcuts from the collection**   Revold's estranged wife Engelka acknowledged involvement in the sale of two prints in Switzerland. As the investigation widened, Revold confessed that in the five years since the museum's opening, he had stolen some forty works by Munch. Museum officials later estimated that many were sold by art dealers in Switzerland. The public was particularly incensed that Revold would forge Munch's signature on unsigned works.

222 **living in Italy**   Revold had applied for the director's position, but lost out to Ragna Thiis Stang, daughter of Jens Thiis—the legendary director of Norway's National Museum who presented Eva Mudocci with the brooch depicted in Munch's portrait.

222 **other Munch scholars**   In "Edvard Munch's Writings," Lasse Jaobsen notes that one of the scholars who was denied access to the archive was Director Langaard's ex-wife, Ingrid Langaard. The Director justified his actions, citing the private character of Munch's writings, the poor condition of many documents, and the lack of space for research. Langaard wrote unapologetically about locking away Munch's papers and argued that he had denied access to all researchers, not just to his ex-wife. Other scholars "hardly have more to be grateful for than the opportunity to check a few precise facts that they wished to verify with certainty," he said.

222 **'book about Munch'**   Ibid.

223 **'vested interests'**   Bjørnstad, "Munch is the State's Responsibility." In "Edvard Munch's Writings," Lasse Jacobsen defended Langaard, arguing that while the Director's attitude might seem arrogant, it was understandable, given the context of a museum and archive devoted to a single artist. Such an institution, he wrote, "provides the opportunity for a deeply felt fascination coupled with the obligation and necessity to study and disseminate this material."

223 **irregularities**   Lasse Jacobsen, personal communication, August 16, 2016.

224 **'should be treasured'**   Mudocci to Stabell, May 7, 1950, 5.

224 **that survived?**   In 2013, Bent Weber showed me two envelopes that Munch addressed to Mudocci, but did not know what had happened to the letters they once contained, *WFP*.

224 **letters from Munch**   Lund to Langaard, September 6, 1963, *MM* administrative files. Lund learned from Isobel Weber that she had sold the entire collection of mail from Munch—with the exception of one card from Erfurt.

224 **for the BBC** Two letters mention Isobel Weber's sale of Munch's letters to Stabell: Poul Rée to Isobel Weber, September 19, 1963, *WFP*; Lund to Langaard, August 18, 1964, *MM* administrative files.

224 **informed Johan Langaard** Lund to Langaard, September 6, 1963, *MM* administrative files.

224 **'a copy of them'** Langaard to Stabell, September 13, 1963, *MM* administrative files.

224 **'handed over to the museum'** Lund to Langaard, September 12, 1964, *MM* administrative files.

224 **'after your review'** Revold to Lund, September 22, 1964, *MM* administrative files.

224 **excerpts from Munch's letters** The *MM* archives also include a document containing excerpts (in German) from Munch's letters that Mudocci apparently translated from German to Danish and sent to Waldemar Stabell in May 1950 as she prepared for their conversation on BBC.

229 **Robinson** Margrete Louis Levy, *Fregnes Dagbog: Fra hans fødsel til hans 2 aars fødselsdag* (Copenhagen: Det Schønbergske Forlag, 1914). The book was represented as the work of both Margrete and Louis Levy.

229 **'entire family'** Margrete Levy, *Fregnes Dagbog III* (manuscript), 5, *LFP*.

231 **family doctor** Lotte Thrane, "Koks I Kulissen," *KVinfo webmagazine*, November 2, 2012. This article mentions that in 1911, after she submitted her first play to the Royal Danish Theatre, Ott wrote to Georg Brandes complaining that "LL" had mocked her, lecturing about the difference between art and entertainment.

233 **nothing to do but wait** During this period, I read an article by genealogist Bruce Durie focusing on a DNA sample taken from another Mudocci descendent and reporting that the "ethnic distribution seen in [the subject's] tested autosomal makeup" revealed European origins, with both Northlands (consistent with Norwegian) and Jewish contributions. He speculated that both contributions would be explained if a "Jewish-Norwegian businessman" named Louis Levy had fathered the twins. In fact, Levy was a Jewish writer and journalist living in Denmark, with no known Norwegian forebears. Durie's article offered interesting genealogical data but did not resolve the question of the twins' paternity, given Durie's unfounded conjecture and the fact that Mudocci herself had been quoted as claiming Jewish roots. See Durie, "Did Edvard Munch Have Children with Eva Mudocci?"

236 **'your heart'** Louis Levy to Anders W. Holm, December 14, 1916, *RDL*.

236 **'breakdown in 1908'** Rée to Tetlie, January 1, 1961, *FM*.

239 **has not survived** Interview with Otto Lund's son and stepdaughter, April 2017. After Dr. Lund's death, his heirs discarded all of his papers related to Eva Mudocci and her twins.

244 **more akin to siblings than lovers** Chang, *Negotiating Modernity*, 18: "Although Mudocci served as his love interest in Salome, the pair was never romantically involved; in a draft of one of his letters to the violinist, Munch told her that he loved her like a sister." Chang's reading overlooks the content and erotic overtones of other letters in the Mudocci-Munch correspondence.

244 **'artist-couple'** Egum, *Munch and Photography*, 77.

246 **'began in our blood'** Mudocci to Munch, [1903], *MM* K 1803.

247 **companionship** In talking to me about his grandmother, Bent Weber described Mudocci as a "new woman" of the type described by H. G. Wells.

249 **censure** See Lillian Faderman, *Surpassing the Love of Men: Romantic Friendship and Love between Women from the Renaissance to the Present* (New York: Morrow and London: Junction, 1981).

249 **'able to find it'** Poul Rée to Isobel Weber, September 19, 1963, *WFP*.

250 **in the process** Rée to Tetlie, January 19, 1961, *FM*. Rée claimed to have seen another painting of Eva, attributed to Munch by Bella Edwards, in the corridor of their London flat in 1947. He described it as "nearly the same size as mine. It was placed in a pitch-dark corridor without windows and very high on the wall over the rack. . . [that] Bella said was painted by Munch. She said, 'I dislike this portrait, we could get a big lot of money for it.' . . . I cannot tell you much about that painting so many years after. I remember that Eva was wandering straight out of the frame like a sleep-walker." According to Rée, Mogens Fog also recalled the painting and "thinks she was in a black gown."

250 **masterpiece** In several letters and documents archived at the Flaten Museum, Richard Tetlie (the collector who bought the Mudocci portrait in 1960) notes that it has been called the Mona Lisa of Expressionism. He does not identify the source of this descriptor. Other works have been referred to in this way, including Munch's *The Scream* and Max Beckmann's *Quappi Beckmann as Victor*.

252 **in Berlin** It appears that Munch succeeded at portraying Eva when he worked from photographs, but was dissatisfied with his efforts to capture the living Eva.

253 **woman violinist [*violinistin*]?** Linde to Munch, February 1, 1904, *MM* K 2792.

253 **1903-04** Waldemar Stabell, "Edvard Munch og Eva Mudocci," *Kunst og Kultur, 56* (1973): 209–36.

254 **Copenhagen auction** Lunøe to Revold, 1959, *MM* administrative files. I have not seen this letter, but its contents were described to me by the Munch Museum's senior curator for paintings, Petra Pettersen, on April 27, 2017.

255 **book on Frederick Delius and Edvard Munch** Smith, *Frederick Delius and Edvard Munch*, 73.

255 **right hand** A photograph of Bella Edwards wearing a ribbon across her hand, in the same fashion, accompanied a 1923 article in a Danish publication. See "En kvindelig Komponist Frk Bella Edwards," 1.

255 **pencil** Rée to Tetlie, December 13, 1960, *FM*. Rée quoted a letter from the actor Valdemar Willumsen, a longtime friend of Eva and Bella, who wrote about the painting: "How well I recognize the cozy diminutive home overfilled with Oriental carpets and recollect the black piano at which I daily spent several hours in 1904 in Paris."

255 **by Munch** Rée to Tetlie, January 19, 1961, *FM*. Lunøe had attended the auction. Rée wrote to Tetlie that in the presence of other museum officials, Lunøe was non-commital about the portrait's origin, unwilling to admit that he had passed up the opportunity to buy a Munch for his museum.

257 **'which Norway needs'** Tetlie to Hildegarde Flanner Monhoff, March 7, 1981, *FM*. The recipient, a writer, was Kay Nielsen's neighbor after Nielsen and his wife settled in California. She wrote an appreciation of Nielsen published in David Larkin, ed., *The Unknown Paintings of Kay Nielsen* (New York: Peacock Press/Bantam Books, 1984).

257 **broke off contact** Mudocci to Munch, [late 1903 or early 1904], *MM* K 1816.

258 **'gifted boy, as a painter'** Mudocci to Munch, [1904], *MM* K 1819.

259 **Munch's paintings** Gerd Woll reviewed a photograph of the portrait, not the original. She apparently had received a summary of Rée's letters to Tetlie prepared by the executor of Tetlie's estate (*FM*). Woll also had access to correspondence about the painting (*MM* administrative files).

259 **woman violinist** In the nineteen forties and fifties, Kay Nielsen worked as an animator at the Walt Disney studios. His correspondence from this period, archived at the Huntington Library in Los Angeles, makes no reference to Mudocci or the painting.

260 **'only one who can paint me'** Mudocci to Munch, April 17, [1906], *MM* K 1842. Mudocci wrote: "But if we could meet in June [in Berlin] and you painted me while I played for you – I think I could play music which would calm your nerves." Mudocci posed for Munch, Matisse, and Heaton. Portraits of Mudocci (or the duo) by other artists or illustrators were based on photographs or were variations on Munch's lithographs.

261 **sophisticated tools** The report listed these analytic methods: visible and ultraviolet light microscopy, Fourier transform infrared spectroscopy, X-ray fluorescence, and micro-Raman spectroscopy.

261 *The Scream* Jennifer L. Mass, Erich Uffelman, Barbara Buckley, et al., "Portable X-ray Fluorescence and Infrared Fluorescence Imaging Studies of Cadmium Yellow Alteration in Paintings by Edward Munch and Henri Matisse in Oslo, Copenhagen, and San Francisco," *Smithsonian Contributions to Museum Conservation* 5, (2016): 53-64.

261 **collaborating scientists** A summary of scientists' findings can be found in Brian Singer, Trond E. Aslaksby, Biljana Topalova-Casadiego and Eva Storevik Tveit, "Investigation of Materials Used by Edvard Munch," *Studies in Conservation* 55, no. 4 (2010): 274-92.

262 **before 1916** These paintings include *The Sick Child*, *Chemistry*, *New Rays*, and *Woman Harvesting*.

262 **timeframe for the Mudocci portrait** Jennifer L. Mass, "Analysis of an Unfinished Portrait of Eva Mudocci Attributed to Edvard Munch (1903-1904)," (unpublished paper, Scientific Analysis of Fine Art Report 1802, New York, NY, November 28, 2018), 1.

262 **not available in 1904** Mass and Finnefrock noted the absence of phthalocyanine blue and phthalocyanine green—pigments found in expressionist paintings beginning in the 1930s.

262 **resembled St. Olaf's portrait** The portrait's painter was evidently familiar with Mudocci dress (i.e., the ribbon she wore on her hand—as did Bella in a photograph that accompanied Gustav Hetsch's article in *Hversdag*), and with the artifacts in her home (statuette, oriental rugs, as reported by visitors Valdemar Willumsen and Janet Weber).

263 **'Famous Composer'** Simon Haydon, "Letters Reveal Passion of Famous Composer," *Albuquerque Journal*, March 31, 1985: 56. Haydon reported that the recipient was seventeen or eighteen at the time Grieg was writing to her. In fact, Bella Edwards was thirty.

264 **forces landed in Denmark** The occupation had been widely anticipated, especially after a mid-February naval incident (the Altman affair) in neutral waters off Norway.

264 **boarding house** Reported in *Rye's Own Magazine*, August 1, 2006, http://ryesown.co.uk/50-year-anniversary/#more-4728.

264 **'leading pianists'** Quoted in Shattuck, *Memoirs*, 245.

265 **'let it die out'** Bergitte Folmer, personal communication, March 2, 2017.

268 **four decades** Photographs show her holding the Emiliani in the early 1890s. The website tarisio.com reports that the violin was owned by "Mme Mudocci in Paris" in the 1920s until it was acquired by dealer William Hill in 1931.

268 **interpretations** The violinists who owned the Emiliani directly before and after Mudocci had similar inclinations and repertoires. Ludwig Straus started out as a soloist but became known primarily as a chamber player. According to the *Encylcopedia Britannica*, "His playing, whether of violin or viola, had very great qualities; he was perfect in ensemble, and his power of self-effacement was of a piece with his gentle disposition and with the pure love of art which distinguished him through life. A more lovable nature never existed, and his quiet influence on the art of his time was very great." The violinist who played the Emiliani between Mudocci and Mutter was Charlene Dilling Brewer of Chicago, Illinois, who acquired the Stradivarius in 1951 and performed on the radio and in smaller venues, often teaming up with her sister, a fine harpist.

268 **'dark in timbre'** Volker Blech, "Schönheit wird aus Schmerz geboren," *Berliner Morgenpost*, July 21, 2011.

Appendix A

Mudocci-Edwards Repertoire

Few programs from the performances of Eva Mudocci and Bella Edwards have survived. The lists below were compiled from advertisements and concert announcements, published reviews, and contemporaries' written recollections. The titles are taken from the original sources.

As their repertoire suggests, Eva Mudocci and Bella Edwards were steeped in the music of romanticism. In particular, they were drawn to the haunting melodies and chromatic complexity of late romanticism. Many of the selections listed below were written during the late nineteenth century. Composers of the baroque and classical eras were largely absent from their programs, as were the musical innovators of their own day. The music of Scandinavia—with emphasis on the work of Edvard Grieg, Christian Sinding, and Emil Sjøgren—was an important focus. Mudocci and Edwards helped to popularize this music in Belle Époque France.

A typical Mudocci-Edwards concert comprised three "acts": a sonata for violin and piano (typically by one of the Norwegian composers, or by Raff or Beethoven); followed by solo pieces showcasing each performer's virtuosity (often a Paganini caprice performed by Mudocci and one or more Chopin etudes or preludes played by Edwards); and ending with the duo reunited, playing a suite, a single movement of a concerto, or a medley of shorter selections. Many of the pieces in the Mudocci-Edwards repertoire are seldom performed today, and in general programs now place less emphasis on variety, aiming instead for coherence.

Violin-Piano Repertoire: Eva Mudocci and Bella Edwards

Eyvind Alnæs	Suite for Violin and Piano, op. 3
Ludwig van Beethoven	Violin Sonata no. 9 ("Kreutzer"), op. 47
Johannes Brahms	Hungarian Dances (arr. for violin by Joseph Joachim)
Jan Brandts-Buys	Sonata for Violin and Piano, op. 26
Frederic Hymen Cowen	The Language of Flowers (from Suite de Ballet no. 5)
Bella Edwards	Danse caractéristique
	Méditation
	Air de fête
Edward Elgar	Variations on an Original Theme ("Enigma"), op. 36
Willem de Fesch	Sonata for Violin and Piano, op. 8a
César Franck	Sonata in A major for Violin and Piano
Benjamin Godard	Légende et Scherzo, op. 3
Karl Goldmark	Suite for Violin and Piano in D major, op. 11
Edvard Grieg	Sonata in C minor for Piano and Violin, op. 45
	To the Spring, op. 43, no. 6 (from Lyric Pieces III)
Joseph Joachim	Violin Concerto no. 2 in D minor ("Hungarian"), op. 11
Éduard Lalo	Andante from Violin Concerto no. 2 in D minor, op. 21
Peter E. Lange-Müller	Three Fantasies for Violin and Piano, op. 39
Jean-Marie Leclair	Violin Sonata in D major (Sarabande and Tamborin), op. 9
Guillaume Lekeu	Sonata for Violin and Piano in G major

Ottokar Nováček · Perpetuum Mobile, op. 5, no. 4
Franz Liszt/Niccolò Paganini
· Etude no. 6 (Liszt-Paganini) &
· Caprice, op. 1, no. 24 (Paganini)
Alexander Mackenzie · Highland Ballad, op. 47, no. 1.
Felix Mendelssohn · Violin Concerto in E minor, op. 64
Gabriel Pierné · Sonata for Violin and Piano, op. 36
Henry Purcell · Two Airs (transcribed for violin and piano)
· Spanish Dance*
Joachim Raff · La Fée d'amour, op. 67
· Violin Sonata no. 2, op. 78
· Prelude (from Suite for Violin and
· Orchestra), op. 180
Camille Saint-Saëns · Le Cygne (from Carnival of the Animals)
Pablo de Sarasate · Sérénade Andaleuse, op. 10
· Gypsy Airs, op. 20
· Habañera, Japateado, Zapateado (from
· Spanish Dances, op. 21)
Franz Schubert · Violin Sonata in A major, op. 162
· Die Biene, op. 13, no. 9 (from Bagatelles)
Anton Simon · Célèbre Berceuse, op. 28
Christian Sinding · Cantus Doloris, op. 78 (dedicated to
· Mudocci), op. 78
· Prelude, op. 43
· Suite for Violin and Piano in G minor, op. 96
· Piano Trio in D major, op. 23
· (performed with cellist Josef Malkin)
Emil Sjøgren · Sonata No. 2 for Violin and Piano, op. 24
· Sonata No. 3 for Violin and Piano, op. 32
Johan Svendsen · Romance, op. 26
Pyotr I. Tchaikovsky · Violin Concerto in D major, op. 35
Henri Vieuxtemps · Rêverie, op. 22, no. 3 (from 6 Morceaux de salon)
William Vincent Wallace · Overture (from the opera Lurline)
Henryk Wieniawski · Two Mazurkas, op. 12
· Légende, op. 17

*Program announcements do not fully identify the selection.

Violin Repertoire: Eva Mudocci

Johann Sebastian Bach	Air (from Orchestral Suite No. 3 in D major), BWV 1068
	Gavotte*
Cécile Chaminade	Sérénade, op. 150.
Ernest Guiraud	Caprice (Andante et Allegro appassionato)
Hubert Léonard	La Fontaine
Niccolò Paganini	24 Caprices, op. 1
	Waterfall
Robert Schumann	Evening Song, op. 85
Christian Sinding	Romance*
Henri Vieuxtemps	Romances, op. 7

Piano Repertoire: Bella Edwards

Alexander Borodin	In the Steppes of Central Asia
Frédéric Chopin	Etudes, op. 10, nos. 3 and 8
	Etude, op. 25, no. 9
	Preludes, op. 28
Edvard Grieg	Berceuse, op. 41, no. 1
	Berceuse, op. 38, no. 1
	Grandmother's Minuet, op. 68, no. 2
	Waltz in D-flat major, op. 64, no. 1
Edward MacDowell	Two Fantastic Pieces, op. 17
Felix Mendelssohn	Six Preludes and Fugues, op. 35
Sergei Rachmaninoff	Thirteen Preludes, op. 32
Joachim Raff	Perpetuum Mobile
Christian Sinding	Variations for Two Pianos, op. 2 (performed with Fridtjof Backer-Grøndahl)

Violin Repertoire of Miss Rose Lynton
(stage name of the young Eva Mudocci)

Johann Sebastian Bach	Chaconne (from Partita no. 2 in D minor)
Ludwig van Beethoven	Violin Concerto in D major, op. 61
Max Bruch	Violin Concerto no. 1 in G minor, op. 26
Frédéric Chopin	Nocturne no. 11 in G minor, op. 37, no. 1 (transcribed for violin)
Ferdinand David	Introduction et variations brillantes sur un thème original, op. 19
Heinrich Ernst	Airs Hongrois Variés, op. 22
Joseph Joachim	Violin Concerto no. 2 ("Hungarian"), op. 11
Felix Mendelssohn	Andante (from Violin Concerto in E minor), op. 64
Pablo de Sarasate	Gypsy Airs, op. 20
Henri Vieuxtemps	Ballade et Polonaise, op. 38
	Caprice based on Old English Airs, op. 42
	Violin Concerto*
Henryk Wieniawski	Souvenir de Moscou, op. 6
	Grand caprice fantastique, op. 1
	Thème original varié, op. 15
Aleksandr Zarzycki	Mazurka in G major, op. 26

Sheet music in Mudocci's personal collection

(*Note: These pieces were not represented in announcements or reports of Mudocci-Edwards programs. Many of them were arranged for violin and piano by Issay Barmas.*)

Semyon Barmotine	Petit Poème
Ernest Chausson	Piano Quartet in A major, op. 30
César Franck	Andantino Quietoso, op. 6
Edvard Grieg	Bridal Procession, op. 19, no. 2
	Erotikon, op. 43, no. 5
	Lyric Piece, op. 43, no. 47

	Solitary Wanderer, op. 43, no. 2
Johan Halvorsen	Chant de Veslemøy (Suite Mosaïque, no. 4)
	An Old-Fashioned Wedding (Suite Mosaïque, no. 5)
Fini Henriques	Dance of the Gnats, op. 20, no. 5
	Religioso Andante, op. 34a
Jean Meyer	Mazurek de Salon (3 Compositions for Violin, no. 3)
Eduard Nápravník	Russian Melody, op. 64, no. 3
Ottokar Nováček	Bulgarian Dances, op. 6
	Bagpipes, Concert Caprice, op. 5, no. 8
Joachim Raff	Cavatine, op. 85, no. 3
Vladimir Rebikov	Lullaby in E-flat major, op. 7, no. 1 (from 3 Morceaux)
Émile Sauret	Nocturne, op. 2, no. 5
Franz Schubert	Six Grandes Marches, op. 40
Jean Sibelius	Scaramouche, op. 71
Christian Sinding,	An Old Air, op. 89, no. 2
	Andantino al Placere, op. 43, no. 3
	Fête, op. 43, no. 3
Leone Sinigaglia	Intermezzo, op. 13, no. 2
Pyotr Tchaikovsky	Melancholoy Serenade, op. 26
Joseph Miroslav Weber	Miniature Suite

Appendix B

Letters and Documents

Mudocci and Munch Letters

A 1903 draft letter from Edvard Munch to Eva Mudocci. Munch Museum, Oslo, N 2382

The text reads: "Dear Eva—A greeting from my house—mental storms and Christiania life have broken off our spiritual connection—do you think of me? I kissed your little letter—and I see your white cliffs in the distance—I almost went to you but my work forces me—and your picture hangs over my bed, you look as though you would protect me from evil spirits."

Letter from Eva Mudocci to Edvard Munch, October 31, [1905]. MUNCH MUSEUM, OSLO, K 1823 / AUTHOR'S PHOTOGRAPHS. A translation of the text is provided on pp. 86-87.

To watch the gradually ebbing out of forces in one one loves, is heart-breaking – When I look at Bella & remember how – only a very few years ago – she was so bright & independent & capable, & now! – some of the helplessness of age is already coming over her, & my heart breaks to see it – knowing there is nothing to be done – except to make the going down hill as smooth for her as possible – & even that I cannot do! my own turn is not far off, & the only thing I have left to hope & pray for is that we may be permitted to keep together to the last – or as near the last as possible. And then I think, how blessed I am in knowing that last to be not the ending of life but only of a phase of life – with all the illimitable future in which to gather up the threads again & again. And that is what I would give anything to be able to help you to feel – That is what all my words are trying & struggling to help you to feel – dearest, dearest Toto – don't mind all my silly, clumsy words – forgive them please, & only know that I am with you heart & soul. That I grieve with you & think of, & pray for you night & day – praying that some light may be shown me for the passing on to you. You do understand, darling?-please. We love you so & thee marcee so. Ever your loving friend

Last page of Mudocci's nine-page letter to Toto Norman, 1937. GERTRUDE NORMAN-MARCIA VAN DRESSER COLLECTION, NEW YORK PUBLIC LIBRARY, NEW YORK CITY /AUTHOR'S PHOTOGRAPH

Letters from Edvard Grieg to Bella Edwards

1

Leipzig, 6 November, 1895

Finally! If only you knew how I longed for this! And how happy you made me just now. It is like every breeze of wind carries your breath towards me! The few lines—far, far too few and too cautious, why?—

Should we be embarrassed by the most noble and beautiful feelings? Yes, far too few [lines]—but still a whole world! But I must be permitted to write without inhibition.

You don't need to thank me for the most wonderful hours of your life—and yet these words sound like no other music on earth! For what should I say? And then it wasn't hours. It was seconds, but with the feeling of eternity. Since we met, I have started believing in hypnotism! Do you know, you have become part of my consciousness, my surroundings are now cold and empty when you are not there. Promise me that I can see you and talk to you when we are both in Denmark. Promise me this!

How sweet you are when you write: <u>we</u> sang the Swan! Yes, you dare say that the tones vibrate in the depth of your soul, that is true. I just wanted the technical expression to be better, and you shall and must acquire this. Couldn't I have the pleasure of playing a bit with you in Copenhagen when you return home in January-February? Because then I shall do everything I can to be there. I believe I could teach you a few things—also pure technicalities, if you so wish—in the interpretation of my own works. And now I let these lines make the journey to you. I hope an amiable star will accompany them, the same star that let us meet in order to become friends! Yes, write to me as a friend,—<u>immediately</u> after receiving this. Write about your life, your plans, about how "we" sing! About everything! Farewell, my darling!

My best regards to Margarethe Petersen, if she knows about our correspondence. I did take the risk of confiding in her that strange day in the hotel. An instinct told me it was safe to confide in her. She would have understood there was something underneath the joking tone. And that would make it sacred to her, right?

Promise: Burn this!

2

Leipzig, 15 November 1895

My dear!

If I am your friend, then please do not call me Master, something I am not and do not want to be. And the Masters are dead—and I am alive, alive to search for something I never find, that is my sorrow and my happiness—both as an artist and as a man.

In your eyes I saw the most beautiful thing I have ever seen. But your letters, however dear they are to me, stubbornly deny the entire marvel I read in those eyes. Why? Are you scared? Or don't you trust me? It is true, why should you trust me when you don't know me? And still I believe in you without knowing you. Don't deprive me of this belief! Or was I wrong? Was it indeed just the harmonies? No, no, those sweet eyes told so very much more. That strange moment when I said: Is it possible? And you didn't answer. But you looked—you looked at me for a very, very long time, with a look in your eyes that was blissful, yes,—this moment was not imaginary, it really did exist! So tell me, with just one single word, that this look in your eyes didn't lie, let me able to read between the lines of your letters, let me believe in what I so much wish would be there—but which is not there! Say it to me in just a short "yes" in a corner of the letter! Because it cannot continue the way it is now. I can't stand it. Each letter will torture me, and that is not something you would wish. But—if you don't say it, then I will understand— and that will be the end of it. Then I will try to forget and in my art move beyond what they call "all sorrows and heavy thoughts." And then you must forgive me that I in an instant could misunderstand a far too tender—woman's glance.

You see there is a storm inside me. But let it storm! If I withstood the previous letter—I can withstand this one. I am a loner and you had become my world. That is the explanation.

And so farewell, my dear!

And warm regards, although not "surrounded by delightful harmonies," but by an even more delightful hope of a "yes"!

Promise me the same as last time: Burn this! And also nobody else must see these lines, not M.P [Margrethe Petersen], no matter how much I like her. You must promise!

But give her my regards and thank her for "The Swan," which I believe she will be able to sing so beautifully that I would want to grab the baton. What a pity I am not there! You never know, maybe some other time.

Tell her that "then it sounded" must be fortissimo till the very end, and not diminuendo, which they mistakenly wrote in the piano version. "Hverken Slag eller Trille lod Sangrøst ane…" must be entirely pp [pianissimo], without any crescendo.

3

Leipzig, 5 December 1895

If you knew how many times I have read and reread your wonderful letter! Did the "yes" please me? No, please is not the word. But it carried me away into a fairy-tale world. I forget that I am middle-aged and feel like a schoolboy in love, blessedly dizzy, thinking about the girl he loves! (Tell me, is this actually what is called "friendship"!?)

So, it took my stormy letter to make you talk. Yes, our "delightful, wonderful three-day relationship with no regrets"! Where did you find such magic words? I wouldn't be able to express myself like that. But let us be realistic; it can't be denied: - if there is no regret, there is still sorrow amid all the happiness. Tell me, is it coincidence that will bring us together again? Is that really what you think? And can you accept that? Impossible! Please give me some hope!

For how long will you stay in England? Tell me about your plans for late winter. There is a Danish man, Folmer Hansen, who (between you and me) very much wants me to conduct in several German cities. He knows you and has travelled with you. Let me therefore ask you: what do you know about him? Is he talented and reliable?—

And also tell me about both "Swans," both about the one whose eyes were concealed lies, but even more about the one whose eyes were not! Send regards to M.P. She is the only one in the younger generation of singers who is brave enough not to be a singer, but—herself. There are certain Nordic Romances, particularly my own, which absolutely require such a personality.

I admit, I had already resigned, but had forgotten the delightful secret of nature, that life renews itself. Yes, the three of us must get together somewhere in the world! If I dare believe this is possible, you must let me know. And I will try to be happy—and write about the "jubilant unattainable happiness." How very strange you should mention this purpose, which is the essence of the deepest part of my own soul! It must be a good omen!

Farewell darling,

Write soon!

(and date your letter)

Tell me your exact new address, and burn this! Tell me honestly if you have done so?????

4

Leipzig, 24 December 1895

Darling! Forgive my silence! I have been too upset to write. That is, I have written at least 4 letters, but tore them up. But today I have to talk. And that shall be from the bottom of my heart. Because I can't stand this exchange of letters any longer! It is shaking the foundation of both me and my art. Because what I sense is that our letters are not in the same language. Every word from you increases my longing for you and tells me that you have captured my heart completely, whereas you only give me a tiny fraction of yours in return. It was different when we met. But now I am not sure what to think anymore. Your letters confuse me, as there is no devotion, no longing! For my sake—and for your own, speak out and tell me from your heart the answer to what I am now asking. I think you very much want to meet again, although you don't write it. But I need to know. And more than anything, I need to see you and talk to you again. Shouldn't we, during the two months you will be back home, meet regularly by the piano and revive the blessed moments from last time? Nobody will know, trust me—wherever I go I have my own workroom which absolutely nobody knows about. Shall we dream the wonderful dream? So I will come to Copenhagen not later than the end of January and cancel all other plans!

If your longing is not strong enough, or you are not brave enough—then be honest! As you see, I am completely honest! Because in that case I will try the impossible: to forget you! There is no in-between for me! It's either-or!

If this is my last letter, then thank you very much for all the beauty I saw in your eyes. It is not your fault if Eros is not capturing you as deeply as me. If this is not my last letter, then I will not risk writing to your address in Copenhagen any more. I will write to poste restante under the name E.G.B.E—I will then let you know when there is a letter. But—now you have to reply fast—and give a complete answer! Talk to me the way your eyes did! Caution, now that you know how I am—[playing with my feelings] would be a sin, and—a game. And you don't want to play with me, do you?

I am a lonely man. That's why I have this eternal longing for deep sympathy. I found it in

Woman, never in life.

—I needed to speak fervently!

Best Christmas greetings!

5

Leipzig, 30 December 1895

Thank you for the marvelous reply! I was living in incredible suspense! So the situation is this: You don't have the courage! Oh, then you don't have that which gives you courage! But to go against your wishes is the last thing I would want. So therefore I throw the dice—and am <u>not</u> coming to Copenhagen before the end of March, when you leave for Norway, and I will be gone again before you return. Now I said it—it took all my strength to say it. The way I now feel, I couldn't stand a day, an hour, being in the same place as you without seeing you and talking to you, just the two of us. The pain of longing would kill me.—You mustn't talk about never parting, you, who don't want us to meet! That just sounds empty! With regard to Copenhagen, I think there would be no need to worry. Over an extended period I have had various workrooms there so hidden away that nobody, not even my closest friends or my wife, have known where they were. I have required this in order to be undisturbed while I am working, and this has been accepted. This is just to inform you. But rest assured, I am not trying to convince you. Your lack of courage has been like a cold bath on my burning passion. And this bath will give me strength to maintain for myself and my art all of my dignity and intensity as an artist and as a man.

How could I be angry! Sorrow, not anger, is what fills my soul! You wouldn't cause sorrow in anyone other than me!

I still want to thank you for everything.

Thank you for the Christmas card and thank you for the incredibly wonderful and bitter year!

From the enclosed piece of envelope you can see how you, my dear light-hearted creature, sealed your last letter!! And you still assure me that I can trust you! It was actually open!!

6

Leipzig, 27 January 1896

I am not able to respond to your letter without reopening all the wounds! So all I want to tell you is: Do not write to me anymore! But—when you so wish—nothing shall be over! Let us then meet again as friends!!

Translated by Lisbeth Dore

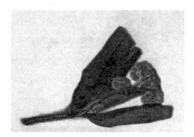

Two enclosures in Grieg's letters to Bella Edwards: a musical greeting and a pressed flower. BERGEN (NORWAY) PUBLIC LIBRARY; AUTHOR'S PHOTOGRAPH

April 1903 letter from Edvard Grieg to Bella Edwards, offering seating to her and Eva Mudocci at a concert marking his sixtieth birthday. See pp. 56-57. ROYAL DANISH LIBRARY, COPENHAGEN

Documentation Related to the
Unfinished Portrait of Eva Mudocci

A letter from Max Linde to Edvard Munch, dated February 1, 1904, asking how it is going with the painting of the woman violinist.
MUNCH MUSEUM, OSLO, K 2792

KUNSTHANDEL

KONSULENT-
VIRKSOMHET

TAKSTFORRETNINGER

UNIVERSITETSGT. 14. T. 33 29 04

PRIV. ELISENBERGVN. 4. T. 56 31 66

SOMMERADR.: SKAATØY. T. 85130

BANK: KRISTIANIA FOLKEBANK

HARALD HOLST HALVORSEN
OSLO–NORW.

Aasgaardstrand 5.okt.1959

Herr gross.Poul Rée,
Holbergsgade 11,
Köbenhavn.

Kjäre herr Rée,
Jeg takker for Deres breve som har
interessert mig meget(brevens av 19.,21.og 27.sept.og 1.okt.)
De inneholder mange ting,som man kunne utdype mere ved en
personlig samtale ved leilighet.Jeg takker ogsaa for fotogra-
fiet og for adresserne,som jeg gaar ut fra jeg kan benytte
med Deres tillatelse.

Idag nevner jeg bare at en av Tulla
Larsens mänd er min meget gode ven,og saasnart jeg treffer
ham skal jeg faa brakt baade "flyktningshistorien" og skuddet
fullstendig paa det rene.Jeg setter ikke Stenersens historier
särlig höit hva troverdighet angaar.Boken er blitt,hva han
tilsiktet,en sensasjonsaffäre,som utkom i Norge efter Munchs
död,men som Inger Munch tok avstand fra i mange stykker.
Stenersen er först og fremst en smart forretningsmand som i
allerhöieste grad har profitert paa sit saakaldte venskap med
Munch.Heller ikke tror jeg Pola G.har dekning for sin historie
om at det var Tulla L.som skjöt og derefter hentet Munch hjem.
Jeg forstaar godt at Stenersen meget gjerne vil kjöpe Deres
billede.

Men jeg tror at De paa enhver maate
vil väre mere tjent med aa benytte mig som Deres mellemmand
-om jeg faar väre saa ubeskjeden at jeg sier det selv.
Jeg er helt sikker paa at vi skal finde en form,som baade vil
gi Dem den fortjeneste De bör ha og som vil frita Dem for aa
bli plyndret av skattevesenet.

Det vil neppe kunne skjules at De
kjöpte maleriet for kr. og ved aa selge det selv,vil det
i vor lille verden heller ikke kunne skjules hva De faar for
det.Og saa er skattevesenet der.Det er derfor jeg mener,at
jeg vil kunne hjelpe Dem overfor skattevesenet og samtidig
selv ogsaa ha fordel avdet.

Blad 2.P.R.Kbhvn.

Men disse spörsmaal bör diskuteres mundtlig og derefter bör en
skriftlig avtale settes op og undertegnes under et möte mellem
os.

Jeg vil kunne bringe maleriet med til Oslo og faa baade
Langaards og Nasjonalgalleriets skriftlige uttalelse og jeg kan
selv skrive en ekspertise,der vel ogsaa vil väre av be-
tydning,for aa opnaa den bedst mulige pris.

Hva Gauguinskulpturer angaar,saa kjender jeg flere slike.Og
er det särlig interessante ting kan man opnaa gode priser.Jeg
kjender saaledes et treskulpturarbeide som bestaar av et skrin
med en liggende kvindelig akt.Det ömeget verdifuldt.Selv har
jeg siet en pottemakerarbeide av Gauguin.Og desuten er jeg blitt
tilbudt et skap med blomsterutskjäringer.

Gjör nu intet overilet med Deres maleria,og jeg tror at jo
mindre der snakkes om det,desto bedre,inntil den dag bomben vil
springe.Da tror jeg den vil gjöre stor virkning.

Hvis De er interessert i at gjöre en avtale med mig om det
videre arbeide og under en form som saavel De,som skatte-vesenet
og jeg er tjent med,kunne jeg gjerne komme til Kb.hvn det jeg
samtidig kan utföre endel forretninger,som riktignok ikke haster
men som allikevel kunne gjöres nu.

Venlig hilsen,
Deres Harald Holst Halvorsen

A two-page letter from art collector and dealer Harald Holst Halvorsen to Poul Rée, dated October 5, 1959. FLATEN MUSEUM, ST. OLAF COLLEGE, NORTHFIELD, MINNESOTA. Halvorsen predicts "an explosion" in the art world when the existence of Rée's Eva Mudocci portrait becomes known. He writes, "I would be able to bring the painting to Oslo and get a written statement from both Langaard and the National Gallery, and I could also write an expert statement myself, which might be valuable in order to get the best possible price." Unwilling to share the profits, Rée declined his help, and Halvorsen dropped the matter. Halvorsen died less than a year later.

40   Malerier

H. YLEMANN

302 Opstilling med syrener. Sign. H. Ylemann. Ovalt.
     68×95.

KRISTIAN ZAHRTMANN

303 Hjørne af kunstnerens atelier. Sign. monogram 1886.
     48×42. S. Danneskjold-Samsøe nr. 579. H. Chr.
     Christensen nr. 312.

Tilhørende boet efter
TEGNEREN KAY NIELSEN
på rekvisition af
overretssagfører H. Hindenburg,
landsretssagfører Bent Himmelstrup
og advokat Claus Pedersen

KAY NIELSEN

304 Kvinde i lang kjole. 78×61.

305 Båd i klitterne, og udsigt over havet. 26×24 og
     31×25.

306 Selvportræt med høj hat. 100×80.

307 Dame i sort kjole. 117×88.

308 En havedør. 27×19.

309 Udsigt mod en by. Sign. Kay N. 1903. 37×23.

310 Udsigt over havet. Sign. monogram. Skagen 1903.
     45×33.

311 En busk. 20×25.

312 Diverse malerier, akvareller, tegninger og raderinger
     samt radering af P. S. Krøyer. U. r.

Page from a 1959 Bruun Rasmussen auction catalogue
showing inclusion of an oil painting (No. 307) called
"Woman in a Black Dress" in a sale of paintings from
Kay Nielsen's estate. The auction house has confirmed
that the painting was bought by Poul Rée for 50 kroner
(about $60 today).

Index

CPSIA information can be obtained
at www.ICGtesting.com
Printed in the USA
FFHW011856140219
50549952-55844FF